Enrichment Masters

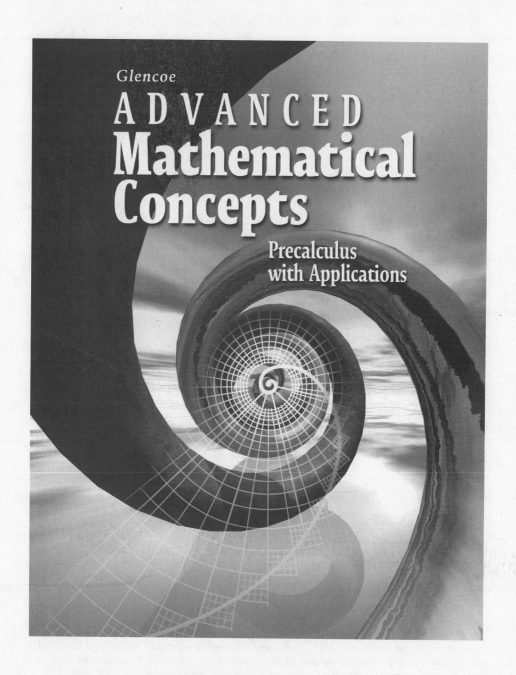

Glencoe

ADVANCED
Mathematical
Concepts

Precalculus
with Applications

**Glencoe
McGraw-Hill**

New York, New York   Columbus, Ohio   Woodland Hills, California   Peoria, Illinois

Glencoe/McGraw-Hill

A Division of The **McGraw·Hill** *Companies*

Send all inquiries to:
Glencoe/McGraw-Hill
8787 Orion Place
Columbus, OH 43240-4027

ISBN: 0-02-834180-5

AMC Enrichment Masters

1 2 3 4 5 6 7 8 9 10 024 08 07 06 05 04 03 02 01 00

Contents

1-1

Enrichment

Rates of Change

Between $x = a$ and $x = b$, the function $f(x)$ changes by $f(b) - f(a)$.
The *average rate of change* of $f(x)$ between $x = a$ and $x = b$ is defined
by the expression
$$\frac{f(b) - f(a)}{(b - a)}.$$

Find the change and the average rate of change of f(x) in the given range.

1. $f(x) = 3x - 4$, from $x = 3$ to $x = 8$

2. $f(x) = x^2 + 6x - 10$, from $x = 2$ to $x = 4$

The average rate of change of a function $f(x)$ over an
interval is the amount the function changes per unit
change in x. As shown in the figure at the right, the
average rate of change between $x = a$ and $x = b$
represents the slope of the line passing through the
two points on the graph of f with abscissas a and b.

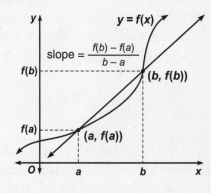

3. Which is larger, the average rate of change of
$f(x) = x^2$ between 0 and 1 or between 4 and 5?

4. Which of these functions has the greatest average rate of change
between 2 and 3: $f(x) = x$; $g(x) = x^2$; $h(x) = x^3$?

5. Find the average rate of change for the function $f(x) = x^2$ in each interval.
   a. $a = 1$ to $b = 1.1$ **b.** $a = 1$ to $b = 1.01$ **c.** $a = 1$ to $b = 1.001$

   d. What value does the average rate of change appear to be
   approaching as the value of b gets closer and closer to 1?

The value you found in Exercise **5d** is the *instantaneous rate of
change* of the function. Instantaneous rate of change has enormous
importance in calculus, the topic of Chapter 15.

6. Find the instantaneous rate of change of the function $f(x) = 3x^2$
   as x approaches 3.

     Advanced Mathematical Concepts

1-2

Enrichment

Applying Composition of Functions

Because the area of a square A is explicitly determined by the length of a side of the square, the area can be expressed as a function of one variable, the length of a side s: $A = f(s) = s^2$. Physical quantities are often functions of numerous variables, each of which may itself be a function of several additional variables. A car's gas mileage, for example, is a function of the mass of the car, the type of gasoline being used, the condition of the engine, and many other factors, each of which is further dependent on other factors. Finding the value of such a quantity for specific values of the variables is often easiest by first finding a single function composed of all the functions and then substituting for the variables.

The *frequency* f of a pendulum is the number of complete swings the pendulum makes in 60 seconds. It is a function of the *period* p of the pendulum, the number of seconds the pendulum requires to make one complete swing: $f(p) = \frac{60}{p}$.

In turn, the period of a pendulum is a function of its length L in centimeters: $p(L) = 0.2\sqrt{L}$.

Finally, the length of a pendulum is a function of its length ℓ at $0°$ Celsius, the Celsius temperature C, and the *coefficient of expansion* e of the material of which the pendulum is made:
$L(\ell, C, e) = \ell(1 + eC)$.

1. a. Find and simplify $f(p(L(\ell, C, e)))$, an expression for the frequency of a brass pendulum, $e = 0.00002$, in terms of its length, in centimeters at $0°C$, and the Celsius temperature.

b. Find the frequency, to the nearest tenth, of a brass pendulum at $300°C$ if the pendulum's length at $0°C$ is 15 centimeters.

2. The volume V of a spherical weather balloon with radius r is given by $V(r) = \frac{4}{3}\pi r^3$. The balloon is being inflated so that the radius increases at a constant rate $r(t) = \frac{1}{2}t + 2$, where r is in meters and t is the number of seconds since inflation began.
a. Find $V(r(t))$

b. Find the volume after 10 seconds of inflation. Use 3.14 for π.

1-3

Enrichment

Inverses and Symmetry

1. Use the coordinate axes at the right to graph the function $f(x) = x$ and the points $A(2, 4)$, $A'(4, 2)$, $B(-1, 3)$, $B'(3, -1)$, $C(0, -5)$, and $C'(-5, 0)$.

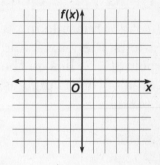

2. Describe the apparent relationship between the graph of the function $f(x) = x$ and any two points with interchanged abscissas and ordinates.

3. Graph the function $f(x) = 2x - 4$ and its inverse $f^{-1}(x)$ on the coordinate axes at the right.

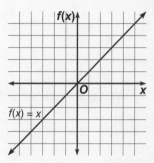

4. Describe the apparent relationship between the graphs you have drawn and the graph of the function $f(x) = x$.

Recall from your earlier math courses that two points P and Q are said to be *symmetric* about line ℓ provided that P and Q are equidistant from ℓ and on a perpendicular through ℓ. The line ℓ is the *axis of symmetry* and P and Q are *images* of each other in ℓ. The image of the point $P(a, b)$ in the line $y = x$ is the point $Q(b, a)$.

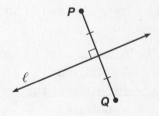

5. Explain why the graphs of a function $f(x)$ and its inverse, $f^{-1}(x)$, are symmetric about the line $y = x$.

1-4

Enrichment

Finding Equations From Area

A right triangle in the first quadrant is bounded by the
x-axis, the y-axis, and a line intersecting both axes. The
point (1, 2) lies on the hypotenuse of the triangle. The
area of the triangle is 4 square units.

*Follow these instructions to find the equation of the line containing
the hypotenuse. Let m represent the slope of the line.*

1. Write the equation, in point-slope form, of the line containing the
hypotenuse of the triangle.

2. Find the x-intercept and the y-intercept of the line.

3. Write the measures of the legs of the triangle.

4. Use your answers to Exercise 3 and the formula for the area of a
triangle to write an expression for the area of the triangle in
terms of the slope of the hypotenuse. Set the expression equal to
4, the area of the triangle, and solve for m .

5. Write the equation of the line, in point-slope form, containing the
hypotenuse of the triangle.

6. Another right triangle in the first quadrant has an area of
4 square units. The point (2, 1) lies on the hypotenuse. Find the
equation of the line, in point-slope form, containing the
hypotenuse.

7. A line with negative slope passes through the point (6, 1). A
triangle bounded by the line and the coordinate axes has an area
of 16 square units. Find the slope of the line.

1-5

Enrichment

Reading Mathematics: Question Assumptions

Students at the elementary level assume that the statements in their textbooks are complete and verifiably true. A lesson on the area of a triangle is assumed to contain everything there is to know about triangle area, and the conclusions reached in the lesson are rock-solid fact. The student's job is to "learn" what textbooks have to say. The better the student does this, the better his or her grade.

By now you probably realize that knowledge is open-ended and that much of what passes for fact—in math and science as well as in other areas— consists of theory or opinion to some degree.

At best, it offers the closest guess at the "truth" that is now possible. Rather than accept the statements of an author blindly, the educated person's job is to read them carefully, critically, and with an open mind, and to then make an independent judgment of their validity. The first task is to question the author's assumptions.

The following statements appear in the best-selling text Mathematics: Trust Me!. Describe the author's assumptions. What is the author trying to accomplish? What did he or she fail to mention? What is another way of looking at the issue?

1. "The study of trigonometry is critically important in today's world."

2. "We will look at the case where $x > 0$. The argument where $x \leq 0$ is similar."

3. "As you recall, the mean is an excellent method of describing a set of data."

4. "Sometimes it is necessary to estimate the solution."

5. "This expression can be written $\frac{1}{x}$."

1-6

Enrichment

Significant Digits

All measurements are approximations. The **significant digits** of an approximate number are those which indicate the results of a measurement.

For example, the mass of an object, measured to the nearest gram, is 210 grams. The measurement 21$\underline{0}$ g has 3 significant digits. The mass of the same object, measured to the nearest 100 g, is 200 g. The measurement 200 g has one significant digit.

Several identifying characteristics of significant digits are listed below, with examples.

1. Non-zero digits and zeros between significant digits are significant. For example, the measurement 9.071 m has 4 significant digits, 9, 0, 7, and 1.
2. Zeros at the end of a decimal fraction are significant. The measurement 0.050 mm has 2 significant digits, 5 and 0.
3. Underlined zeros in whole numbers are significant. The measurement 104,0$\underline{0}$0 km has 5 significant digits, 1, 0, 4, 0, and 0.

In general, a computation involving multiplication or division of measurements *cannot* be more accurate than the least accurate measurement of the computation. Thus, the result of computation involving multiplication or division of measurements should be rounded to the number of significant digits in the least accurate measurement.

Example   **The mass of 37 quarters is 21$\underline{0}$ g. Find the mass of one quarter.**

mass of 1 quarter $= 21\underline{0} \text{ g} \div 37$ *21$\underline{0}$ has 3 significant digits.*
                          $= 5.68 \text{ g}$ *37 does not represent a measurement. Round the result to 3 significant digits. Why?*

Write the number of significant digits for each measurement.

1. 8314.20 m   **2.** 30.70 cm   **3.** 0.01 mm   **4.** 0.0605 mg

5. 37$\underline{0}$,000 km   **6.** 370,0$\underline{0}$0 km   **7.** 9.7×10^4 g   **8.** 3.20×10^{-2} g

Solve each problem. Round each result to the correct number of significant digits.

9. 23 m × 1.54 m   **10.** 12,0$\underline{0}$0 ft ÷ 52$\underline{0}$ ft   **11.** 2.5 cm × 25

12. 11.01 mm × 11   **13.** 908 yd ÷ 0.5   **14.** 38.6 m × 4.0 m

1-7

Enrichment

Modus Ponens

A **syllogism** is a deductive argument in which a conclusion is inferred from two premises. Whether a syllogistic argument is valid or invalid is determined by its form. Consider the following syllogism.

Premise 1: If a line is perpendicular to line m, then the slope of that line is $-\frac{3}{5}$.

Premise 2: Line ℓ is perpendicular to line m.

Conclusion: ∴ The slope of line ℓ is $-\frac{3}{5}$.

Any statement of the form, "if p, then q," such as the statement in premise 1, can be written symbolically as $p \rightarrow q$. We read this "p implies q."

The syllogism above is valid because the argument form,

Premise 1: $p \rightarrow q$ (This argument says that if p implies q

Premise 2: p is true and p is true, then q must

Conclusion: ∴ q be true.)

is a valid argument form.

The argument form above has the Latin name **modus ponens**, which means "a manner of affirming." Any *modus ponens* argument is a valid argument.

Decide whether each argument is a modus ponens argument.

1. If the graph of a relation passes the vertical line test, then the relation is a function. The graph of the relation $f(x)$ does not pass the vertical line test. Therefore, $f(x)$ is not a function.

2. If you know the Pythagorean Theorem, you will appreciate Shakespeare. You do know the Pythagorean Theorem. Therefore, you will appreciate Shakespeare.

3. If the base angles of a triangle are congruent, then the triangle is isosceles. The base angles of triangle ABC are congruent. Therefore, triangle ABC is isosceles.

4. When $x = -3$, $x^2 = 9$. Therefore, if $t = -3$, it follows that $t^2 = 9$.

5. Since $x > 10$, $x > 0$. It is true that $x > 0$. Therefore, $x > 10$.

1-8

Enrichment

Line Designs: Art and Geometry

Iteration paths that spiral in toward an attractor or spiral out from
a repeller create interesting designs. By inscribing polygons within
polygons and using the techniques of line design, you can create
your own interesting spiral designs that create an illusion of curves.

1. Mark off equal units on the sides of a square.

2. Connect two points that are equal distances from adjacent vertices.

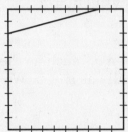

3. Draw the second (adjacent) side of the inscribed square.

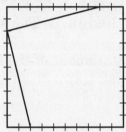

4. Draw the other two sides of the inscribed square

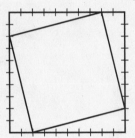

5. Repeat Step 1 for the inscribed square. (Use the same number of divisions).

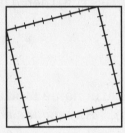

6. Repeat Steps 2, 3, and 4 for the inscribed square.

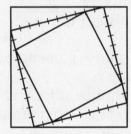

7. Repeat Step 1 for the new square.

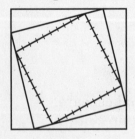

8. Repeat Steps 2, 3, and 4, for the third inscribed square.

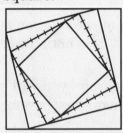

9. Repeat the procedure as often as you wish.

10. Suppose your first inscribed square is a clockwise rotation
like the one at the right. How will the design you create
compare to the design created above, which used a
counterclockwise rotation?

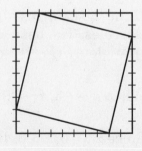

11. Create other spiral designs by inscribing triangles within
triangles and pentagons within pentagons.

1-1

Enrichment

Rates of Change

Between $x = a$ and $x = b$, the function $f(x)$ changes by $f(b) - f(a)$. The *average rate of change* of $f(x)$ between $x = a$ and $x = b$ is defined by the expression $\frac{f(b) - f(a)}{(b - a)}$.

Find the change and the average rate of change of f(x) in the given range.

1. $f(x) = 3x - 4$, from $x = 3$ to $x = 8$
change: **15**; average rate of change: **3**

2. $f(x) = x^2 + 6x - 10$, from $x = 2$ to $x = 4$
change: **24**; average rate of change: **12**

The average rate of change of a function $f(x)$ over an interval is the amount the function changes per unit change in x. As shown in the figure at the right, the average rate of change between $x = a$ and $x = b$ represents the slope of the line passing through the two points on the graph of f with abscissas a and b.

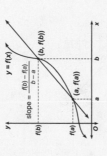

$$\text{slope} = \frac{f(b) - f(a)}{b - a}$$

3. Which is larger, the average rate of change of $f(x) = x^2$ between 0 and 1 or between 4 and 5?
between 4 and 5

4. Which of these functions has the greatest average rate of change between 2 and 3: $f(x) = x$; $g(x) = x^2$; $h(x) = x^3$?
h(x)

5. Find the average rate of change for the function $f(x) = x^2$ in each interval.
   a. $a = 1$ to $b = 1.1$ b. $a = 1$ to $b = 1.01$ c. $a = 1$ to $b = 1.001$
   2.1   **2.01**   **2.001**

   d. What value does the average rate of change appear to be approaching as the value of b gets closer and closer to 1?   **2**

The value you found in Exercise **5d** is the *instantaneous rate of change* of the function. Instantaneous rate of change has enormous importance in calculus, the topic of Chapter 15.

6. Find the instantaneous rate of change of the function $f(x) = 3x^2$ as x approaches 3.   **18**

1-2

Enrichment

Applying Composition of Functions

Because the area of a square A is explicitly determined by the length of a side of the square, the area can be expressed as a function of one variable, the length of a side s: $A = f(s) = s^2$. Physical quantities are often functions of numerous variables, each of which may itself be a function of several additional variables. A car's gas mileage, for example, is a function of the mass of the car, the type of gasoline being used, the condition of the engine, and many other factors, each of which is further dependent on other factors. Finding the value of such a quantity for specific values of the variables is often easiest by first finding a single function composed of all the functions and then substituting for the variables.

The *frequency* f of a pendulum is the number of complete swings the pendulum makes in 60 seconds. It is a function of the *period* p of the pendulum, the number of seconds the pendulum requires to make one complete swing: $f(p) = \frac{60}{p}$.

In turn, the period p of a pendulum is a function of its length L in centimeters: $p(L) = 0.2\sqrt{L}$.

Finally, the length of a pendulum is a function of its length ℓ at $0°$ Celsius, the Celsius temperature C, and the *coefficient of expansion* e of the material of which the pendulum is made: $L(\ell, C, e) = \ell(1 + eC)$.

1. a. Find and simplify $f(p(L(\ell, C, e)))$, an expression for the frequency of a brass pendulum, $e = 0.00002$, in terms of its length, in centimeters at $0°C$, and the Celsius temperature.
$$f(p(L(\ell, C, e))) = \frac{300\sqrt{\ell(1 + 0.00002C)}}{\ell(1 + 0.00002C)}$$

   b. Find the frequency, to the nearest tenth, of a brass pendulum at $300°C$ if the pendulum's length at $0°C$ is 15 centimeters.
77.2 swings per minute

2. The volume V of a spherical weather balloon with radius r is given by $V(r) = \frac{4}{3}\pi r^3$. The balloon is being inflated so that the radius increases at a constant rate $r(t) = \frac{1}{2}t + 2$, where r is in meters and t is the number of seconds since inflation began.

   a. Find $V(r(t))$
$$V(r(t)) = \frac{\pi t^3}{6} + 2\pi t^2 + 8\pi t + \frac{32}{3}\pi$$

   b. Find the volume after 10 seconds of inflation. Use 3.14 for π.   **1436.0 m³**

1-3 Enrichment

Inverses and Symmetry

1. Use the coordinate axes at the right to graph the function $f(x) = x$ and the points $A(2, 4)$, $A'(4, 2)$, $B(-1, 3)$, $B'(3, -1)$, $C(0, -5)$, and $C'(-5, 0)$.

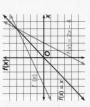

2. Describe the apparent relationship between the graph of the function $f(x) = x$ and any two points with interchanged abscissas and ordinates.
Sample answers: The points are mirror images of each other in the graph of $f(x) = x$; the points are symmetric to each other with respect to the graph of $f(x) = x$; the points are the same distance from but on opposite sides of the graph of $f(x) = x$.

3. Graph the function $f(x) = 2x - 4$ and its inverse $f^{-1}(x)$ on the coordinate axes at the right.

4. Describe the apparent relationship between the graphs you have drawn and the graph of the function $f(x) = x$.
Sample answers: They are mirror images of each other in the graph of $f(x) = x$; they intersect $f(x) = x$ at the same point and at the same angle.

Recall from your earlier math courses that two points P and Q are said to be *symmetric* about line ℓ provided that P and Q are equidistant from ℓ and on a perpendicular through ℓ. The line ℓ is the *axis of symmetry* and P and Q are *images* of each other in ℓ. The image of the point $P(a, b)$ in the line $y = x$ is the point $Q(b, a)$.

5. Explain why the graphs of a function $f(x)$ and its inverse, $f^{-1}(x)$, are symmetric about the line $y = x$.
The graph of $f^{-1}(x)$ consists of ordered pairs formed by interchanging the coordinates of the ordered pairs of $f(x)$. Therefore, each point $P(a, b)$ in $f(x)$ has an image $Q(b, a)$ in $f^{-1}(x)$ that is symmetric with it about the line $y = x$.

1-4 Enrichment

Finding Equations From Area

A right triangle in the first quadrant is bounded by the x-axis, the y-axis, and a line intersecting both axes. The point $(1, 2)$ lies on the hypotenuse of the triangle. The area of the triangle is 4 square units.

Follow these instructions to find the equation of the line containing the hypotenuse. Let m represent the slope of the line.

1. Write the equation, in point-slope form, of the line containing the hypotenuse of the triangle.
$y - 2 = m(x - 1)$

2. Find the x-intercept and the y-intercept of the line.
x–intercept: $\frac{m-2}{m}$ y–intercept: $2 - m$

3. Write the measures of the legs of the triangle.
$\frac{m-2}{m}$ and $2 - m$

4. Use your answers to Exercise 3 and the formula for the area of a triangle to write an expression for the area of the triangle in terms of the slope of the hypotenuse. Set the expression equal to 4, the area of the triangle, and solve for m.
$m = -2$

5. Write the equation of the line, in point-slope form, containing the hypotenuse of the triangle.
$y - 2 = -2(x - 1)$

6. Another right triangle in the first quadrant has an area of 4 square units. The point $(2, 1)$ lies on the hypotenuse. Find the equation of the line, in point-slope form, containing the hypotenuse.
$y - 1 = -\frac{1}{2}(x - 2)$

7. A line with negative slope passes through the point $(6, 1)$. A triangle bounded by the line and the coordinate axes has an area of 16 square units. Find the slope of the line.
$m = -\frac{1}{2}$ or $m = -\frac{1}{18}$

1-5 Enrichment

Reading Mathematics: Question Assumptions

Students at the elementary level assume that the statements in their textbooks are complete and verifiably true. A lesson on the area of a triangle is assumed to contain everything there is to know about triangle area, and the conclusions reached in the lesson are rock-solid fact. The student's job is to "learn" what textbooks have to say. The better the student does this, the better his or her grade.

By now you probably realize that knowledge is open-ended and that much of what passes for fact—in math and science as well as in other areas—consists of theory or opinion to some degree.

At best, it offers the closest guess at the "truth" that is now possible. Rather than accept the statements of an author blindly, the educated person's job is to read them carefully, critically, and with an open mind, and to then make an independent judgment of their validity. The first task is to question the author's assumptions. **Answers will vary. Sample answers are given.**

The following statements appear in the best-selling text Mathematics: Trust Me!.
Describe the author's assumptions. What is the author trying to accomplish? What did he or she fail to mention? What is another way of looking at the issue?

1. "The study of trigonometry is critically important in today's world." That's an opinion. Critically important to whom? The author should back this statement up. It sounds like the author is trying to justify including this topic in the book.

2. "We will look at the case where $x > 0$. The argument where $x \leq 0$ is similar." Is it? I would like to hear the argument. Perhaps it gets into some sticky issues or raises some interesting points. The author assumes that I am not interested, but I am.

3. "As you recall, the mean is an excellent method of describing a set of data." I do not recall that. Where and when was that established? What does "excellent" mean? Perhaps at certain times the mean is excellent but there are times when it is not.

4. "Sometimes it is necessary to estimate the solution." When is it necessary? Why is it necessary? It sounds as though the author is trying to avoid saying that there are no good methods for solving this problem, or that there are some methods but the author thinks I am not capable of understanding them.

5. "This expression can be written $\frac{1}{x}$." How is it done? Why is the author writing the expression in this form rather than another?

1-6 Enrichment

Significant Digits

All measurements are approximations. The **significant digits** of an approximate number are those which indicate the results of a measurement.

For example, the mass of an object, measured to the nearest gram, is 210 grams. The measurement 210 g has 3 significant digits. The mass of the same object, measured to the nearest 100 g, is 200 g. The measurement 200 g has one significant digit.

Several identifying characteristics of significant digits are listed below, with examples.

1. Non-zero digits and zeros between significant digits are significant. For example, the measurement 9.071 m has 4 significant digits, 9, 0, 7, and 1.

2. Zeros at the end of a decimal fraction are significant. The measurement 0.050 mm has 2 significant digits, 5 and 0.

3. Underlined zeros in whole numbers are significant. The measurement 104,0̲00 km has 5 significant digits, 1, 0, 4, 0, and 0.

In general, a computation involving multiplication or division of measurements *cannot* be more accurate than the least accurate measurement of the computation. Thus, the result of computation involving multiplication or division of measurements should be rounded to the number of significant digits in the least accurate measurement.

Example The mass of 37 quarters is 210 g. **Find the mass of one quarter.**

mass of 1 quarter $= 210 \text{ g} \div 37$ *210 has 3 significant digits.*
$= 5.68 \text{ g}$ *37 does not represent a measurement.*
Round the result to 3 significant digits.
Why?

Write the number of significant digits for each measurement.

1. 8314.20 m
   6
2. 30.70 cm
   4
3. 0.01 mm
   1
4. 0.0605 mg
   3

5. 37̲0,000 km
   3
6. 370,0̲00 km
   5
7. 9.7×10^4 g
   2
8. 3.20×10^{-2} g
   3

Solve each problem. Round each result to the correct number of significant digits.

9. 23 m × 1.54 m
   35 m²
10. 12,0̲00 ft ÷ 520 ft
    23.1
11. 2.5 cm × 25
    63 cm

12. 11.01 mm × 11
    121.1 mm
13. 908 yd ÷ 0.5
    1,820 yd
14. 38.6 m × 4.0 m
    150 m²

1-7

Enrichment

Modus Ponens

A **syllogism** is a deductive argument in which a conclusion is inferred from two premises. Whether a syllogistic argument is valid or invalid is determined by its form. Consider the following syllogism.

Premise 1: If a line is perpendicular to line m, then the slope of that line is $-\frac{3}{5}$.

Premise 2: Line ℓ is perpendicular to line m.

Conclusion: ∴ The slope of line ℓ is $-\frac{3}{5}$.

Any statement of the form, "if p, then q," such as the statement in premise 1, can be written symbolically as $p \to q$. We read this "p implies q."

The syllogism above is valid because the argument form,

Premise 1: $p \to q$ (This argument says that if p implies q
Premise 2: p is true and p is true, then q must
Conclusion: ∴ q be true.)

is a valid argument form.

The argument form above has the Latin name **modus ponens**, which means "a manner of affirming." Any *modus ponens* argument is a valid argument.

Decide whether each argument is a modus ponens argument.

1. If the graph of a relation passes the vertical line test, then the relation is a function. The graph of the relation $f(x)$ does not pass the vertical line test. Therefore, $f(x)$ is not a function.
no

2. If you know the Pythagorean Theorem, you will appreciate Shakespeare. You do know the Pythagorean Theorem. Therefore, you will appreciate Shakespeare.
yes

3. If the base angles of a triangle are congruent, then the triangle is isosceles. The base angles of triangle ABC are congruent. Therefore, triangle ABC is isosceles.
yes

4. When $x = -3$, $x^2 = 9$. Therefore, if $t = -3$, it follows that $t^2 = 9$.
yes

5. Since $x > 10$, $x > 0$. It is true that $x > 0$. Therefore, $x > 10$.
no

T7   *Advanced Mathematical Concepts*

1-8

Enrichment

Line Designs: Art and Geometry

Iteration paths that spiral in toward an attractor or spiral out from a repeller create interesting designs. By inscribing polygons within polygons and using the techniques of line design, you can create your own interesting spiral designs that create an illusion of curves.

1. Mark off equal units on the sides of a square.

2. Connect two points that are equal distances from adjacent vertices.

3. Draw the second (adjacent) side of the inscribed square.
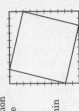

4. Draw the other two sides of the inscribed square.

5. Repeat Step 1 for the inscribed square. (Use the same number of divisions).

6. Repeat Steps 2, 3, and 4 for the inscribed square.
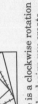

7. Repeat Step 1 for the new square.

8. Repeat Steps 2, 3, and 4, for the third inscribed square.

9. Repeat the procedure as often as you wish.

10. Suppose your first inscribed square is a clockwise rotation like the one at the right. How will the design you create compare to the design created above, which used a counterclockwise rotation? **One design is the mirror reflection of the other.**

11. Create other spiral designs by inscribing triangles within triangles and pentagons within pentagons. **See students' work.**

T8   *Advanced Mathematical Concepts*

2-1

Enrichment

Set Theory and Venn Diagrams

Set theory, which was developed by the nineteenth century German logician and mathematician, Georg Cantor, became a fundamental unifying principle in the study of mathematics in the middle of the twentieth century. The use of sets permits the precise description of mathematical concepts.

The intersection of two sets determines the elements common to the two sets. Thus, the intersection of two lines in a system of equations refers to the point or points that are common to the sets of points belonging to each of the lines. We can use Venn diagrams, which are named for the British logician, John Venn, to visually represent the intersection of two sets.

Example Let U = the set of all points in the Cartesian coordinate plane.
Let A = the set of all points that satisfy the equation $x = 4$.
Let B = the set of all points that satisfy the equation $y = -2$.
Draw a Venn diagram to represent U, A, and B.

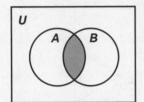

The shaded region represents the intersection of sets A and B, written $A \cap B$. In this example, $A \cap B = \{(4, -2)\}$.

Since the solution sets of two parallel lines have no points in common, the sets are called **disjoint sets**. In a Venn diagram, such sets are drawn as circles that do not overlap.

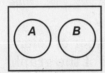 $A \cap B = \varnothing.$

Use the diagram at the right to answer the following questions.

Let A = the set of all points that satisfy the equation for line p.

Let B = the set of all points that satisfy the equation for line q.

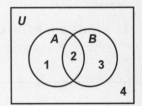

1. In which numbered region do the points that satisfy only the equation for line p lie?

2. In which numbered region do the points that satisfy only the equation for line q lie?

3. In which numbered region do the points that satisfy the equations for neither line p nor line q lie?

4. If the equation of line p is $2x - y = 4$ and the equation of line q is $3x + y = 6$, which point lies in region 2?

2-2

Enrichment

Graph Coloring

The student council is scheduling a volleyball tournament for teams from all four classes. They want each class team to play every other class team exactly once. How should they schedule the tournament?

If we call the teams A, B, C, and D, all of the possible games among the four teams can be represented as AB, AC, AD, BC, BD, and CD.

Draw a graph to represent the problem. Then color the graph. To **color** a graph means to color the vertices of that graph so that no two vertices connected by an edge have the same color.

Let the vertices represent the possible games. Let the edges represent games that cannot be scheduled at the same time. For example, if team B is playing team C, then team C cannot play team D.

Choose a vertex at which to begin.

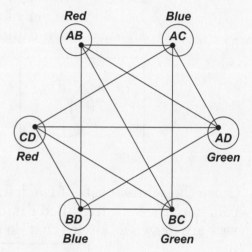

- Color AB red. Since CD is not connected to AB, color it red as well. All of the other vertices are connected to AB, so do not color them red.
- Color AC blue. Since BD is not connected to AC, color it blue.
- Color AD green. Since BC is not connected to AD, color it green.

The colored graph shows that pairs of games can be scheduled as follows

AB with CD; AC with BD; AD with BC

The **chromatic number** of a graph is the least number of colors necessary to color the graph. The chromatic number of the graph above is 3.

1. What does the chromatic number of the graph in the example above represent?

2. Draw and color a graph to represent the same type of tournament, but with 6 teams playing.

3. What is the chromatic number for your graph?

2-3

Enrichment

Elementary Matrix Transformations

Elementary row transformations can be made by multiplying a matrix on the left by the appropriate transformation matrix. For example, to interchange rows 2 and 3 in a 3×3 matrix, multiply the

matrix on the left by the matrix $\begin{bmatrix} 1 & 0 & 0 \\ 0 & 0 & 1 \\ 0 & 1 & 0 \end{bmatrix}$.

Example   Let $C = \begin{bmatrix} -5 & 3 & 1 \\ 1 & 5 & 0 \\ 10 & -6 & -2 \end{bmatrix}$. **Multiply on the left by** $\begin{bmatrix} 1 & 0 & 0 \\ 0 & 0 & 1 \\ 0 & 1 & 0 \end{bmatrix}$.

$$\begin{bmatrix} 1 & 0 & 0 \\ 0 & 0 & 1 \\ 0 & 1 & 0 \end{bmatrix}\begin{bmatrix} -5 & 3 & 1 \\ 1 & 5 & 0 \\ 10 & -6 & -2 \end{bmatrix} = \begin{bmatrix} -5 & 3 & 1 \\ 10 & -6 & -2 \\ 1 & 5 & 0 \end{bmatrix}$$

More complicated row transformations can also be made by a matrix multiplier.

Example   **Find the elementary matrix that, when matrix A is multiplied by it on the left, row 1 will be replaced by the sum of 2 times row 1 and row 3.**

Let $A = \begin{bmatrix} a_{11} & a_{12} & a_{13} \\ a_{21} & a_{22} & a_{23} \\ a_{31} & a_{32} & a_{33} \end{bmatrix}$. Find M such that $M \begin{bmatrix} a_{11} & a_{12} & a_{13} \\ a_{21} & a_{22} & a_{23} \\ a_{31} & a_{32} & a_{33} \end{bmatrix} =$

$\begin{bmatrix} 2a_{11} + a_{31} & 2a_{12} + a_{32} & 2a_{13} + a_{33} \\ a_{21} & a_{22} & a_{23} \\ a_{31} & a_{32} & a_{33} \end{bmatrix}$. Try $M = \begin{bmatrix} 2 & 0 & 1 \\ 0 & 1 & 0 \\ 0 & 0 & 1 \end{bmatrix}$.

Check to see that the product MA meets the required conditions.

1. Find the elementary matrix that will interchange rows 1 and 3 of matrix A.

2. Find the elementary matrix that will multiply row 2 of matrix A by 5.

3. Find the elementary matrix that will multiply the elements of the first row of matrix A by -2 and add the results to the corresponding elements of the third row.

4. Find the elementary matrix that will interchange rows 2 and 3 of matrix A and multiply row 1 by -2.

5. Find the elementary matrix that will multiply the elements of the second row of matrix A by -3 and add the results to the corresponding elements of row 1.

2-4

Enrichment

Map Coloring

Each of the graphs below is drawn on a plane with no accidental crossings of its edges. This kind of graph is called a planar graph. A planar graph separates the plane into **regions**. A very famous rule called the *four-color theorem* states that every planar graph can be colored with at most four colors, without any adjacent regions having the same color.

Graph A
one region
one color

Graph B
two regions
two colors

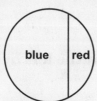

Graph C
three regions
two colors

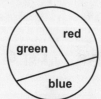

Graph D
three regions
three colors

If there are four or more regions, two, three, or four colors may be required.

Example   **Color the map at the right using the least number of colors.**

Look for the greatest number of isolated states or regions. Virginia, Georgia, and Mississippi are isolated. Color them pink.

Alabama and North Carolina are also isolated. Color them blue.

South Carolina and Tennessee are remaining. Because they do not share a common edge, they may be colored with the same color. Color them both green.

Thus, three colors are needed to color this map.

Color each map with the least number of colors.

1.

2.

2-5

Enrichment

Area of a Triangle

Determinants can be used to find the area of a triangle on the coordinate plane. For a triangle with vertices $P_1(x_1, y_1)$, $P_2(x_2, y_2)$, and $P_3(x_3, y_3)$, the area is given by the following formula.

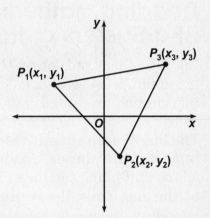

$$\text{Area} = \pm \frac{1}{2} \begin{vmatrix} x_1 & y_1 & 1 \\ x_2 & y_2 & 1 \\ x_3 & y_3 & 1 \end{vmatrix}$$

The sign is chosen so that the result is positive.

Example   **Find the area of the triangle with vertices**
$A(3, 8)$, $B(-2, 5)$, and $C(0, -1)$.

$$\text{Area} = \pm \frac{1}{2} \begin{vmatrix} 3 & 8 & 1 \\ -2 & 5 & 1 \\ 0 & -1 & 1 \end{vmatrix} = \pm \frac{1}{2} \left[3 \begin{vmatrix} 5 & 1 \\ -1 & 1 \end{vmatrix} - 8 \begin{vmatrix} -2 & 1 \\ 0 & 1 \end{vmatrix} + 1 \begin{vmatrix} -2 & 5 \\ 0 & -1 \end{vmatrix} \right]$$

$$= \pm \frac{1}{2} [3(5 - (-1)) - 8(-2 - 0) + 1(2 - 0)]$$

$$= \pm \frac{1}{2} [36] = 18$$

The area is 18 square units.

Find the area of the triangle having vertices with the given coordinates.

1. $A(0, 6)$, $B(0, -4)$, $C(0, 0)$

2. $A(5, 1)$, $B(-3, 7)$, $C(-2, -2)$

3. $A(8, -2)$, $B(0, -4)$, $C(-2, 10)$

4. $A(12, 4)$, $B(-6, 4)$, $C(3, 16)$

5. $A(-1, -3)$, $B(7, -5)$, $C(-3, 9)$

6. $A(1.2, 3.1)$, $B(5.7, 6.2)$, $C(8.5, 4.4)$

7. What is the sign of the determinant in the formula when the points are taken in clockwise order? in counterclockwise order?

2-6

Enrichment

Reading Mathematics: Reading the Graph of a System of Inequalities

Like all other kinds of graphs, the graph of a system of linear inequalities is useful to us only as long as we are able to "read" the information presented on it.

The line of each equation separates the xy-plane into two **half-planes**. Shading is used to tell which half-plane satisfies the inequality bounded by the line. Thus, the shading below the boundary line $y = 4$ indicates the solution set of $y \leq 4$. By drawing horizontal or vertical shading lines or lines with slopes of 1 or -1, and by using different colors, you will make it easier to "read" your graph.

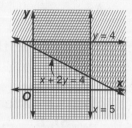

$$0 \leq x \leq 5$$
$$y \leq 4$$
$$x + 2y \geq 7$$

The shading in between the boundary lines $x \geq 0$ and $x \leq 5$, indicate that the inequality $0 \leq x \leq 5$ is equivalent to the *intersection* $x \geq 0 \cap x \leq 5$.

Similarly, the solution set of the system, indicated by the cross-hatching, is the intersection of the solutions of all the inequalities in the system. We can use set notation to write a description of this solution set:

$$\{(x, y) \mid 0 \leq x \leq 5 \cap y \leq 4 \cap x + 2y \geq 7\}.$$

We read this " The set of all ordered pairs, (x, y), such that x is greater than or equal to 0 *and* x is less than or equal to 5 *and* y is less than or equal to 4 *and* $x + 2y$ is greater than or equal to 7."

The graph also shows where any maximum and minimum values of the function f occur. Notice, however, that these values occur only at points belonging to the set containing the *union* of the vertices of the convex polygonal region.

Use the graph at the right to show which numbered region or regions belong to the graph of the solution set of each system.

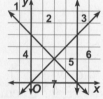

1. $x \geq 0$
$\quad y \leq x$

2. $0 \leq x \leq 4$
$\quad y \leq x$
$\quad x + y \geq 4$

3. The domain of $f(x, y) = 2x + y$ is the xy-plane. If we graphed this function, where would we represent its range?

Enrichment

Convex Polygons

You have already learned that over a closed convex polygonal region, the maximum and minimum values of any linear function occur at the vertices of the polygon. To see why the values of the function at any point on the boundary of the region must be between the values at the vertices, consider the convex polygon with vertices P and Q.

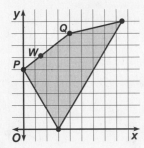

Let W be a point on $\overline{PQ}$.

If W lies between P and Q, let $\dfrac{PW}{PQ} = w$.

Then $0 < w < 1$ and the coordinates of W are $((1 - w)x_1 + wx_2, (1 - w)y_1 + wy_2)$. Now consider the function $f(x, y) = 3x - 5y$.

$$
\begin{aligned}
f(W) &= 3[(1-w)x_1 + wx_2] - 5[(1-w)y_1 + wy_2] \\
&= (1-w)(3x_1) + 3wx_2 + (1-w)(-5y_1) - 5wy_2 \\
&= (1-w)(3x_1 - 5y_1) + w(3x_2 - 5y_2) \\
&= (1-w)f(P) + wf(Q)
\end{aligned}
$$

This means that $f(W)$ is between $f(P)$ and $f(Q)$, or that the greatest and least values of $f(x, y)$ must occur at P or Q.

Example   **If $f(x, y) = 3x + 2y$, find the maximum value of the function over the shaded region at the right.**

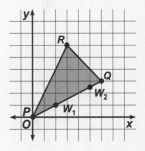

The maximum value occurs at the vertex $(6, 3)$. The minimum value occurs at $(0, 0)$. The values of $f(x, y)$ at W_1 and W_2 are between the maximum and minimum values.

$f(Q) = f(6, 3) = 24$
$f(W_1) = f(2, 1) = 8$
$f(W_2) = f(5, 2.5) = 20$
$f(P) = f(0, 0) = 0$

Let P and Q be vertices of a closed convex polygon, and let W lie on $\overline{PQ}$. Let $f(x, y) = ax + by$.

1. If $f(Q) = f(P)$, what is true of f? of $f(W)$?

2. If $f(Q) = f(P)$, find an equation of the line containing P and Q.

2-1

Enrichment

Set Theory and Venn Diagrams

Set theory, which was developed by the nineteenth century German logician and mathematician, Georg Cantor, became a fundamental unifying principle in the study of mathematics in the middle of the twentieth century. The use of sets permits the precise description of mathematical concepts.

The intersection of two sets determines the elements common to the two sets. Thus, the intersection of two lines in a system of equations refers to the point or points that are common to the sets of points belonging to each of the lines. We can use Venn diagrams, which are named for the British logician, John Venn, to visually represent the intersection of two sets.

Example   Let U = the set of all points in the Cartesian coordinate plane.
Let A = the set of all points that satisfy the equation $x = 4$.
Let B = the set of all points that satisfy the equation $y = -2$.
Draw a Venn diagram to represent U, A, and B.

The shaded region represents the intersection of sets A and B, written $A \cap B$. In this example, $A \cap B = \{(4, -2)\}$.

Since the solution sets of two parallel lines have no points in common, the sets are called **disjoint sets.** In a Venn diagram, such sets are drawn as circles that do not overlap.

$A \cap B = \varnothing$.

Use the diagram at the right to answer the following questions.
Let A = the set of all points that satisfy the equation for line p.
Let B = the set of all points that satisfy the equation for line q.

1. In which numbered region do the points that satisfy only the equation for line p lie? **1**

2. In which numbered region do the points that satisfy only the equation for line q lie? **3**

3. In which numbered region do the points that satisfy the equations for neither line p nor line q lie? **4**

4. If the equation of line p is $2x - y = 4$ and the equation of line q is $3x + y = 6$, which point lies in region 2? **(2,0)**

2-2

Enrichment

Graph Coloring

The student council is scheduling a volleyball tournament for teams from all four classes. They want each class team to play every other class team exactly once. How should they schedule the tournament?

If we call the teams A, B, C, and D, all of the possible games among the four teams can be represented as AB, AC, AD, BC, BD, and CD.

Draw a graph to represent the problem. Then color the graph. To **color** a graph means to color the vertices of that graph so that no two vertices connected by an edge have the same color.

Let the vertices represent the possible games. Let the edges represent games that cannot be scheduled at the same time. For example, if team B is playing team C, then team C cannot play team D.

Choose a vertex at which to begin.

• Color AB red. Since CD is not connected to AB, color it red as well. All of the other vertices are connected to AB, so do not color them red.

• Color AC blue. Since BD is not connected to AC, color it blue.

• Color AD green. Since BC is not connected to AD, color it green.

The colored graph shows that pairs of games can be scheduled as follows

AB with CD; AC with BD; AD with BC

The **chromatic number** of a graph is the least number of colors necessary to color the graph. The chromatic number of the graph above is 3.

1. What does the chromatic number of the graph in the example above represent?
the number of game times scheduled

2. Draw and color a graph to represent the same type of tournament, but with 6 teams playing.
See students' graphs.

3. What is the chromatic number for your graph? **5**

2-3 Enrichment

NAME _____ DATE _____ PERIOD _____

Elementary Matrix Transformations

Elementary row transformations can be made by multiplying a matrix on the left by the appropriate transformation matrix. For example, to interchange rows 2 and 3 in a 3×3 matrix, multiply the matrix on the left by the matrix $\begin{bmatrix} 1 & 0 & 0 \\ 0 & 0 & 1 \\ 0 & 1 & 0 \end{bmatrix}$.

Example Let $C = \begin{bmatrix} -5 & 3 & 1 \\ 1 & 5 & 0 \\ 10 & -6 & -2 \end{bmatrix}$. Multiply on the left by $\begin{bmatrix} 1 & 0 & 0 \\ 0 & 0 & 1 \\ 0 & 1 & 0 \end{bmatrix}$.

$$\begin{bmatrix} 1 & 0 & 0 \\ 0 & 0 & 1 \\ 0 & 1 & 0 \end{bmatrix} \begin{bmatrix} -5 & 3 & 1 \\ 1 & 5 & 0 \\ 10 & -6 & -2 \end{bmatrix} = \begin{bmatrix} -5 & 3 & 1 \\ 10 & -6 & -2 \\ 1 & 5 & 0 \end{bmatrix}$$

More complicated row transformations can also be made by a matrix multiplier.

Example Find the elementary matrix that, when matrix A is multiplied by it on the left, row 1 will be replaced by the sum of 2 times row 1 and row 3.

Let $A = \begin{bmatrix} a_{11} & a_{12} & a_{13} \\ a_{21} & a_{22} & a_{23} \\ a_{31} & a_{32} & a_{33} \end{bmatrix}$. Find M such that $M \begin{bmatrix} a_{11} & a_{12} & a_{13} \\ a_{21} & a_{22} & a_{23} \\ a_{31} & a_{32} & a_{33} \end{bmatrix} =$

$\begin{bmatrix} 2a_{11} + a_{31} & 2a_{12} + a_{32} & 2a_{13} + a_{33} \\ a_{21} & a_{22} & a_{23} \\ a_{31} & a_{32} & a_{33} \end{bmatrix}$. Try $M = \begin{bmatrix} 2 & 0 & 1 \\ 0 & 1 & 0 \\ 0 & 0 & 1 \end{bmatrix}$.

Check to see that the product MA meets the required conditions.

1. Find the elementary matrix that will interchange rows 1 and 3 of matrix A.

$\begin{bmatrix} 0 & 0 & 1 \\ 0 & 1 & 0 \\ 1 & 0 & 0 \end{bmatrix}$

2. Find the elementary matrix that will multiply row 2 of matrix A by 5.

$\begin{bmatrix} 1 & 0 & 0 \\ 0 & 5 & 0 \\ 0 & 0 & 1 \end{bmatrix}$

3. Find the elementary matrix that will multiply the elements of the first row of matrix A by -2 and add the results to the corresponding elements of the third row.

$\begin{bmatrix} 1 & 0 & 0 \\ 0 & 1 & 0 \\ -2 & 0 & 1 \end{bmatrix}$

4. Find the elementary matrix that will interchange rows 2 and 3 of matrix A and multiply row 1 by -2.

$\begin{bmatrix} -2 & 0 & 0 \\ 0 & 0 & 1 \\ 0 & 1 & 0 \end{bmatrix}$

5. Find the elementary matrix that will multiply the elements of the second row of matrix A by -3 and add the results to the corresponding elements of row 1.

$\begin{bmatrix} 1 & -3 & 0 \\ 0 & 1 & 0 \\ 0 & 0 & 1 \end{bmatrix}$

2-4 Enrichment

NAME _____ DATE _____ PERIOD _____

Map Coloring

Each of the graphs below is drawn on a plane with no accidental crossings of its edges. This kind of graph is called a planar graph. A planar graph separates the plane into **regions**. A very famous rule called the *four-color theorem* states that every planar graph can be colored with at most four colors, without any adjacent regions having the same color.

Graph A
one region
one color

Graph B
two regions
two colors

Graph C
three regions
two colors

Graph D
three regions
three colors

If there are four or more regions, two, three, or four colors may be required.

Example Color the map at the right using the least number of colors.

Look for the greatest number of isolated states or regions. Virginia, Georgia, and Mississippi are isolated. Color them pink. Alabama and North Carolina are also isolated. Color them blue. South Carolina and Tennessee are remaining. Because they do not share a common edge, they may be colored with the same color. Color them both green. Thus, three colors are needed to color this map.

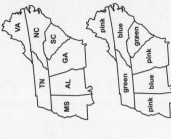

Color each map with the least number of colors. See students' maps.

1.

2.

2-5

NAME _____ DATE _____ PERIOD _____

Enrichment

Area of a Triangle

Determinants can be used to find the area of a triangle on the coordinate plane. For a triangle with vertices $P_1(x_1, y_1)$, $P_2(x_2, y_2)$, and $P_3(x_3, y_3)$, the area is given by the following formula.

$$\text{Area} = \pm \frac{1}{2} \begin{vmatrix} x_1 & y_1 & 1 \\ x_2 & y_2 & 1 \\ x_3 & y_3 & 1 \end{vmatrix}$$

The sign is chosen so that the result is positive.

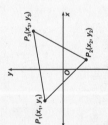

Example   Find the area of the triangle with vertices $A(3, 8)$, $B(-2, 5)$, and $C(0, -1)$.

$$\text{Area} = \pm \frac{1}{2} \begin{vmatrix} 3 & 8 & 1 \\ -2 & 5 & 1 \\ 0 & -1 & 1 \end{vmatrix} = \pm \frac{1}{2} \left[3 \begin{vmatrix} 5 & 1 \\ -1 & 1 \end{vmatrix} - 8 \begin{vmatrix} -2 & 1 \\ 0 & 1 \end{vmatrix} + 1 \begin{vmatrix} -2 & 5 \\ 0 & -1 \end{vmatrix} \right]$$

$$= \pm \frac{1}{2} [3(5 - (-1)) - 8(-2 - 0) + 1(2 - 0)]$$

$$= \pm \frac{1}{2} [36] = 18$$

The area is 18 square units.

Find the area of the triangle having vertices with the given coordinates.

1. $A(0, 6)$, $B(0, -4)$, $C(0, 0)$
   Points are collinear; there is no triangle.

2. $A(5, 1)$, $B(-3, 7)$, $C(-2, -2)$
   33 units^2

3. $A(8, -2)$, $B(0, -4)$, $C(-2, 10)$
   58 units^2

4. $A(12, 4)$, $B(-6, 4)$, $C(3, 16)$
   108 units^2

5. $A(-1, -3)$, $B(7, -5)$, $C(-3, 9)$
   46 units^2

6. $A(1.2, 3.1)$, $B(5.7, 6.2)$, $C(8.5, 4.4)$
   8.39 units^2

7. What is the sign of the determinant in the formula when the points are taken in clockwise order? in counterclockwise order?
   negative; positive

© Glencoe/McGraw-Hill   T17   *Advanced Mathematical Concepts*

2-6

NAME _____ DATE _____ PERIOD _____

Enrichment

Reading Mathematics: Reading the Graph of a System of Inequalities

Like all other kinds of graphs, the graph of a system of linear inequalities is useful to us only as long as we are able to "read" the information presented on it.

The line of each equation separates the xy-plane into two **half-planes**. Shading is used to tell which half-plane satisfies the inequality bounded by the line. Thus, the shading below the boundary line $y = 4$ indicates the solution set of $y \le 4$. By drawing horizontal or vertical shading lines or lines with slopes of 1 or -1, and by using different colors, you will make it easier to "read" your graph.

$$0 \le x \le 5$$
$$y \le 4$$
$$x + 2y \ge 7$$

The shading in between the boundary lines $x \ge 0$ and $x \le 5$, indicate that the inequality $0 \le x \le 5$ is equivalent to the *intersection* $x \ge 0 \cap x \le 5$.

Similarly, the solution set of the system, indicated by the cross-hatching, is the intersection of the solutions of all the inequalities in the system. We can use set notation to write a description of this solution set:

$$\{(x, y) \mid 0 \le x \le 5 \cap y \le 4 \cap x + 2y \ge 7\}.$$

We read this " The set of all ordered pairs, (x, y), such that x is greater than or equal to 0 *and* x is less than or equal to 5 *and* y is less than or equal to 4 *and* $x + 2y$ is greater than or equal to 7."

The graph also shows where any maximum and minimum values of the function f occur. Notice, however, that these values occur only at points belonging to the set containing the *union* of the vertices of the convex polygonal region.

Use the graph at the right to show which numbered region or regions belong to the graph of the solution set of each system.

1. $x \ge 0$
   $y \le x$
   5, 6, 7

2. $0 \le x \le 4$
   $y \le x$
   $x + y \ge 4$
   5

3. The domain of $f(x, y) = 2x + y$ is the xy-plane. If we graphed this function, where would we represent its range? **On a 3rd axis, perpendicular to the xy-plane.**

© Glencoe/McGraw-Hill   T18   *Advanced Mathematical Concepts*

NAME _____ DATE _____ PERIOD _____

2-7 Enrichment

Convex Polygons

You have already learned that over a closed convex polygonal region, the maximum and minimum values of any linear function occur at the vertices of the polygon. To see why the values of the function at any point on the boundary of the region must be between the values at the vertices, consider the convex polygon with vertices P and Q.

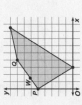

Let W be a point on $\overline{PQ}$.

If W lies between P and Q, let $\dfrac{PW}{PQ} = w$.

Then $0 < w < 1$ and the coordinates of W are $((1 - w)x_1 + wx_2, (1 - w)y_1 + wy_2)$. Now consider the function $f(x, y) = 3x - 5y$.

$$
\begin{aligned}
f(W) &= 3[(1-w)x_1 + wx_2] - 5[(1-w)y_1 + wy_2] \\
&= (1-w)(3x_1) + 3wx_2 + (1-w)(-5y_1) - 5wy_2 \\
&= (1-w)(3x_1 - 5y_1) + w(3x_2 - 5y_2) \\
&= (1-w)f(P) + wf(Q)
\end{aligned}
$$

This means that $f(W)$ is between $f(P)$ and $f(Q)$, or that the greatest and least values of $f(x, y)$ must occur at P or Q.

Example If $f(x, y) = 3x + 2y$, find the maximum value of the function over the shaded region at the right.

The maximum value occurs at the vertex $(6, 3)$.
The minimum value occurs at $(0, 0)$. The values of $f(x, y)$ at W_1 and W_2 are between the maximum and minimum values.

$$
\begin{aligned}
f(Q) &= f(6, 3) = 24 \\
f(W_1) &= f(2, 1) = 8 \\
f(W_2) &= f(5, 2.5) = 20 \\
f(P) &= f(0, 0) = 0
\end{aligned}
$$

Let P and Q be vertices of a closed convex polygon, and let W lie on $\overline{PQ}$. Let $f(x, y) = ax + by$.

1. If $f(Q) = f(P)$, what is true of f? of $f(W)$? **It produces alternate optimal solutions;** $f(W) = f(P)$.

2. If $f(Q) = f(P)$, find an equation of the line containing P and Q.
Sample answer: $ax + by = f(P)$

T19

Advanced Mathematical Concepts

3-1

Enrichment

Symmetry in Three-Dimensional Figures

A solid figure that can be superimposed, point for point, on its mirror image has a *plane of symmetry*. A symmetrical solid object may have a finite or infinite number of planes of symmetry. The chair in the illustration at the right has just one plane of symmetry; the doughnut has infinitely many planes of symmetry, three of which are shown.

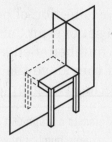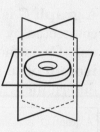

Determine the number of planes of symmetry for each object and describe the planes.

1. a brick

2. a tennis ball

3. a soup can

4. a square pyramid

5. a cube

Solid figures can also have *rotational symmetry*. For example, the axis drawn through the cube in the illustration is a fourfold axis of symmetry because the cube can be rotated about this axis into four different positions that are exactly alike.

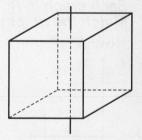

6. How many four-fold axes of symmetry does a cube have? Use a die to help you locate them.

7. A cube has 6 two-fold axes of symmetry. In the space at the right, draw one of these axes.

Advanced Mathematical Concepts

Enrichment

Isomorphic Graphs

A **graph** G is a collection of points in which a pair of points, called **vertices**, are connected by a set of segments or arcs, called **edges**. The **degree** of vertex C, denoted deg (C), is the number of edges connected to that vertex. We say two graphs are **isomorphic** if they have the same structure. The definition below will help you determine whether two graphs are isomorphic.

A graph G' is isomorphic to a graph G if the following conditions hold.

1. G and G' have the same number of vertices and edges.

2. The degree of each vertex in G is the same as the degree of each corresponding vertex in G'.

3. If two vertices in G are joined by $k\,(k \geq 0)$ edges, then the two corresponding vertices in G' are

---

Example In the graphs below *HIJKLMN*   *TUVWXYZ*.
Determine whether the graphs are isomorphic.

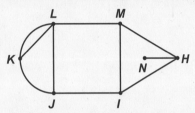 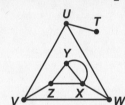

Number of vertices in G: 7   Number of vertices in G': 7
Number of edges in G: 10   Number of edges in G': 10
deg (H): 3   deg (I): 3   deg (T): 1   deg (U): 3
deg (J): 3   deg (K): 3   deg (V): 3   deg (W): 3
deg (L): 4   deg (M): 3   deg (X): 4   deg (Y): 3
deg (N): 1   deg (Z): 3

Since there are the same number of vertices and the same number of edges and there are five vertices of degree 3, one vertex of degree 4, and one vertex of degree 1 in both graphs, we can assume they are isomorphic.

Each graph in Row A is isomorphic to one graph in Row B.
Match the graphs that are isomorphic.

Row A

1.   2.   3.

Row B

a.   b.   c.

3-3

Enrichment

Some Parametric Graphs

For some curves, the coordinates x and y can be written as functions of a third variable. The conditions determining the curve are given by two equations, rather than by a single equation in x and y. The third variable is called a *parameter*, and the two equations are called *parametric equations* of the curve.

For the curves you will graph on this page, the parameter is t and the parametric equations of each curve are in the form $x = f(t)$ and $y = g(t)$.

Example **Graph the curve associated with the parametric equations $x = 48t$ and $y = 64t - 16t^2$.**

Choose values for t and make a table showing the values of all three variables. Then graph the x- and y-values.

t	x	y
−1	−48	−80
0	0	0
0.5	24	28
1	48	48
2	96	64
3	144	48
4	192	0

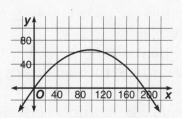

Graph each curve.

1. $x = 3t, \quad y = \dfrac{12}{t}$

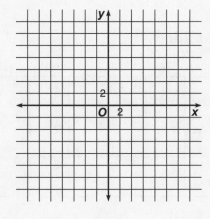

2. $x = t^2 + 1, \quad y = t^3 - 1$

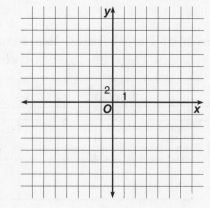

3-4

Enrichment

An Inverse Acrostic

The puzzle on this page is called an acrostic. To solve the puzzle, work back and forth between the clues and the puzzle box. You may need a math dictionary to help with some of the clues.

1. If a relation contains the element (e, v), then the inverse of the relation must contain the element $(\_\,,\_\,)$.

$\overline{}\ \overline{}$
17 28

2. The inverse of the function $2x$ is found by computing __ of x.

$\overline{}\ \overline{}\ \overline{}\ \overline{}$
2 29 6 27

3. The first letter and the last two letters of the meaning of the symbol f^{-1} are __ .

$\overline{}\ \overline{}\ \overline{}$
31 33 14

4. This is the product of a number and its multiplicative inverse.

$\overline{}\ \overline{}\ \overline{}$
20 11 34

5. If the second coordinate of the inverse of $(x, f(x))$ is y, then the first coordinate is read "__ of __".

$\overline{}\ \overline{}$
36 7

6. The inverse ratio of two numbers is the __ of the reciprocals of the numbers.

$\overline{}\ \overline{}\ \overline{}\ \overline{}\ \overline{}$
24 16 19 10 4

7. If · is a binary operation on set S and $x \cdot e = e \cdot x = x$ for all x in S, then an identity element for the operation is __.

$\overline{}$
18

8. To solve a matrix equation, multiply each side of the matrix equation on the __ by the inverse matrix.

$\overline{}\ \overline{}\ \overline{}\ \overline{}$
35 3 21 8

9. Two variables are inversely proportional __ their product is constant.

$\overline{}\ \overline{}\ \overline{}\ \overline{}$
13 9 22 5

10. The graph of the inverse of a linear function is a __ line.

$\overline{}\ \overline{}\ \overline{}\ \overline{}\ \overline{}\ \overline{}\ \overline{}\ \overline{}$
26 32 30 23 25 12 15 1

From President Franklin D. Roosevelt's inaugural address during the Great Depression; delivered March 4, 1933.

	1	2	3		4	5	6	7		8	9	10	11	12	
13	14		15	16	17	18		19	20		21	22	23	24	
	25	26		27	28	29	30		31	32	33	34	35	36	

Advanced Mathematical Concepts

3-5

Enrichment

Reading Mathematics

The following selection gives a definition of a continuous function as it might be defined in a college-level mathematics textbook. Notice that the writer begins by explaining the notation to be used for various types of intervals. It is a common practice for college authors to explain their notation, since, although a great deal of the notation is standard, each author usually chooses the notation he or she wishes to use.

Throughout this book, the set S, called the domain of definition of a function, will usually be an interval. An interval is a set of numbers satisfying one of the four inequalities $a < x < b$, $a \leq x < b$, $a < x \leq b$, or $a \leq x \leq b$. In these inequalities, $a \leq b$. The usual notations for the intervals corresponding to the four inequalities are, respectively, (a, b), $[a, b)$, $(a, b]$, and $[a, b]$.

An interval of the form (a, b) is called *open*, an interval of the form $[a, b)$ or $(a, b]$ is called *half-open* or *half-closed*, and an interval of the form $[a, b]$ is called *closed*.

Suppose I is an interval that is either open, closed, or half-open. Suppose $f(x)$ is a function defined on I and x_0 is a point in I. We say that the function $f(x)$ is continuous at the point x_0 if the quantity $|f(x) - f(x_0)|$ becomes small as $x \in I$ approaches x_0.

Use the selection above to answer these questions.

1. What happens to the four inequalities in the first paragraph when $a = b$?

2. What happens to the four intervals in the first paragraph when $a = b$?

3. What mathematical term makes sense in this sentence?
   If $f(x)$ is not ___?___ at x_0, it is said to be discontinuous at x_0.

4. What notation is used in the selection to express the fact that a number x is contained in the interval I?

5. In the space at the right, sketch the graph of the function $f(x)$ defined as follows:
$$f(x) = \begin{cases} \frac{1}{2} \text{ if } x \in \left[0, \frac{1}{2}\right) \\ 1, \text{ if } x \in \left[\frac{1}{2}, 1\right] \end{cases}$$

6. Is the function given in Exercise 5 continuous on the interval $[0, 1]$? If not, where is the function discontinuous?

3-6

Enrichment

"Unreal" Equations

There are some equations that cannot be graphed on the real-number coordinate system. One example is the equation $x^2 - 2x + 2y^2 + 8y + 14 = 0$. Completing the squares in x and y gives the equation $(x - 1)^2 + 2(y + 2)^2 = -5$.

For any real numbers, x and y, the values of $(x - 1)^2$ and $2(y + 2)^2$ are nonnegative. So, their sum cannot be -5. Thus, no real values of x and y satisfy the equation; only imaginary values can be solutions.

Determine whether each equation can be graphed on the real-number plane. Write yes or no.

1. $(x + 3)^2 + (y - 2)^2 = -4$

2. $x^2 - 3x + y^2 + 4y = -7$

3. $(x + 2)^2 + y^2 - 6y + 8 = 0$

4. $x^2 + 16 = 0$

5. $x^4 + 4y^2 + 4 = 0$

6. $x^2 + 4y^2 + 4xy + 16 = 0$

In Exercises 7 and 8, for what values of k :

a. will the solutions of the equation be imaginary?

b. will the graph be a point?

c. will the graph be a curve?

d. Choose a value of k for which the graph is a curve and sketch the curve on the axes provided.

7. $x^2 - 4x + y^2 + 8y + k = 0$

8. $x^2 + 4x + y^2 - 6y - k = 0$

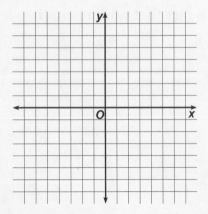

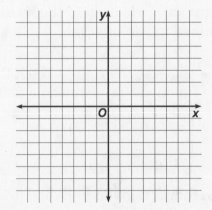

30

3-7

Enrichment

Slant Asymptotes

The graph of $y = ax + b$, where $a \neq 0$, is called a slant asymptote of $y = f(x)$ if the graph of $f(x)$ comes closer and closer to the line as $x \to \infty$ or $x \to -\infty$.

For $f(x) = 3x + 4 + \dfrac{2}{x}$, $y = 3x + 4$ is a slant asymptote because

$f(x) - (3x + 4) = \dfrac{2}{x}$, and $\dfrac{2}{x} \to 0$ as $x \to \infty$ or $x \to -\infty$.

Example   Find the slant asymptote of $f(x) = \dfrac{x^2 + 8x + 15}{x + 2}$.

$$\begin{array}{r|rrr} -2 & 1 & 8 & 15 \\ & & -2 & -12 \\ \hline & 1 & 6 & |3 \end{array}$$ *Use synthetic division.*

$y = \dfrac{x^2 + 8x + 15}{x + 2} = x + 6 + \dfrac{3}{x + 2}$

Since $\dfrac{3}{x + 2} \to 0$ as $x \to \infty$ or $x \to -\infty$,

$y = x + 6$ is a slant asymptote.

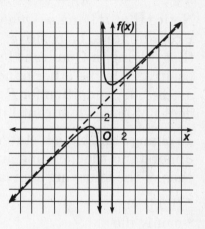

Use synthetic division to find the slant asymptote for each of the following.

1. $y = \dfrac{8x^2 - 4x + 11}{x + 5}$

2. $y = \dfrac{x^2 + 3x - 15}{x - 2}$

3. $y = \dfrac{x^2 - 2x - 18}{x - 3}$

4. $y = \dfrac{ax^2 + bx + c}{x - d}$

5. $y = \dfrac{ax^2 + bx + c}{x + d}$

Enrichment

Reading Mathematics: Interpreting Conditional Statements

The conditional statement below is written in "if-then" form. It has the form $p \rightarrow q$ where p is the hypothesis and q is the consequent.

If a matrix A has a determinant of 0, then A^{-1} does not exist.

It is important to recognize that a conditional statement need not appear in "if-then" form. For example, the statement

Any point that lies in Quadrant I has a positive x-coordinate.

can be rewritten as

If the point $P(x, y)$ lies in Quadrant I, then x is positive.

Notice that P lying in Quadrant I is a *sufficient* condition for its x-coordinate to be positive. Another way to express this is to say that P lying in Quadrant I *guarantees* that its x-coordinate is positive. On the other hand, we can also say that x being positive is a *necessary* condition for P to lie in Quadrant I. In other words, P does not lie in Quadrant I if x is not positive.

To change an English statement into "if-then" form requires that you understand the meaning and syntax of the English statement. Study each of the following equivalent ways of expressing $p \rightarrow q$.

- If p then q
- p only if q
- p is a sufficient condition for q
- q is a necessary condition for p.

- p implies q
- only if q, p
- not p unless q

Rewrite each of the following statements in "if-then" form.

1. A consistent system of equations has at least one solution.

2. When the region formed by the inequalities in a linear programming application is unbounded, an optimal solution for the problem may not exist.

3. Functions whose graphs are symmetric with respect to the y-axis are called even functions.

4. In order for a function to be continuous on an interval, it is necessary and sufficient that $f(x)$ be continuous at each number x in the interval.

         Advanced Mathematical Concepts

3-1

Enrichment

Symmetry in Three-Dimensional Figures

A solid figure that can be superimposed, point for point, on its mirror image has a *plane of symmetry*. A symmetrical solid object may have a finite or infinite number of planes of symmetry. The chair in the illustration at the right has just one plane of symmetry; the doughnut has infinitely many planes of symmetry, three of which are shown.

Determine the number of planes of symmetry for each object and describe the planes.

1. a brick
3 planes of symmetry; each plane is parallel to a pair of opposite faces.

2. a tennis ball
An infinite number of planes; each plane passes through the center.

3. a soup can
an infinite number of planes passing through the central axis, plus one plane cutting the center of the axis at right angles

4. a square pyramid
4 planes all passing through the top vertex: 2 planes are parallel to a pair of opposite edges of the base and the other 2 cut along the diagonals of the square base.

5. a cube
9 planes: 3 planes are parallel to pairs of opposite faces and the other 6 pass through pairs of opposite edges.

Solid figures can also have *rotational symmetry*. For example, the axis drawn through the cube in the illustration is a fourfold axis of symmetry because the cube can be rotated about this axis into four different positions that are exactly alike.

6. How many four-fold axes of symmetry does a cube have? Use a die to help you locate them.
3; each axis passes through the centers of a pair of opposite faces.

7. A cube has 6 two-fold axes of symmetry. In the space at the right, draw one of these axes.

3-2

Enrichment

Isomorphic Graphs

A **graph** G is a collection of points in which a pair of points, called **vertices**, are connected by a set of segments or arcs, called **edges**. The **degree** of vertex C, denoted deg (C), is the number of edges connected to that vertex. We say two graphs are **isomorphic** if they have the same structure. The definition below will help you determine whether two graphs are isomorphic.

A graph G' is isomorphic to a graph G if the following conditions hold.
1. G and G' have the same number of vertices and edges.
2. The degree of each vertex in G is the same as the degree of each corresponding vertex in G'.
3. If two vertices in G are joined by $k (k \geq 0)$ edges, then the two corresponding vertices in G' are also joined by k edges.

Example   In the graphs below $HIJKLMN$ $TUVWXYZ$.
Determine whether the graphs are isomorphic.

Number of vertices in G: 7
Number of edges in G: 10
deg (H): 3   deg (I): 3
deg (J): 3   deg (K): 3
deg (L): 4   deg (M): 3
deg (N): 1

Number of vertices in G': 7
Number of edges in G': 10
deg (T): 1   deg (U): 3
deg (V): 3   deg (W): 3
deg (X): 4   deg (Y): 3
deg (Z): 3

Since there are the same number of vertices and the same number of edges and there are five vertices of degree 3, one vertex of degree 4, and one vertex of degree 1 in both graphs, we can assume they are isomorphic.

Each graph in Row A is isomorphic to one graph in Row B. Match the graphs that are isomorphic.

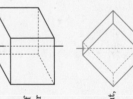

Row A
1.   2.   3.
Row B
a.   b.   c.

3-3 Enrichment

NAME _____ **DATE** _____ **PERIOD** _____

Some Parametric Graphs

For some curves, the coordinates x and y can be written as functions of a third variable. The conditions determining the curve are given by two equations, rather than by a single equation in x and y. The third variable is called a *parameter*, and the two equations are called *parametric equations* of the curve.

For the curves you will graph on this page, the parameter is t and the parametric equations of each curve are in the form $x = f(t)$ and $y = g(t)$.

Example **Graph the curve associated with the parametric equations $x = 48t$ and $y = 64t - 16t^2$.**

Choose values for t and make a table showing the values of all three variables. Then graph the x- and y-values.

t	x	y
-1	-48	-80
0	0	0
0.5	24	28
1	48	48
2	96	64
3	144	48
4	192	0

Graph each curve.

1. $x = 3t$, $y = \dfrac{12}{t}$

2. $x = t^2 + 1$, $y = t^3 - 1$

3-4 Enrichment

NAME _____ **DATE** _____ **PERIOD** _____

An Inverse Acrostic

The puzzle on this page is called an acrostic. To solve the puzzle, work back and forth between the clues and the puzzle box. You may need a math dictionary to help with some of the clues.

1. If a relation contains the element (e, v), then the inverse of the relation must contain the element
(___ , ___).
$\underset{17}{V}\ \underset{28}{E}$

2. The inverse of the function $2x$ is found by computing ___ of x.
$\underset{2}{H}\ \underset{29}{A}\ \underset{6}{L}\ \underset{27}{F}$

3. The first letter and the last two letters of the meaning of the symbol f^{-1} are ___.
$\underset{31}{I}\ \underset{33}{S}\ \underset{14}{E}$

4. This is the product of a number and its multiplicative inverse.
$\underset{20}{O}\ \underset{11}{N}\ \underset{34}{E}$

5. If the second coordinate of the inverse of $(x, f(x))$ is y, then the first coordinate is read " ___ of ___ ".
$\underset{36}{F}\ \underset{7}{Y}$

6. The inverse ratio of two numbers is the ___ of the reciprocals of the numbers.
$\underset{24}{R}\ \underset{16}{A}\ \underset{19}{T}\ \underset{10}{I}\ \underset{4}{O}$

7. If $\cdot$ is a binary operation on set S and $x \cdot e = e \cdot x = x$ for all x in S, then an identity element for the operation is ___.
$\underset{18}{E}$

8. To solve a matrix equation, multiply each side of the matrix equation on the ___ by the inverse matrix.
$\underset{35}{L}\ \underset{3}{E}\ \underset{21}{F}\ \underset{8}{T}$

9. Two variables are inversely proportional ___ their product is constant.
$\underset{13}{W}\ \underset{9}{H}\ \underset{22}{E}\ \underset{5}{N}$

10. The graph of the inverse of a linear function is a ___ line.
$\underset{26}{S}\ \underset{32}{T}\ \underset{30}{R}\ \underset{23}{A}\ \underset{25}{I}\ \underset{12}{G}\ \underset{15}{H}\ \underset{1}{T}$

From President Franklin D. Roosevelt's inaugural address during the Great Depression; delivered March 4, 1933.

1 T	2 H	3 E		4 T	5 H	6 E	7 O	8 N	9 L	10 Y		11 T	12 H		

(puzzle box: THE ONLY THING ... WE HAVE TO FEAR ... IS FEAR ITSELF)

| 13 W | 14 E | | 15 H | 16 A | 17 V | 18 E | | 19 T | 20 O | | 21 F | 22 E | 23 A | 24 R | |
| 25 I | 26 S | | 27 F | 28 E | 29 A | 30 R | | 31 I | 32 T | 33 S | 34 E | 35 L | 36 F | | |

NAME _____ DATE _____ PERIOD _____

3-5 Enrichment

Reading Mathematics

The following selection gives a definition of a continuous function as it might be defined in a college-level mathematics textbook. Notice that the writer begins by explaining the notation to be used for various types of intervals. It is a common practice for college authors to explain their notation, since, although a great deal of the notation is standard, each author usually chooses the notation he or she wishes to use.

Throughout this book, the set S, called the domain of definition of a function, will usually be an interval. An interval is a set of numbers satisfying one of the four inequalities $a < x < b$, $a \le x < b$, $a < x \le b$, or $a \le x \le b$. In these inequalities, $a \le b$. The usual notations for the intervals corresponding to the four inequalities are, respectively, (a, b), $[a, b)$, $(a, b]$, and $[a, b]$.

An interval of the form (a, b) is called *open*, an interval of the form $[a, b)$ or $(a, b]$ is called *half-open* or *half-closed*, and an interval of the form $[a, b]$ is called *closed*.

Suppose I is an interval that is either open, closed, or half-open. Suppose $f(x)$ is a function defined on I and x_0 is a point in I. We say that the function $f(x)$ is continuous at the point x_0 if the quantity $|f(x) - f(x_0)|$ becomes small as $x \in I$ approaches x_0.

Use the selection above to answer these questions.

1. What happens to the four inequalities in the first paragraph when $a = b$?

   Only the last inequality can be satisfied.

2. What happens to the four intervals in the first paragraph when $a = b$?

   The intervals reduce to a single point.

3. What mathematical term makes sense in this sentence?

   If $f(x)$ is not ___?___ at x_0, it is said to be discontinuous at x_0.

   continuous

4. What notation is used in the selection to express the fact that a number x is contained in the interval I?

   $x \in I$

5. In the space at the right, sketch the graph of the function $f(x)$ defined as follows:

   $$f(x) = \begin{cases} \frac{1}{2} & \text{if } x \in \left[0, \frac{1}{2}\right) \\ 1 & \text{if } x \in \left[\frac{1}{2}, 1\right] \end{cases}$$

   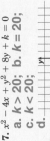

6. Is the function given in Exercise 5 continuous on the interval $[0, 1]$? If not, where is the function discontinuous?

   No; it is discontinuous at $x = \frac{1}{2}$.

NAME _____ DATE _____ PERIOD _____

3-6 Enrichment

"Unreal" Equations

There are some equations that cannot be graphed on the real-number coordinate system. One example is the equation $x^2 - 2x + 2y^2 + 8y + 14 = 0$. Completing the squares in x and y gives the equation $(x - 1)^2 + 2(y + 2)^2 = -5$.

For any real numbers, x and y, the values of $(x - 1)^2$ and $2(y + 2)^2$ are nonnegative. So, their sum cannot be -5. Thus, no real values of x and y satisfy the equation; only imaginary values can be solutions.

Determine whether each equation can be graphed on the real-number plane. Write yes or no.

1. $(x + 3)^2 + (y - 2)^2 = -4$
   no

2. $x^2 - 3x + y^2 + 4y = -7$
   no

3. $(x + 2)^2 + y^2 - 6y + 8 = 0$
   yes

4. $x^2 + 16 = 0$
   no

5. $x^4 + 4y^2 + 4 = 0$
   no

6. $x^2 + 4y^2 + 4xy + 16 = 0$
   no

In Exercises 7 and 8, for what values of k:

a. will all the solutions of the equation be imaginary?
b. will the graph be a point?
c. will the graph be a curve?
d. Choose a value of k for which the graph is a curve and sketch the curve on the axes provided.

7. $x^2 - 4x + y^2 + 8y + k = 0$
   a. $k > 20$; b. $k = 20$;
   c. $k < 20$;
   d.

8. $x^2 + 4x + y^2 - 6y - k = 0$
   a. $k < -13$; b. $k = -13$;
   c. $k > -13$;
   d.

3-7

NAME _____ DATE _____ PERIOD _____

Enrichment

Slant Asymptotes

The graph of $y = ax + b$, where $a \neq 0$, is called a slant asymptote of $y = f(x)$ if the graph of $f(x)$ comes closer and closer to the line as $x \to \infty$ or $x \to -\infty$.

For $f(x) = 3x + 4 + \frac{2}{x}$, $y = 3x + 4$ is a slant asymptote because $f(x) - (3x + 4) = \frac{2}{x}$, and $\frac{2}{x} \to 0$ as $x \to \infty$ or $x \to -\infty$.

Example   Find the slant asymptote of $f(x) = \frac{x^2 + 8x + 15}{x + 2}$.

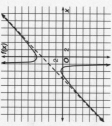

Use synthetic division.

$$\begin{array}{r} -2 \,\lfloor\, 1 \quad 8 \quad 15 \\ \underline{-2 \;-12} \\ 1 \quad 6 \quad \lfloor 3 \end{array}$$

$y = \frac{x^2 + 8x + 15}{x + 2} = x + 6 + \frac{3}{x + 2}$

Since $\frac{3}{x + 2} \to 0$ as $x \to \infty$ or $x \to -\infty$,

$y = x + 6$ is a slant asymptote.

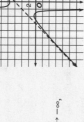

Use synthetic division to find the slant asymptote for each of the following.

1. $y = \frac{8x^2 - 4x + 11}{x + 5}$

     $y = 8x - 44$

2. $y = \frac{x^2 + 3x - 15}{x - 2}$

     $y = x + 5$

3. $y = \frac{x^2 - 2x - 18}{x - 3}$

     $y = x + 1$

4. $y = \frac{ax^2 + bx + c}{x - d}$

     $y = ax + b + ad$

5. $y = \frac{ax^2 + bx + c}{x + d}$

     $y = ax + b - ad$

3-8

NAME _____ DATE _____ PERIOD _____

Enrichment

Reading Mathematics: Interpreting Conditional Statements

The conditional statement below is written in "if-then" form. It has the form $p \to q$ where p is the hypothesis and q is the consequent.

     If a matrix A has a determinant of 0, then A^{-1} does not exist.

It is important to recognize that a conditional statement need not appear in "if-then" form. For example, the statement

     Any point that lies in Quadrant I has a positive x-coordinate.

can be rewritten as

     If the point $P(x, y)$ lies in Quadrant I, then x is positive.

Notice that P lying in Quadrant I is a *sufficient* condition for its x-coordinate to be positive. Another way to express this is to say that P lying in Quadrant I *guarantees* that its x-coordinate is positive. On the other hand, we can also say that x being positive is a *necessary* condition for P to lie in Quadrant I. In other words, P does not lie in Quadrant I if x is not positive.

To change an English statement into "if-then" form requires that you understand the meaning and syntax of the English statement. Study each of the following equivalent ways of expressing $p \to q$.

- If p then q
- p only if q
- p is a sufficient condition for q
- q is a necessary condition for p.

- p implies q
- only if q, p
- not p unless q

Rewrite each of the following statements in "if-then" form.

1. A consistent system of equations has at least one solution.

     If a system of equations is consistent, then the system has at least one solution.

2. When the region formed by the inequalities in a linear programming application is unbounded, an optimal solution for the problem may not exist.

     If the region formed by the inequalities in a linear programming application is unbounded, then an optimal solution for the problem may not exist.

3. Functions whose graphs are symmetric with respect to the y-axis are called even functions.

     If the graph of a function is symmetric with respect to the y-axis, then the function is even.

4. In order for a function to be continuous on an interval, it is necessary and sufficient that $f(x)$ be continuous at each number x in the interval.

     If a function $f(x)$ is continuous at each number x in an interval, then $f(x)$ is continuous on that interval.

4-1

Enrichment

Graphic Addition

One way to sketch the graphs of some polynomial functions is to use *addition of ordinates*. This method is useful when a polynomial function $f(x)$ can be written as the sum of two other functions, $g(x)$ and $h(x)$, that are easier to graph. Then, each $f(x)$ can be found by mentally adding the corresponding $g(x)$ and $h(x)$. The graph at the right shows how to construct the graph of $f(x) = -\frac{1}{2}x^3 + \frac{1}{2}x^2 - 8$ from the graphs of $g(x) = -\frac{1}{2}x^3$ and $h(x) = \frac{1}{2}x^2 - 8$.

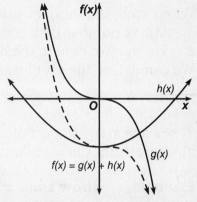

In each problem, the graphs of g(x) and h(x) are shown. Use addition of ordinates to graph a new polynomial function f(x), such that f(x) = g(x) + h(x). Then write the equation for f(x).

1.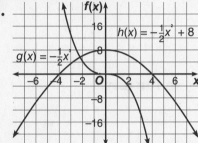

2.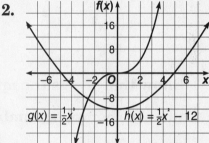

3.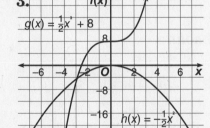

4.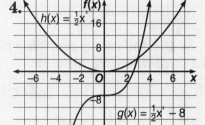

5.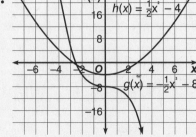

6.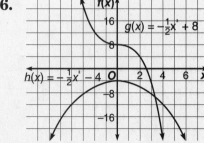

4-2

Enrichment

Conjugates and Absolute Value

When studying complex numbers, it is often convenient to represent a complex number by a single variable. For example, we might let $z = x + yi$. We denote the conjugate of z by $\bar{z}$. Thus, $\bar{z} = x - yi$. We can define the absolute value of a complex number as follows.

$$|z| = |x + yi| = \sqrt{x^2 + y^2}$$

There are many important relationships involving conjugates and absolute values of complex numbers.

Example   **Show that $z^2 = z\bar{z}$ for any complex number z.**

Let $z = x + yi$. Then,

$$z\bar{z} = (x + yi)(x - yi)$$
$$= x^2 + y^2$$
$$= \left(\sqrt{x^2 + y^2}\right)^2$$
$$= |z|^2$$

Example   **Show that $\dfrac{\bar{z}}{|z|^2}$ is the multiplicative inverse for any**

nonzero complex number z.

We know that $|z|^2 = z\bar{z}$. If $z \neq 0$, then we have

$z\left(\dfrac{\bar{z}}{|z|^2}\right) = 1$. Thus, $\dfrac{\bar{z}}{|z|^2}$ is the multiplicative

inverse of z.

For each of the following complex numbers, find the absolute value and multiplicative inverse.

1. $2i$

2. $-4 - 3i$

3. $12 - 5i$

4. $5 - 12i$

5. $1 + i$

6. $\sqrt{3} - i$

7. $\dfrac{\sqrt{3}}{3} + \dfrac{\sqrt{3}}{3}i$

8. $\dfrac{\sqrt{2}}{2} - \dfrac{\sqrt{2}}{2}i$

9. $\dfrac{1}{2} - \dfrac{\sqrt{3}}{2}i$

4-3

Enrichment

The Secret Cubic Equation

You might have supposed that there existed simple formulas for solving higher-degree equations. After all, there is a simple formula for solving quadratic equations. Might there not be formulas for cubics, quartics, and so forth?

There are formulas for some higher-degree equations, but they are certainly not "simple" formulas!

Here is a method for solving a reduced cubic of the form $x^3 + ax + b = 0$ published by Jerome Cardan in 1545. Cardan was given the formula by another mathematician, Tartaglia. Tartaglia made Cardan promise to keep the formula secret, but Cardan published it anyway. He did, however, give Tartaglia the credit for inventing the formula!

Let $R = \left(\dfrac{1}{2}b\right)^2 + \dfrac{a^3}{27}$

Then, $x = \left[-\dfrac{1}{2}b + \sqrt{R}\right]^{\frac{1}{3}} + \left[-\dfrac{1}{2}b - \sqrt{R}\right]^{\frac{1}{3}}$

Use Cardan's method to find the real root of each cubic equation. Round answers to three decimal places. Then sketch a graph of the corresponding function on the grid provided.

1. $x^3 + 8x + 3 = 0$

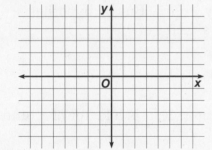

2. $x^3 - 2x - 5 = 0$

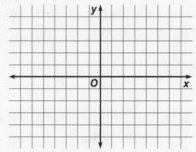

3. $x^3 + 4x - 1 = 0$

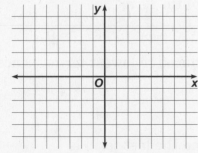

4. $x^3 - x + 2 = 0$

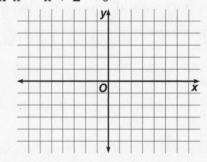

4-4

Enrichment

Scrambled Proofs

The proofs on this page have been scrambled. Number the
statements in each proof so that they are in a logical order.

The Remainder Theorem

☐ Thus, if a polynomial $f(x)$ is divided by $x - a$, the remainder is $f(a)$.

☐ In any problem of division the following relation holds:

dividend = quotient × divisor + remainder. In symbols, this may be written as:

☐ Equation (2) tells us that the remainder R is equal to the value $f(a)$; that is, $f(x)$ with a substituted for x.

☐ For $x = a$, Equation (1) becomes:

Equation (2) $f(a) = R$,

since the first term on the right in Equation (1) becomes zero.

☐ Equation (1) $f(x) = Q(x)(x - a) + R$,

in which $f(x)$ denotes the original polynomial, $Q(x)$ is the quotient, and R the
constant remainder. Equation (1) is true for all values of x, and in particular,
it is true if we set $x = a$.

The Rational Root Theorem

☐ Each term on the left side of Equation (2) contains the factor a; hence, a
must be a factor of the term on the right, namely, $-c_n b^n$. But by hypothesis,
a is not a factor of b unless $a = \pm 1$. Hence, a is a factor of c_n.

☐ $f\left(\dfrac{a}{b}\right)^n = c_0\left(\dfrac{a}{b}\right)^n + c_1\left(\dfrac{a}{b}\right)^{n-1} + \ldots + c_{n-1}\left(\dfrac{a}{b}\right) + c_n = 0$

☐ Thus, in the polynomial equation given in Equation (1), a is a factor of c_n and
b is a factor of c_0.

☐ In the same way, we can show that b is a factor of c_0.

☐ A polynomial equation with integral coefficients of the form

Equation (1) $f(x) = c_0 x^n + c_1 x^{n-1} + \ldots + c_{n-1} x + c_n = 0$

has a rational root $\dfrac{a}{b}$, where the fraction $\dfrac{a}{b}$ is reduced to lowest terms. Since

$\dfrac{a}{b}$ is a root of $f(x) = 0$, then

☐ If each side of this equation is multiplied by b^n and the last term is
transposed, it becomes

Equation (2) $c_0 a^n + c_1 a^{n-1} b + \ldots + c_{n-1} a b^{n-1} = -c_n b^n$

4-5

Enrichment

The Bisection Method for Approximating Real Zeros

The bisection method can be used to approximate zeros of polynomial functions like $f(x) = x^3 + x^2 - 3x - 3$. Since $f(1) = -4$ and $f(2) = 3$, there is at least one real zero between 1 and 2. The midpoint of this interval is $\frac{1+2}{2} = 1.5$. Since $f(1.5) = -1.875$, the zero is between 1.5 and 2. The midpoint of this interval is $\frac{1.5+2}{2} = 1.75$. Since $f(1.75) = 0.172$, the zero is between 1.5 and 1.75. $\frac{1.5+1.75}{2} = 1.625$ and $f(1.625) = -0.94$. The zero is between 1.625 and 1.75. The midpoint of this interval is $\frac{1.625+1.75}{2} = 1.6875$. Since $f(1.6875) = -0.41$, the zero is between 1.6875 and 1.75. Therefore, the zero is 1.7 to the nearest tenth. The diagram below summarizes the bisection method.

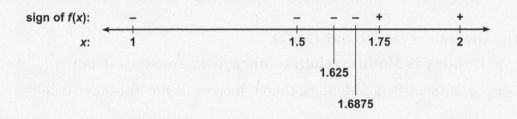

Using the bisection method, approximate to the nearest tenth the zero between the two integral values of each function.

1. $f(x) = x^3 - 4x^2 - 11x + 2, f(0) = 2, f(1) = -12$

2. $f(x) = 2x^4 + x^2 - 15, f(1) = -12, f(2) = 21$

3. $f(x) = x^5 - 2x^3 - 12, f(1) = -13, f(2) = 4$

4. $f(x) = 4x^3 - 2x + 7, f(-2) = -21, f(-1) = 5$

5. $f(x) = 3x^3 - 14x^2 - 27x + 126, f(4) = -14, f(5) = 16$

4-6

Enrichment

Inverses of Conditional Statements

In the study of formal logic, the compound statement "*if p, then q*" where *p* and *q* represent any statements, is called a *conditional* or an *implication*. The symbolic representation of a conditional is

$$p \to q.$$

p	q

If the determinant of a 2×2 matrix is 0, then the matrix does not have an inverse.

If both *p* and *q* are negated, the resulting compound statement is called the **inverse** of the original conditional. The symbolic notation for the negation of *p* is $\sim p$.

Conditional	**Inverse**	*If a conditional is true, its inverse*
$p \to q$	$\sim p \to \sim q$	*may be either true or false.*

Example **Find the inverse of each conditional.**

　　　a. *p*　*q*: If today is Monday, then tomorrow is Tuesday. (true)

　　　　$\sim p \to \sim q$ If today is not Monday, then tomorrow is not Tuesday. (true)

　　　b. *p*　*q* If *ABCD* is a square, then *ABCD* is a rhombus. (true)

　　　　$\sim p \to \sim q$ If *ABCD* is not a square, then *ABCD* is not a rhombus. (false)

Write the inverse of each conditional.

1. $q \to p$　　　　　**2.** $\sim p \to q$　　　　　**3.** $\sim q \to \sim p$

4. If the base angles of a triangle are congruent, then the triangle is isosceles.

5. If the moon is full tonight, then we'll have frost by morning.

Tell whether each conditional is true or false. Then write the inverse of the conditional and tell whether the inverse is true or false.

6. If this is October, then the next month is December.

7. If $x > 5$, then $x > 6$, $x \in R$.

8. If $x = 0$, then $x^{\frac{1}{2}} = 0$, $x \in R$.

9. Make a conjecture about the truth value of an inverse if the conditional is false.

4-7

Enrichment

Discriminants and Tangents

The diagram at the right shows that through a point P outside of a circle C, there are lines that do not intersect the circle, lines that intersect the circle in one point (tangents), and lines that intersect the circle in two points (secants).

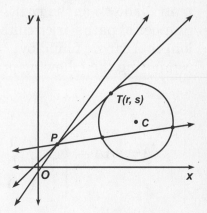

Given the coordinates for P and an equation for the circle C, how can we find the equation of a line tangent to C that passes through P?

Suppose P has coordinates $P(0, 0)$ and $\odot C$ has equation $(x - 4)^2 + y^2 = 4$. Then a line tangent through P has equation $y = mx$ for some real number m.

Thus, if $T(r, s)$ is a point of tangency, then
$s = mr$ and $(r - 4)^2 + s^2 = 4$.
Therefore, $(r - 4)^2 + (mr)^2 = 4$.
$$r^2 - 8r + 16 + m^2r^2 = 4$$
$$(1 + m^2)r^2 - 8r + 16 = 4$$
$$(1 + m^2)r^2 - 8r + 12 = 0$$

The equation above has exactly one real solution for r if the discriminant is 0, that is, when $(-8)^2 - 4(1 + m^2)(12) = 0$. Solve this equation for m and you will find the slopes of the lines through P that are tangent to circle C.

1. a. Refer to the discussion above. Solve $(-8)^2 - 4(1 + m^2)(12) = 0$ to find the slopes of the two lines tangent to circle C through point P.

b. Use the values of m from part **a** to find the coordinates of the two points of tangency.

2. Suppose P has coordinates $(0, 0)$ and circle C has equation $(x + 9)^2 + y^2 = 9$. Let m be the slope of the tangent line to C through P.

a. Find the equations for the lines tangent to circle C through point P.

b. Find the coordinates of the points of tangency.

4-8

Enrichment

Number of Paths

For the figure and adjacency matrix shown at the right, the number of paths or circuits of length 2 can be found by computing the following product.

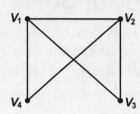

$$V_1\ V_2\ V_3\ V_4$$

$$A = \begin{array}{c} V_1 \\ V_2 \\ V_3 \\ V_4 \end{array} \begin{bmatrix} 0 & 1 & 1 & 1 \\ 1 & 0 & 1 & 1 \\ 1 & 1 & 0 & 0 \\ 1 & 1 & 0 & 0 \end{bmatrix}$$

$$A^2 = AA = \begin{bmatrix} 0 & 1 & 1 & 1 \\ 1 & 0 & 1 & 1 \\ 1 & 1 & 0 & 0 \\ 1 & 1 & 0 & 0 \end{bmatrix} \cdot \begin{bmatrix} 0 & 1 & 1 & 1 \\ 1 & 0 & 1 & 1 \\ 1 & 1 & 0 & 0 \\ 1 & 1 & 0 & 0 \end{bmatrix} = \begin{bmatrix} 3 & 2 & 1 & 1 \\ 2 & 3 & 1 & 1 \\ 1 & 1 & 2 & 2 \\ 1 & 1 & 2 & 2 \end{bmatrix}$$

In row 3 column 4, the entry 2 in the product matrix means that there are 2 paths of length 2 between V_3 and V_4. The paths are $V_3 \to V_1 \to V_4$ and $V_3 \to V_2 \to V_4$. Similarly, in row 1 column 3, the entry 1 means there is only 1 path of length 2 between V_1 and V_3.

Name the paths of length 2 between the following.

1. V_1 and V_2

2. V_1 and V_3

3. V_1 and V_1

For Exercises 4-6, refer to the figure below.

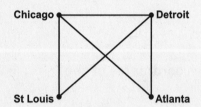

4. The number of paths of length 3 is given by the product $A \cdot A \cdot A$ or A^3. Find the matrix for paths of length 3.

5. How many paths of length 3 are there between Atlanta and St. Louis? Name them.

6. How would you find the number of paths of length 4 between the cities?

4-1 Enrichment

NAME _____ DATE _____ PERIOD _____

Graphic Addition

One way to sketch the graphs of some polynomial functions is to use *addition of ordinates*. This method is useful when a polynomial function $f(x)$ can be written as the sum of two other functions, $g(x)$ and $h(x)$, that are easier to graph. Then, each $f(x)$ can be found by mentally adding the corresponding $g(x)$ and $h(x)$. The graph at the right shows how to construct the graph of $f(x) = -\frac{1}{2}x^3 + \frac{1}{2}x^2 - 8$ from the graphs of $g(x) = -\frac{1}{2}x^3$

and $h(x) = \frac{1}{2}x^2 - 8$.

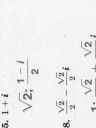

In each problem, the graphs of $g(x)$ and $h(x)$ are shown. Use addition of ordinates to graph a new polynomial function f(x), such that f(x) = g(x) + h(x). Then write the equation for f(x).

1.
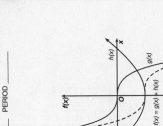

$f(x) = -\frac{1}{2}x^3 - \frac{1}{2}x^2 + 8$

3.
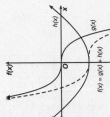

$f(x) = \frac{1}{2}x^3 - \frac{1}{2}x^2 + 8$

5.
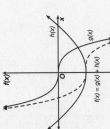

$f(x) = -\frac{1}{2}x^3 + \frac{1}{2}x^2 - 12$

2.

$f(x) = \frac{1}{2}x^3 + \frac{1}{2}x^2 - 12$

4.
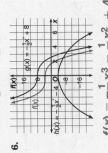

$f(x) = \frac{1}{2}x^3 + \frac{1}{2}x^2 - 8$

6.
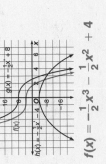

$f(x) = -\frac{1}{2}x^3 - \frac{1}{2}x^2 + 4$

T37

Advanced Mathematical Concepts

4-2 Enrichment

NAME _____ DATE _____ PERIOD _____

Conjugates and Absolute Value

When studying complex numbers, it is often convenient to represent a complex number by a single variable. For example, we might let $z = x + yi$. We denote the conjugate of z by $\bar{z}$. Thus, $\bar{z} = x - yi$. We can define the absolute value of a complex number as follows.

$$|z| = |x + yi| = \sqrt{x^2 + y^2}$$

There are many important relationships involving conjugates and absolute values of complex numbers.

Example Show that $z^2 = z\bar{z}$ for any complex number z.

Let $z = x + yi$. Then,

$$z\bar{z} = (x + yi)(x - yi)$$
$$= x^2 + y^2$$
$$= \left(\sqrt{x^2 + y^2}\right)^2$$
$$= |z|^2$$

Example Show that $\dfrac{\bar{z}}{|z|^2}$ is the multiplicative inverse for any nonzero complex number z.

We know that $|z|^2 = z\bar{z}$. If $z \neq 0$, then we have $z\left(\dfrac{\bar{z}}{|z|^2}\right) = 1$. Thus, $\dfrac{\bar{z}}{|z|^2}$ is the multiplicative inverse of z.

For each of the following complex numbers, find the absolute value and multiplicative inverse.

1. $2i$

   $2; \dfrac{-i}{2}$

2. $-4 - 3i$

   $5; \dfrac{-4 + 3i}{25}$

3. $12 - 5i$

   $13; \dfrac{12 + 5i}{169}$

4. $5 - 12i$

   $13; \dfrac{5 + 12i}{169}$

5. $1 + i$

   $\sqrt{2}; \dfrac{1 - i}{2}$

6. $\sqrt{3} - i$

   $2; \dfrac{\sqrt{3} + i}{4}$

7. $\dfrac{\sqrt{3}}{3} + \dfrac{\sqrt{3}}{3}i$

   $\dfrac{\sqrt{6}}{3}; \dfrac{\sqrt{3} - i\sqrt{3}}{2}$

8. $\dfrac{\sqrt{2}}{2} - \dfrac{\sqrt{2}}{2}i$

   $1; \dfrac{\sqrt{2}}{2} + \dfrac{\sqrt{2}}{2}i$

9. $\dfrac{1}{2} - \dfrac{\sqrt{3}}{2}i$

   $1; \dfrac{1}{2} + \dfrac{\sqrt{3}}{2}i$

T38

Advanced Mathematical Concepts

4-3

Enrichment

The Secret Cubic Equation

You might have supposed that there existed simple formulas for solving higher-degree equations. After all, there is a simple formula for solving quadratic equations. Might there not be formulas for cubics, quartics, and so forth?

There are formulas for some higher-degree equations, but they are certainly not "simple" formulas!

Here is a method for solving a reduced cubic of the form $x^3 + ax + b = 0$ published by Jerome Cardan in 1545. Cardan was given the formula by another mathematician, Tartaglia. Tartaglia made Cardan promise to keep the formula secret, but Cardan published it anyway. He did, however, give Tartaglia the credit for inventing the formula!

Let $R = \left(\frac{1}{2}b\right)^2 + \frac{a^3}{27}$.

Then, $x = \left[-\frac{1}{2}b + \sqrt{R}\right]^{\frac{1}{3}} + \left[-\frac{1}{2}b - \sqrt{R}\right]^{\frac{1}{3}}$

Use Cardan's method to find the real root of each cubic equation. Round answers to three decimal places. Then sketch a graph of the corresponding function on the grid provided.

1. $x^3 + 8x + 3 = 0$ $x = -0.369$

$y = x^3 + 8x + 3$

2. $x^3 - 2x - 5 = 0$ $x = 2.095$

$y = x^3 - 2x - 5$

3. $x^3 + 4x - 1 = 0$ $x = 0.246$

$y = x^3 + 4x - 1$

4. $x^3 - x + 2 = 0$ $x = -1.521$

$y = x^3 - x + 2$

4-4

Enrichment

Scrambled Proofs

The proofs on this page have been scrambled. Number the statements in each proof so that they are in a logical order.

The Remainder Theorem

5 Thus, if a polynomial $f(x)$ is divided by $x - a$, the remainder is $f(a)$.

1 In any problem of division the following relation holds:

dividend = quotient × divisor + remainder. In symbols, this may be written as:

4 Equation (2) tells us that the remainder R is equal to the value $f(a)$; that is, $f(x)$ with a substituted for x.

3 For $x = a$, Equation (1) becomes:

Equation (2) $f(a) = R$,

since the first term on the right in Equation (1) becomes zero.

2 Equation (1) $f(x) = Q(x)(x - a) + R$,

in which $f(x)$ denotes the original polynomial, $Q(x)$ is the quotient, and R the constant remainder. Equation (1) is true for all values of x, and in particular, it is true if we set $x = a$.

The Rational Root Theorem

4 Each term on the left side of Equation (2) contains the factor a; hence, a must be a factor of the term on the right, namely, $-c_n b^n$. But by hypothesis, a is not a factor of b unless $a = \pm 1$. Hence, a is a factor of c_n.

2 $f\left(\frac{a}{b}\right)^n = c_0\left(\frac{a}{b}\right)^n + c_1\left(\frac{a}{b}\right)^{n-1} + \ldots + c_{n-1}\left(\frac{a}{b}\right) + c_n = 0$

6 Thus, in the polynomial equation given in Equation (1), a is a factor of c_n and b is a factor of c_0.

5 In the same way, we can show that b is a factor of c_0.

A polynomial equation with integral coefficients of the form

1 Equation (1) $f(x) = c_0 x^n + c_1 x^{n-1} + \ldots + c_{n-1}x + c_n = 0$

has a rational root $\frac{a}{b}$, where the fraction $\frac{a}{b}$ is reduced to lowest terms. Since $\frac{a}{b}$ is a root of $f(x) = 0$, then

3 If each side of this equation is multiplied by b^n and the last term is transposed, it becomes

Equation (2) $c_0 a^n + c_1 a^{n-1}b + \ldots + c_{n-1}ab^{n-1} = -c_n b^n$

NAME _____ DATE _____ PERIOD _____

4-5 Enrichment

The Bisection Method for Approximating Real Zeros

The bisection method can be used to approximate zeros of polynomial functions like $f(x) = x^3 + x^2 - 3x - 3$. Since $f(1) = -4$ and $f(2) = 3$, there is at least one real zero between 1 and 2. The midpoint of this interval is $\frac{1+2}{2} = 1.5$. Since $f(1.5) = -1.875$, the zero is between 1.5 and 2. The midpoint of this interval is $\frac{1.5+2}{2} = 1.75$. Since $f(1.75) = 0.172$, the zero is between 1.5 and 1.75. $\frac{1.5+1.75}{2} = 1.625$ and $f(1.625) = -0.94$. The zero is between 1.625 and 1.75. The midpoint of this interval is $\frac{1.625+1.75}{2} = 1.6875$. Since $f(1.6875) = -0.41$, the zero is between 1.6875 and 1.75. Therefore, the zero is 1.7 to the nearest tenth. The diagram below summarizes the bisection method.

sign of f(x):   −   −   +   −   +   +
x: 1   1.5   1.625   1.75   2
                    1.6875

Using the bisection method, approximate to the nearest tenth the zero between the two integral values of each function.

1. $f(x) = x^3 - 4x^2 - 11x + 2$, $f(0) = 2$, $f(1) = -12$
   0.2

2. $f(x) = 2x^4 + x^2 - 15$, $f(1) = -12$, $f(2) = 21$
   1.6

3. $f(x) = x^5 - 2x^3 - 12$, $f(1) = -13$, $f(2) = 4$
   1.9

4. $f(x) = 4x^3 - 2x + 7$, $f(-2) = -21$, $f(-1) = 5$
   −1.3

5. $f(x) = 3x^3 - 14x^2 - 27x + 126$, $f(4) = -14$, $f(5) = 16$
   4.7

© Glencoe/McGraw-Hill   T41   Advanced Mathematical Concepts

NAME _____ DATE _____ PERIOD _____

4-6 Enrichment

Inverses of Conditional Statements

In the study of formal logic, the compound statement "*if p, then q*" where *p* and *q* represent any statements, is called a *conditional* or an *implication*. The symbolic representation of a conditional is $p \to q$.

$$p \qquad q$$

If the determinant of a 2×2 matrix is 0, then the matrix does not have an inverse.

If both *p* and *q* are negated, the resulting compound statement is called the **inverse** of the original conditional. The symbolic notation for the negation of *p* is $\sim p$.

Conditional	Inverse	
$p \to q$	$\sim p \to \sim q$	*If a conditional is true, its inverse may be either true or false.*

Example Find the inverse of each conditional.

a. **p**   **q:** If today is Monday, then tomorrow is Tuesday. (true)
   $\sim p \to \sim q$ If today is not Monday, then tomorrow is not Tuesday. (true)

b. **p**   **q** If ABCD is a square, then ABCD is a rhombus. (true)
   $\sim p \to \sim q$ If ABCD is not a square, then ABCD is not a rhombus. (false)

Write the inverse of each conditional.

1. $q \to p$ $\sim q \to \sim p$ 2. $\sim p \to q$ $p \to \sim q$ 3. $\sim q \to \sim p$ $q \to p$

4. If the base angles of a triangle are congruent, then the triangle is isosceles. **If the base angles of a triangle are not congruent, then the triangle is not isosceles.**

5. If the moon is full tonight, then we'll have frost by morning. **If the moon is not full tonight, then we won't have frost by morning.**

Tell whether each conditional is true or false. Then write the inverse of the conditional and tell whether the inverse is true or false.

6. If this is October, then the next month is December. **false; If this is not October, then the next month is not December; false**

7. If $x > 5$, then $x > 6$, $x \in R$. **false; if $x \le 5$, then $x \le 6$, $x \in R$; true**

8. If $x = 0$, then $x^{\frac{1}{2}} = 0$, $x \in R$. **true; if $x \ne 0$, then $x^{\frac{1}{2}} \ne 0$, $x \in R$; true**

9. Make a conjecture about the truth value of an inverse if the conditional is false. **The inverse is sometimes true.**

© Glencoe/McGraw-Hill   T42   Advanced Mathematical Concepts

4-7 Enrichment

Discriminants and Tangents

The diagram at the right shows that through a point P outside of a circle C, there are lines that do not intersect the circle, lines that intersect the circle in one point (tangents), and lines that intersect the circle in two points (secants).

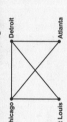

Given the coordinates for P and an equation for the circle C, how can we find the equation of a line tangent to C that passes through P?

Suppose P has coordinates $P(0, 0)$ and $\odot C$ has equation $(x - 4)^2 + y^2 = 4$. Then a line tangent through P has equation $y = mx$ for some real number m.

Thus, if $T(r, s)$ is a point of tangency, then
$s = mr$ and $(r - 4)^2 + s^2 = 4$.
Therefore, $(r - 4)^2 + (mr)^2 = 4$.
$r^2 - 8r + 16 + m^2r^2 = 4$
$(1 + m^2)r^2 - 8r + 16 = 4$
$(1 + m^2)r^2 - 8r + 12 = 0$

The equation above has exactly one real solution for r if the discriminant is 0, that is, when $(-8)^2 - 4(1 + m^2)(12) = 0$. Solve this equation for m and you will find the slopes of the lines through P that are tangent to circle C.

1. a. Refer to the discussion above. Solve $(-8)^2 - 4(1 + m^2)(12) = 0$ to find the slopes of the two lines tangent to circle C through point P. $\pm\dfrac{\sqrt{3}}{3}$

b. Use the values of m from part **a** to find the coordinates of the two points of tangency. $(3, \pm\sqrt{3})$

2. Suppose P has coordinates $(0, 0)$ and circle C has equation $(x + 9)^2 + y^2 = 9$. Let m be the slope of the tangent line to C through P.

a. Find the equations for the lines tangent to circle C through point P. $y = \pm\dfrac{\sqrt{2}}{4}x$

b. Find the coordinates of the points of tangency. $(-8, \pm 2\sqrt{2})$

4-8 Enrichment

Number of Paths

For the figure and adjacency matrix shown at the right, the number of paths or circuits of length 2 can be found by computing the following product.

$$A = \begin{bmatrix} & V_1 & V_2 & V_3 & V_4 \\ V_1 & 0 & 1 & 1 & 1 \\ V_2 & 1 & 0 & 1 & 1 \\ V_3 & 1 & 1 & 0 & 0 \\ V_4 & 1 & 1 & 0 & 0 \end{bmatrix}$$

$$A^2 = AA = \begin{bmatrix} 0 & 1 & 1 & 1 \\ 1 & 0 & 1 & 1 \\ 1 & 1 & 0 & 0 \\ 1 & 1 & 0 & 0 \end{bmatrix} \cdot \begin{bmatrix} 0 & 1 & 1 & 1 \\ 1 & 0 & 1 & 1 \\ 1 & 1 & 0 & 0 \\ 1 & 1 & 0 & 0 \end{bmatrix} = \begin{bmatrix} 3 & 2 & 1 & 1 \\ 2 & 3 & 1 & 1 \\ 1 & 1 & 2 & 2 \\ 1 & 1 & 2 & 2 \end{bmatrix}$$

In row 3 column 4, the entry 2 in the product matrix means that there are 2 paths of length 2 between V_3 and V_4. The paths are $V_3 \to V_1 \to V_4$ and $V_3 \to V_2 \to V_4$. Similarly, in row 1 column 3, the entry 1 means there is only 1 path of length 2 between V_1 and V_3.

Name the paths of length 2 between the following.

1. V_1 and V_2 $V_1, V_3, V_2; V_1, V_4, V_2$

2. V_1 and V_3 V_1, V_2, V_3

3. V_1 and V_1 $V_1, V_2, V_1; V_1, V_3, V_1; V_1, V_4, V_1$

For Exercises 4–6, refer to the figure below.

Detroit   Atlanta
Chicago   St Louis

4. The number of paths of length 3 is given by the product $A \cdot A \cdot A$ or A^3. Find the matrix for paths of length 3.
$$\begin{bmatrix} 4 & 5 & 5 & 5 \\ 5 & 4 & 5 & 5 \\ 5 & 5 & 2 & 2 \\ 5 & 5 & 2 & 2 \end{bmatrix}$$

5. How many paths of length 3 are there between Atlanta and St. Louis? Name them.   **2; A, D, C, S and A, C, D, S**

6. How would you find the number of paths of length 4 between the cities?   **Find Matrix A^4.**

5-1

Enrichment

Reading Mathematics: If and Only If Statements

If p and q are interchanged in a conditional statement so that p becomes the conclusion and q becomes the hypothesis, the new statement, $q \rightarrow p$, is called the **converse** of $p \rightarrow q$.

If $p \rightarrow q$ is true, $q \rightarrow p$ may be either true or false.

Example   **Find the converse of each conditional.**

    a. p q: All squares are rectangles. (true)
        $q \rightarrow p$: All rectangles are squares. (false)

    b. p q: If a function $f(x)$ is increasing on an
        interval I, then for every a and b contained in
        I, $f(a) < f(b)$ whenever $a < b$. (true)
        $q \rightarrow p$: If for every a and b contained in an interval I,
        $f(a) < f(b)$ whenever $a < b$ then function $f(x)$ is
        increasing on I. (true)

In Lesson 3-5, you saw that the two statements in Example 2 can be combined in a single statement using the words "if and only if."

    A function $f(x)$ is increasing on an interval I *if and only if* for
    every a and b contained in I, $f(a) < f(b)$ whenever $a < b$.

The statement "p if and only if q" means that p implies q and q implies p.

State the converse of each conditional. Then tell if the converse is true or false. If it is true, combine the statement and its converse into a single statement using the words "if and only if."

1. All integers are rational numbers.

2. If for all x in the domain of a function $f(x)$, $f(-x) = -f(x)$, then the graph of $f(x)$ is symmetric with respect to the origin.

3. If $f(x)$ and $f^{-1}(x)$ are inverse functions, then $[f \circ f^{-1}](x) = [f^{-1} \circ f](x) = x$.

5-2

Enrichment

Using Right Triangles to Find the Area of Another Triangle

You can find the area of a right triangle by using the formula $A = \frac{1}{2}bh$. In the formula, one leg of the right triangle can be used as the base, and the other leg can be used as the height.

The vertices of a triangle can be represented on the coordinate plane by three ordered pairs. In order to find the area of a general triangle, you can **encase** the triangle in a rectangle as shown in the diagram below.

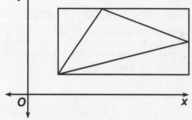

A rectangle is placed around the triangle so that the vertices of the triangle all touch the sides of the rectangle.

Example **Find the area of a triangle whose vertices are $A(-1, 3)$, $B(4, 8)$, and $C(8, 5)$.**

Plot the points and draw the triangle. Encase the triangle in a rectangle whose sides are parallel to the axes, then find the coordinates of the vertices of the rectangle.

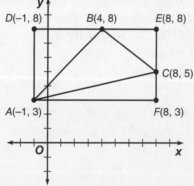

Area $\triangle ABC$ = area $ADEF$ − area $\triangle ADB$ −
   area $\triangle BEC$ − area $\triangle CFA$, where $\triangle ADB$, $\triangle BEC$,
   and $\triangle CFA$ are all right triangles.

Area $\triangle ABC$ = $5(9) - \frac{1}{2}(5)(5) - \frac{1}{2}(4)(3) - \frac{1}{2}(2)(9)$

         = 17.5 square units

Find the area of the triangle having vertices with each set of coordinates.

1. $A(4, 6)$, $B(-1, 2)$, $C(6, -5)$ **2.** $A(-2, -4)$, $B(4, 7)$, $C(6, -1)$

3. $A(4, 2)$, $B(6, 9)$, $C(-1, 4)$ **4.** $A(2, -3)$, $B(6, -8)$, $C(3, 5)$

5-3

Enrichment

Areas of Polygons and Circles

A regular polygon has sides of equal length and angles of equal measure. A regular polygon can be inscribed in or circumscribed about a circle. For n-sided regular polygons, the following area formulas can be used.

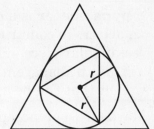

Area of circle $\qquad\qquad\qquad A_C = \pi r^2$

Area of inscribed polygon $\qquad A_I = \dfrac{nr^2}{2} \times \sin \dfrac{360°}{n}$

Area of circumscribed polygon $\quad A_C = nr^2 \times \tan \dfrac{180°}{n}$

Use a calculator to complete the chart below for a unit circle (a circle of radius 1).

	Number of Sides	Area of Inscribed Polygon	Area of Circle less Area of Polygon	Area of Circumscribed Polygon	Area of Polygon less Area of Circle
	3	1.2990381	1.8425545	5.1961524	2.0545598
1.	4				
2.	8				
3.	12				
4.	20				
5.	24				
6.	28				
7.	32				
8.	1000				

9. What number do the areas of the circumscribed and inscribed polygons seem to be approaching as the number of sides of the polygon increases?

5-4

Enrichment

Making and Using a Hypsometer

A **hypsometer** is a device that can be used to measure the height of an object. To construct your own hypsometer, you will need a rectangular piece of heavy cardboard that is at least 7 cm by 10 cm, a straw, transparent tape, a string about 20 cm long, and a small weight that can be attached to the string.

Mark off 1-cm increments along one short side and one long side of the cardboard. Tape the straw to the other short side. Then attach the weight to one end of the string, and attach the other end of the string to one corner of the cardboard, as shown in the figure below. The diagram below shows how your hypsometer should look.

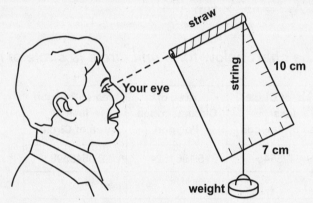

To use the hypsometer, you will need to measure the distance from the base of the object whose height you are finding to where you stand when you use the hypsometer.

Sight the top of the object through the straw. Note where the free-hanging string crosses the bottom scale. Then use similar triangles to find the height of the object.

1. Draw a diagram to illustrate how you can use similar triangles and the hypsometer to find the height of a tall object.

Use your hypsometer to find the height of each of the following.

2. your school's flagpole

3. a tree on your school's property

4. the highest point on the front wall of your school building

5. the goal posts on a football field

6. the hoop on a basketball court

7. the top of the highest window of your school building

8. the top of a school bus

9. the top of a set of bleachers at your school

10. the top of a utility pole near your school

5-5

Enrichment

Disproving Angle Trisection

Most geometry texts state that it is impossible to trisect an arbitrary angle using only a compass and straightedge. This fact has been known since ancient times, but since it is usually stated without proof, some geometry students do not believe it. If the students set out to find a method for trisecting angles, they will probably try the following method. It is based on the familiar construction which allows a segment to be divided into any desired number of congruent segments. You can use inverse trigonometric functions to show that application of the method to the trisection of angles is not valid.

Given: $\angle A$

Claim: $\angle A$ can be trisected using the following method.

Method: Choose point C on one ray of $\angle A$. Through C construct a perpendicular to the other ray, intersecting it at B. Construct M and N, the points that divide $\overline{CB}$ into three congruent segments. Draw $\overline{AM}$ and $\overline{AN}$, which trisect $\angle CAB$ into the congruent angles $\angle 1$, $\angle 2$, and $\angle 3$.

The proposed method has been used to construct the figure below. $CM = MN = NB = 1$. $AB = 5$. Follow the instructions to show that the three angles $\angle 1$, $\angle 2$, and $\angle 3$, are not congruent. Find angle measures to the nearest tenth of a degree.

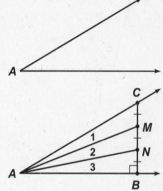

1. Express $m\angle 3$ as an inverse function.

2. Find the measure of $\angle 3$.

3. Write $m\angle MAB$ as an inverse function.

4. Find the measure of $\angle MAB$.

5. Find the measure of $\angle 2$.

6. Find $m\angle CAB$ and use it to find $m\angle 1$.

7. Explain why the proposed method for trisecting an angle fails.

5-6

Enrichment

Triangle Challenge

A surveyor took the following measurements from two irregularly-shaped pieces of land. Some of the lengths and angle measurements are missing. Find all missing lengths and angle measurements. Round lengths to the nearest tenth and angle measurements to the nearest minute.

1.

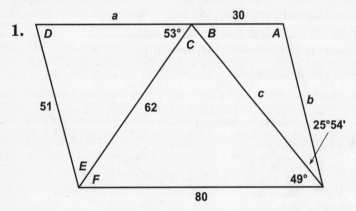

2.

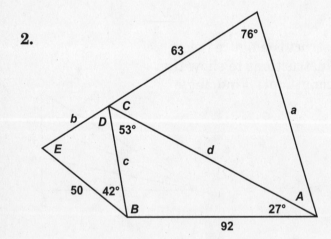

5-7

Enrichment

Spherical Triangles

Spherical trigonometry is an extension of plane trigonometry. Figures are drawn on the surface of a sphere. Arcs of great circles correspond to line segments in the plane. The arcs of three great circles intersecting on a sphere form a spherical triangle. Angles have the same measure as the tangent lines drawn to each great circle at the vertex. Since the sides are arcs, they too can be measured in degrees.

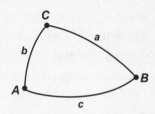

The sum of the sides of a spherical triangle is less than 360°.
The sum of the angles is greater than 180° and less than 540°.
The Law of Sines for spherical triangles is as follows.

$$\frac{\sin a}{\sin A} = \frac{\sin b}{\sin B} = \frac{\sin c}{\sin C}$$

There is also a Law of Cosines for spherical triangles.

$$\cos a = \cos b \cos c + \sin b \sin c \cos A$$
$$\cos b = \cos a \cos c + \sin a \sin c \cos B$$
$$\cos c = \cos a \cos b + \sin a \sin b \cos C$$

Example **Solve the spherical triangle given $a = 72°$, $b = 105°$, and $c = 61°$.**

Use the Law of Cosines.

$$0.3090 = (-0.2588)(0.4848) + (0.9659)(0.8746) \cos A$$
$$\cos A = 0.5143$$
$$A = 59°$$

$$-0.2588 = (0.3090)(0.4848) + (0.9511)(0.8746) \cos B$$
$$\cos B = -0.4912$$
$$B = 119°$$

$$0.4848 = (0.3090)(-0.2588) + (0.9511)(0.9659) \cos C$$
$$\cos C = 0.6148$$
$$C = 52°$$

Check by using the Law of Sines.

$$\frac{\sin 72°}{\sin 59°} = \frac{\sin 105°}{\sin 119°} = \frac{\sin 61°}{\sin 52°} = 1.1$$

Solve each spherical triangle.

1. $a = 56°$, $b = 53°$, $c = 94°$

2. $a = 110°$, $b = 33°$, $c = 97°$

3. $a = 76°$, $b = 110°$, $C = 49°$

4. $b = 94°$, $c = 55°$, $A = 48°$

   Advanced Mathematical Concepts

5-8

Enrichment

The Law of Cosines and the Pythagorean Theorem

The law of cosines bears strong similarities to the Pythagorean Theorem. According to the Law of Cosines, if two sides of a triangle have lengths a and b and if the angle between them has a measure of x, then the length, y, of the third side of the triangle can be found by using the equation

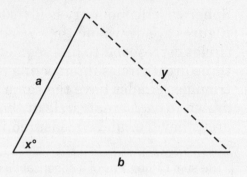

$$y^2 = a^2 + b^2 - 2ab \cos (x°).$$

Answer the following questions to clarify the relationship between the Law of Cosines and the Pythagorean Theorem.

1. If the value of x becomes less and less, what number is $\cos (x°)$ close to?

2. If the value of x is very close to zero but then increases, what happens to $\cos (x°)$ as x approaches 90?

3. If x equals 90, what is the value of $\cos (x°)$? What does the equation of $y^2 = a^2 + b^2 - 2ab \cos (x°)$ simplify to if x equals 90?

4. What happens to the value of $\cos (x°)$ as x increases beyond 90 and approaches 180?

5. Consider some particular values of a and b, say 7 for a and 19 for b. Use a graphing calculator to graph the equation you get by solving $y^2 = 7^2 + 19^2 - 2(7)(19) \cos (x°)$ for y.

   a. In view of the geometry of the situation, what range of values should you use for X on a graphing calculator?

   b. Display the graph and use the TRACE function. What do the maximum and minimum values appear to be for the function?

   c. How do the answers for part **b** relate to the lengths 7 and 19? Are the maximum and minimum values from part **b** ever actually attained in the geometric situation?

NAME _____ DATE _____ PERIOD _____

5-1

Enrichment

Reading Mathematics: If and Only If Statements

If p and q are interchanged in a conditional statement so that p becomes the conclusion and q becomes the hypothesis, the new statement, $q \rightarrow p$, is called the **converse** of $p \rightarrow q$.

If $p \rightarrow q$ is true, $q \rightarrow p$ may be either true or false.

Example Find the converse of each conditional.

a. p q: **All squares are rectangles.** (true)
   $q \rightarrow p$: All rectangles are squares. (false)

b. p q: **If a function $f(x)$ is increasing on an interval I, then for every a and b contained in I, $f(a) < f(b)$ whenever $a < b$.** (true)
   $q \rightarrow p$: If for every a and b contained in an interval I, $f(a) < f(b)$ whenever $a < b$ then function $f(x)$ is increasing on I. (true)

In Lesson 3-5, you saw that the two statements in Example 2 can be combined in a single statement using the words "if and only if."

A function $f(x)$ is increasing on an interval I *if and only if* for every a and b contained in I, $f(a) < f(b)$ whenever $a < b$.

The statement "p if and only if q" means that p implies q and q implies p.

State the converse of each conditional. Then tell if the converse is true or false. If it is true, combine the statement and its converse into a single statement using the words "if and only if."

1. All integers are rational numbers.

All rational numbers are integers; false

2. If for all x in the domain of a function $f(x)$, $f(-x) = -f(x)$, then the graph of $f(x)$ is symmetric with respect to the origin.

If a function has a graph that is symmetric with respect to the origin, then $f(-x) = -f(x)$ for all x in the domain of $f(x)$; true. A function has a graph that is symmetric with respect to the origin if and only if $f(-x) = -f(x)$ for all x in the domain of $f(x)$.

3. If $f(x)$ and $f^{-1}(x)$ are inverse functions, then $[f \circ f^{-1}](x) = [f^{-1} \circ f](x) = x$.

If $[f \circ f^{-1}](x) = [f^{-1} \circ f](x) = x$, then $f(x)$ and $f^{-1}(x)$ are inverse functions; true. Two functions, $f(x)$ and $f^{-1}(x)$, are inverse functions if and only if $[f \circ f^{-1}](x) = [f^{-1} \circ f](x) = x$.

NAME _____ DATE _____ PERIOD _____

5-2

Enrichment

Using Right Triangles to Find the Area of Another Triangle

You can find the area of a right triangle by using the formula $A = \frac{1}{2}bh$. In the formula, one leg of the right triangle can be used as the base, and the other leg can be used as the height.

The vertices of a triangle can be represented on the coordinate plane by three ordered pairs. In order to find the area of a general triangle, you can **encase** the triangle in a rectangle as shown in the diagram below.

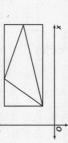

A rectangle is placed around the triangle so that the vertices of the triangle all touch the sides of the rectangle.

Example **Find the area of a triangle whose vertices are $A(-1, 3)$, $B(4, 8)$, and $C(8, 5)$.**

Plot the points and draw the triangle. Encase the triangle in a rectangle whose sides are parallel to the axes, then find the coordinates of the vertices of the rectangle.

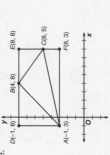

Area $\triangle ABC =$ area $ADEF -$ area $\triangle ADB -$
   area $\triangle BEC -$ area $\triangle CFA$, where $\triangle ADB$, $\triangle BEC$,
   and $\triangle CFA$ are all right triangles.

Area $\triangle ABC = 5(9) - \frac{1}{2}(5)(5) - \frac{1}{2}(4)(3) - \frac{1}{2}(2)(9)$
   $= 17.5$ square units

Find the area of the triangle having vertices with each set of coordinates.

1. $A(4, 6)$, $B(-1, 2)$, $C(6, -5)$ **31.5**   **2.** $A(-2, -4)$, $B(4, 7)$, $C(6, -1)$ **35**

3. $A(4, 2)$, $B(6, 9)$, $C(-1, 4)$ **19.5**   **4.** $A(2, -3)$, $B(6, -8)$, $C(3, 5)$ **18.5**

5-3

NAME _____ **DATE** _____ **PERIOD** _____

Enrichment

Areas of Polygons and Circles

A regular polygon has sides of equal length and angles of equal measure. A regular polygon can be inscribed in or circumscribed about a circle. For n-sided regular polygons, the following area formulas can be used.

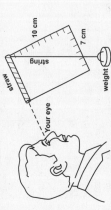

Area of circle $A_C = \pi r^2$

Area of inscribed polygon $A_I = \dfrac{nr^2}{2} \times \sin \dfrac{360°}{n}$

Area of circumscribed polygon $A_C = nr^2 \times \tan \dfrac{180°}{n}$

Use a calculator to complete the chart below for a unit circle (a circle of radius 1).

	Number of Sides	Area of Inscribed Polygon	Area of Circle less Area of Polygon	Area of Circumscribed Polygon	Area of Polygon less Area of Circle
	3	1.2990381	1.8425545	5.1961524	2.0545598
1.	4	2	1.1415927	4	0.8584073
2.	8	2.8284271	0.3131655	3.3137085	0.1721158
3.	12	3	0.1415927	3.2153903	0.0737977
4.	20	3.0901699	0.0514227	3.1676888	0.0260962
5.	24	3.1058285	0.0357641	3.1596599	0.0180673
6.	28	3.1152931	0.0262996	3.1548423	0.0132497
7.	32	3.1214452	0.0201475	3.1517249	0.0101323
8.	1000	3.1415720	0.0000207	3.1416030	0.0000103

9. What number do the areas of the circumscribed and inscribed polygons seem to be approaching as the number of sides of the polygon increases?
π

5-4

NAME _____ **DATE** _____ **PERIOD** _____

Enrichment

Making and Using a Hypsometer

A **hypsometer** is a device that can be used to measure the height of an object. To construct your own hypsometer, you will need a rectangular piece of heavy cardboard that is at least 7 cm by 10 cm, a straw, transparent tape, a string about 20 cm long, and a small weight that can be attached to the string.

Mark off 1-cm increments along one short side and one long side of the cardboard. Tape the straw to the other short side. Then attach the weight to one end of the string, and attach the other end of the string to one corner of the cardboard, as shown in the figure below. The diagram below shows how your hypsometer should look.

10 cm · string · 7 cm · straw · Your eye · weight

To use the hypsometer, you will need to measure the distance from the base of the object whose height you are finding to where you stand when you use the hypsometer.

Sight the top of the object through the straw. Note where the free-hanging string crosses the bottom scale. Then use similar triangles to find the height of the object.

1. Draw a diagram to illustrate how you can use similar triangles and the hypsometer to find the height of a tall object.
See students' diagrams.

Use your hypsometer to find the height of each of the following. **See students' work.**

2. your school's flagpole
3. a tree on your school's property
4. the highest point on the front wall of your school building
5. the goal posts on a football field
6. the hoop on a basketball court
7. the top of the highest window of your school building
8. the top of a school bus
9. the top of a set of bleachers at your school
10. the top of a utility pole near your school

5-5

Enrichment

Disproving Angle Trisection

Most geometry texts state that it is impossible to trisect an arbitrary angle using only a compass and straightedge. This fact has been known since ancient times, but since it is usually stated without proof, some geometry students do not believe it. If the students set out to find a method for trisecting angles, they will probably try the following method. It is based on the familiar construction which allows a segment to be divided into any desired number of congruent segments. You can use inverse trigonometric functions to show that application of the method to the trisection of angles is not valid.

Given: ∠A

Claim: ∠A can be trisected using the following method.

Method: Choose point C on one ray of ∠A.
Through C construct a perpendicular to the other ray, intersecting it at B.
Construct M and N, the points that divide $\overline{CB}$ into three congruent segments. Draw $\overline{AM}$ and $\overline{AN}$, which trisect ∠CAB into the congruent angles ∠1, ∠2, and ∠3.

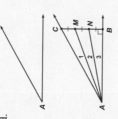

The proposed method has been used to construct the figure below. $CM = MN = NB = 1$, $AB = 5$. Follow the instructions to show that the three angles ∠1, ∠2, and ∠3, are not congruent. Find angle measures to the nearest tenth of a degree.

1. Express $m∠3$ as an inverse function.

   $m∠3 = \arctan\dfrac{1}{5}$

2. Find the measure of ∠3.

   $m∠3 ≈ 11.3°$

3. Write $m∠MAB$ as an inverse function. $m∠MAB = \arctan\dfrac{2}{5}$

4. Find the measure of ∠MAB. $m∠MAB ≈ 21.8°$

5. Find the measure of ∠2. $m∠2 ≈ 10.5°$

6. Find $m∠CAB$ and use it to find $m∠1$. $m∠1 ≈ 9.2°$

7. Explain why the proposed method for trisecting an angle fails.
   The tangent function is not linear. The ratio of the measures of two angles is not equal to the ratio of the tangents of the angles.

5-6

Enrichment

Triangle Challenge

A surveyor took the following measurements from two irregularly-shaped pieces of land. Some of the lengths and angle measurements are missing. Find all missing lengths and angle measurements. Round lengths to the nearest tenth and angle measurements to the nearest minute.

1.

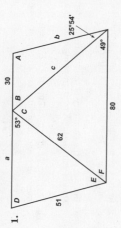

$a ≈ 49.5$; $b ≈ 52.7$; $c ≈ 66.7$
$A ≈ 103°58'$; $B ≈ 50°8'$; $C ≈ 76°52'$;
$D ≈ 76°8'$; $E ≈ 50°52'$; $F ≈ 54°8'$

2.

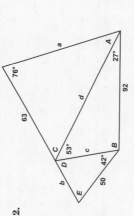

$a ≈ 110.8$; $b ≈ 40.5$; $c ≈ 52.3$; $d ≈ 113.4$
$A ≈ 32°37'$; $B ≈ 100°$; $C ≈ 71°23'$;
$D ≈ 55°37'$; $E ≈ 82°23'$;

5-7

Enrichment

Spherical Triangles

Spherical trigonometry is an extension of plane trigonometry. Figures are drawn on the surface of a sphere. Arcs of great circles correspond to line segments in the plane. The arcs of three great circles intersecting on a sphere form a spherical triangle. Angles have the same measure as the tangent lines drawn to each great circle at the vertex. Since the sides are arcs, they too can be measured in degrees.

The sum of the sides of a spherical triangle is less than 360°.
The sum of the angles is greater than 180° and less than 540°.
The Law of Sines for spherical triangles is as follows.

$$\frac{\sin a}{\sin A} = \frac{\sin b}{\sin B} = \frac{\sin c}{\sin C}$$

There is also a Law of Cosines for spherical triangles.

$$\cos a = \cos b \cos c + \sin b \sin c \cos A$$
$$\cos b = \cos a \cos c + \sin a \sin c \cos B$$
$$\cos c = \cos a \cos b + \sin a \sin b \cos C$$

Example   Solve the spherical triangle given $a = 72°$, $b = 105°$, and $c = 61°$.

Use the Law of Cosines.

$0.3090 = (-0.2588)(0.4848) + (0.9659)(0.8746) \cos A$
$\cos A = 0.5143$
$\qquad A = 59°$

$-0.2588 = (0.3090)(0.4848) + (0.9511)(0.8746) \cos B$
$\cos B = -0.4912$
$\qquad B = 119°$

$0.4848 = (0.3090)(-0.2588) + (0.9511)(0.9659) \cos C$
$\cos C = 0.6148$
$\qquad C = 52°$

Check by using the Law of Sines.

$$\frac{\sin 72°}{\sin 59°} \stackrel{?}{=} \frac{\sin 105°}{\sin 119°} \stackrel{?}{=} \frac{\sin 61°}{\sin 52°} = 1.1$$

Solve each spherical triangle.

1. $a = 56°$, $b = 53°$, $c = 94°$
   $A = 41°$, $B = 39°$, $C = 128°$
2. $a = 110°$, $b = 33°$, $c = 97°$
   $A = 116°$, $B = 31°$, $C = 71°$
3. $a = 76°$, $b = 110°$, $C = 49°$
   $A = 59°$, $B = 124°$, $c = 59°$
4. $b = 94°$, $c = 55°$, $A = 48°$
   $a = 60°$, $B = 121°$, $C = 45°$

5-8

Enrichment

The Law of Cosines and the Pythagorean Theorem

The law of cosines bears strong similarities to the Pythagorean Theorem. According to the Law of Cosines, if two sides of a triangle have lengths a and b and if the angle between them has a measure of x, then the length, y, of the third side of the triangle can be found by using the equation

$$y^2 = a^2 + b^2 - 2ab \cos (x°).$$

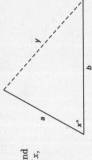

Answer the following questions to clarify the relationship between the Law of Cosines and the Pythagorean Theorem.

1. If the value of x becomes less and less, what number is $\cos (x°)$ close to? **1**

2. If the value of x is very close to zero but then increases, what happens to $\cos (x°)$ as x approaches 90? **decreases, approaches 0**

3. If x equals 90, what is the value of $\cos (x°)$? What does the equation of $y^2 = a^2 + b^2 - 2ab \cos (x°)$ simplify to if x equals 90? **0, $y^2 = a^2 + b^2$**

4. What happens to the value of $\cos (x°)$ as x increases beyond 90 and approaches 180? **decreases to −1**

5. Consider some particular values of a and b, say 7 for a and 19 for b. Use a graphing calculator to graph the equation you get by solving $y^2 = 7^2 + 19^2 - 2(7)(19) \cos (x°)$ for y. **See students' graphs.**

   a. In view of the geometry of the situation, what range of values should you use for X on a graphing calculator?
   Xmin = 0; Xmax = 360

   b. Display the graph and use the TRACE function. What do the maximum and minimum values appear to be for the function?
   See students' graphs; Ymin = 12, Ymax = 26

   c. How do the answers for part **b** relate to the lengths 7 and 19? Are the maximum and minimum values from part **b** ever actually attained in the geometric situation?
   min = (19 − 7); max = (19 + 7); no

6-1

Enrichment

Angle Measurement: The Mil

The **mil** is an angle measurement used by the military. The military uses the mil because it is easy and accurate for measurements involving long distances. Determining the angle to use to hit a target in long-range artillery firing is one example.

In ordinary measurement, 1 mil = $\frac{1}{1000}$ inch. For angle measurement, this means that an angle measuring one mil would subtend an arc of length 1 unit, with the entire circle being 1000 mils around. So, the circumference becomes $2\pi \cdot 1000$, or about 6283.18 units. The military rounds this number to 6400 for convenience. Thus,

$$1 \text{ mil} = \frac{1}{6400} \text{ revolution around a circle}$$

So, 6400 mil = 2π radians.

Example   **Change 3200 mil to radian measure.**

$$\frac{6400 \text{ mil}}{3200 \text{ mil}} = \frac{2\pi}{x}$$
$$x = \pi$$

Change each mil measurement to radian measure.

1. 1600 mil

2. 800 mil

3. 4800 mil

4. 2400 mil

Change each radian measure to mil measurement. Round your answers to the nearest tenth, where necessary.

5. $\frac{\pi}{8}$

6. $\frac{5\pi}{4}$

7. $\frac{\pi}{12}$

8. $\frac{\pi}{6}$

6-2

Enrichment

Angular Acceleration

An object traveling in a circular path experiences linear velocity and angular velocity. It may also experience **angular acceleration**. Angular acceleration is the rate of change in angular velocity with respect to time.

At time $t = 0$, there is an **initial angular velocity**. At the end of time t, there is a **final angular velocity**. Then the angular acceleration α of the object can be defined as

$$\alpha = \frac{\text{final angular velocity} - \text{initial angular velocity}}{\text{time}}.$$

The units for angular acceleration are usually rad/s^2 or rev/min^2.

Example   **A record has a small chip on its edge. If the record begins at rest and then goes to 45 revolutions per minute in 30 seconds, what is the angular acceleration of the chip?**

The record starts at rest, so the initial angular velocity is 0. The final angular velocity is 45 revolutions/minute. Thus, the angular acceleration is

$$\alpha = \frac{45 - 0}{\frac{1}{2}}$$

$$= 90 \text{ rev/min}^2.$$

Solve.

1. The record in the example was playing at 45 rev/min. A power surge lasting 2 seconds caused the record to speed up to 80 rev/min. What was the angular acceleration of the chip then?

2. When a car enters a curve in the road, the tires are turning at an angular velocity of 50 ft/s. At the end of the curve, the angular velocity of the tires is 60 ft/s. If the curve is an arc of a circle with radius 2000 feet and central angle $\theta = \frac{\pi}{4}$, and the car travels at a constant linear velocity of 40 mph, what is the angular acceleration?

6-3

Enrichment

Periodic Phenomena

Periodic phenomena are common in everyday life. The first graph portrays the loudness of a foghorn as a function of time. The sound rises quickly to its loudest level, holds for about two seconds, drops off a little more quickly than it rose, then remains quiet for about four seconds before beginning a new cycle. The **period** of the cycle is eight seconds.

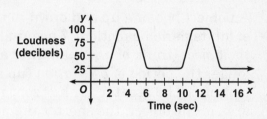

1. Give three examples of periodic phenomena, together with a typical period for each.

2. Sunrise is at 8 A.M. on December 21 in Function Junction and at 6 A.M. on June 21. Sketch a two-year graph of sunrise times in Function Junction.

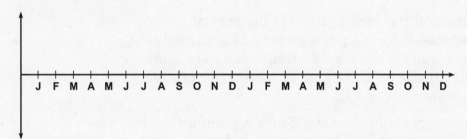

State whether each function is periodic. If it is, give its period.

3.

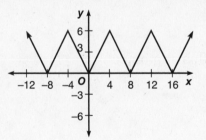

4.

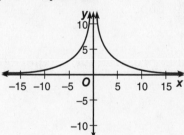

5.

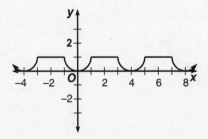

6.

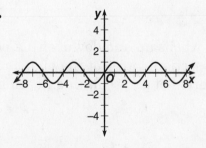

7. A student graphed a periodic function with a period of n. The student then translated the graph c units to the right and obtained the original graph. Describe the relationship between c and n.

6-4

Enrichment

Mass of a Floating Object

An object bobbing up and down in the water exhibits periodic motion. The greater the mass of the object (think of an ocean liner and a buoy), the longer the period of *oscillation* (up and down motion). The greater the horizontal cross-sectional area of the object, the shorter the period. If you know the period and the cross-sectional area, you can find the mass of the object.

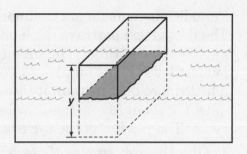

Imagine a point on the waterline of a stationary floating object. Let y represent the vertical position of the point above or below the waterline when the object begins to oscillate. ($y = 0$ represents the waterline.) If we neglect air and water resistance, the equation of motion of the object is

$$y = A \sin\left(\sqrt{\frac{9800C}{M}}\, t \right),$$

where A is the amplitude of the oscillation, C is the horizontal cross-sectional area of the object in square meters, M is the mass of the object in kilograms, and t is the elapsed time since the beginning of the oscillation. The argument of the sine is measured in radians and y is measured in meters.

1. A 4-kg log has a cross-sectional area of 0.2 m². A point on the log has a maximum displacement of 0.4 m above or below the water line. Find the vertical position of the point 5 seconds after the log begins to bob.

2. Find an expression for the period of an oscillating floating object.

3. Find the period of the log described in Exercise 1.

4. A buoy bobs up and down with a period of 0.6 seconds. The mean cross-sectional area of the buoy is 1.3 m². Use your expression for the period of an oscillating floating object to find the mass of the buoy.

5. Write an equation of motion of the buoy described in Exercise 4 if the amplitude is 0.45 m.

6-5

Enrichment

Translating Graphs of Trigonometric Functions

In Lesson 3-2, you learned how changes in a polynomial function affect the graph of the function. If $a > 0$, the graph of $y \pm a = f(x)$ translates the graph of $f(x)$ downward or upward a units. The graph of $y = f(x \pm a)$ translates the graph of $f(x)$ left or right a units. These results apply to trigonometric functions as well.

Example 1   **Graph $y = 3 \sin 2\theta$, $y = 3 \sin 2(\theta - 30°)$, and $y + 4 = 3 \sin 2\theta$ on the same coordinate axes.**

Obtain the graph of $y = 3 \sin 2(\theta - 30°)$ by translating the graph of $y = 3 \sin 2\theta$ 30° to the right. Obtain the graph of $y + 4 = 3 \sin 2\theta$ by translating the graph of $y = 3 \sin 2\theta$ downward 4 units.

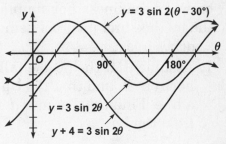

Example 2   **Graph one cycle of $y = 6 \cos (5\theta + 80°) + 2$.**

Step 1   Isolate the term involving the trigonometric function.
$y - 2 = 6 \cos (5\theta + 80°)$

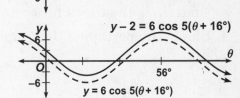

Step 2   Factor out the coefficient of θ.
$y - 2 = 6 \cos 5(\theta + 16°)$

Step 3   Sketch $y = 6 \cos 5\theta$.

Step 4   Translate $y = 6 \cos 5\theta$ to obtain the graph of $y - 2 = 6 \cos 5(\theta + 16°)$.

Sketch these graphs on the same coordinate axes.

1. $y = 3 \sin 2(\theta + 45°)$

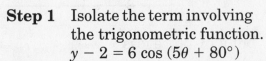

2. $y + 5 = 3 \sin 2(\theta + 90°)$

Graph one cycle of each curve on the same coordinate axes.

3. $y = 6 \cos (4\theta + 360°) + 3$

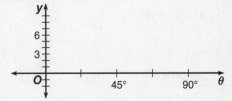

4. $y = 6 \cos 4\theta + 3$

6-6

Enrichment

Approximating π

During the eighteenth century, the French scientist
George de Buffon developed an experimental method for
approximating π using probability. Buffon's method
requires tossing a needle randomly onto an array of
parallel and equidistant lines. If the needle intersects a
line, it is a "hit." Otherwise, it is a "miss." The length of
the needle must be less than or equal to the distance
between the lines. For simplicity, we will demonstrate
the method and its proof using a 2-inch needle and lines
2 inches apart.

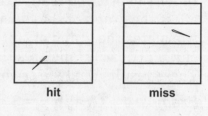

hit   miss

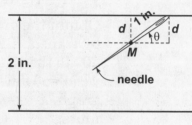

1. Assume that the needle falls at an angle θ with the
   horizontal, and that the tip of the needle just touches
   a line. Find the distance d of the needle's midpoint M
   from the line.

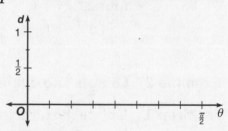

2. Graph the function that relates
   θ and d for $0 \le \theta \le \dfrac{\pi}{2}$.

3. Suppose that the needle lands at an angle θ but a distance less
   than d. Is the toss a hit or a miss?

4. Shade the portion of the graph containing points that represent
   hits.

5. The area A under the curve you have drawn between $x = a$
   and $x = b$ is given by $A = \cos a - \cos b$. Find the area of the
   shaded region of your graph.

6. Draw a rectangle around the graph in Exercise 2 for $d = 0$ to 1
   and $\theta = 0$ to $\dfrac{\pi}{2}$. The area of the rectangle is $1 \times \dfrac{\pi}{2} = \dfrac{\pi}{2}$.

   The probability P of a hit is the area of the set of all "hit" points
   divided by the area of the set of all possible landing points.
   Complete the final fraction:

   $$P = \frac{\text{hit points}}{\text{all points}} = \frac{\text{shaded area}}{\text{total area}} = \frac{1}{\dfrac{\pi}{2}}.$$

7. Use the first and last expressions in the above equation to write π
   in terms of P.

8. The Italian mathematician Lazzerini made 3408 needle tosses,
   scoring 2169 hits. Calculate Lazzerini's experimental value of π.

6-7

Enrichment

Reading Mathematics: Understanding Graphs

Technically, a graph is a set of points where pairs of points are connected by a set of segments and/or arcs. If the graph is the graph of an equation, the set of points consists of those points whose coordinates satisfy the equation.

Practically speaking, to see a graph this way is as useless as seeing a word as a collection of letters. The full meaning of a graph and its value as a tool of understanding can be grasped only by viewing the graph as a whole. It is more useful to see a graph not just as a set of points, but as a picture of a function. The following suggestions, based on the idea of a graph as a picture, may help you reach a deeper understanding of the meaning of graphs.

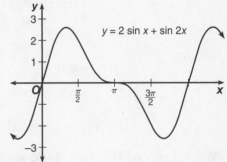

a. **Read the equation of the graph as a title.** Get a sense of the behavior of the function by describing its characteristics to yourself in general terms. The graph shown depicts the function $y = 2 \sin x + \sin 2x$. In the region shown, the function increases, decreases, then increases again. It looks a bit like a sine curve but with steeper sides, sharper peaks and valleys, and a point of inflection at $x = \pi$.

b. **Focus on the details.** View them not as isolated or unrelated facts but as traits of the function that distinguish it from other functions. Think of the graph as a point that moves through the coordinate plane sketching a profile of the function. Use the function to guess the behavior of the graph beyond the region shown. The graph of $y = 2 \sin x + \sin 2x$ appears to exhibit point symmetry about the point of inflection $x = \pi$. It intersects the x-axis at 0, π, and 2π, and reaches a relative maximum of $y \approx 2.6$ at $x = \dfrac{\pi}{3}$ and a relative minimum of $y \approx -2.6$ at $x = \dfrac{5\pi}{3}$. Since the maximum value of $2 \sin x$ is 2 and the maximum value of $\sin 2x$ is 1, $y = 2 \sin x + \sin 2x$ will never exceed 3.

Discuss the graph at the right. Use the above discussion as a model. You should discuss the graph's shape, critical points, and symmetry.

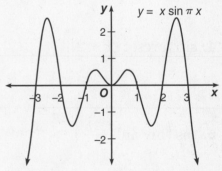

Enrichment

Algebraic Trigonometric Expressions

In Lesson 6-4, you learned how to use right triangles to find exact values of functions of inverse trigonometric functions. In calculus it is sometimes necessary to convert trigonometric expressions into algebraic ones. You can use the same method to do this.

Example **Write $\sin (\arccos 4x)$ as an algebraic expression in x.**

Let $y = \arccos 4x$ and let $z =$ side opposite $\angle y$.

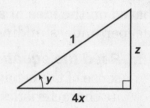

$$(4x)^2 + z^2 = 1^2 \qquad \textit{Pythagorean Theorem}$$
$$16x^2 + z^2 = 1$$
$$z^2 = 1 - 16x^2$$
$$z = \sqrt{1 - 16x^2} \quad \textit{Take the square root of each side.}$$
$$\sin y = \frac{z}{1} \qquad \textit{Definition of sine}$$
$$\sin y = \sqrt{1 - 16x^2}$$

Therefore, $\sin (\arccos 4x) = \sqrt{1 - 16x^2}$.

Write each of the following as an algebraic expression in x .

1. $\cot (\arccos 4x)$

2. $\sin (\arctan x)$

3. $\cos \left(\arctan \dfrac{x}{3} \right)$

4. $\sin [\arcsec (x - 2)]$

5. $\cos \left(\arcsin \dfrac{x - h}{r} \right)$

Answers (Lessons 6-1 and 6-2)

6-1 Enrichment

Angle Measurement: The Mil

The **mil** is an angle measurement used by the military. The military uses the mil because it is easy and accurate for measurements involving long distances. Determining the angle to use to hit a target in long-range artillery firing is one example.

In ordinary measurement, 1 mil = $\frac{1}{1000}$ inch. For angle measurement, this means that an angle measuring one mil would subtend an arc of length 1 unit, with the entire circle being 1000 mils around. So, the circumference becomes $2\pi \cdot 1000$, or about 6283.18 units. The military rounds this number to 6400 for convenience. Thus,

$$1 \text{ mil} = \frac{1}{6400} \text{ revolution around a circle}$$

So, 6400 mil = 2π radians.

Example   Change 3200 mil to radian measure.

$$\frac{6400 \text{ mil}}{3200 \text{ mil}} = \frac{2\pi}{x}$$
$$x = \pi$$

Change each mil measurement to radian measure.

1. 1600 mil $\dfrac{\pi}{2}$

2. 800 mil $\dfrac{\pi}{4}$

3. 4800 mil $\dfrac{3\pi}{2}$

4. 2400 mil $\dfrac{3\pi}{4}$

Change each radian measure to mil measurement. Round your answers to the nearest tenth, where necessary.

5. $\dfrac{\pi}{8}$ **400 mil**

6. $\dfrac{5\pi}{4}$ **4000 mil**

7. $\dfrac{\pi}{12}$ **266.7 mil**

8. $\dfrac{\pi}{6}$ **533.3 mil**

6-2 Enrichment

Angular Acceleration

An object traveling in a circular path experiences linear velocity and angular velocity. It may also experience **angular acceleration**. Angular acceleration is the rate of change in angular velocity with respect to time.

At time $t = 0$, there is an **initial angular velocity**. At the end of time t, there is a **final angular velocity**. Then the angular acceleration α of the object can be defined as

$$\alpha = \frac{\text{final angular velocity} - \text{initial angular velocity}}{\text{time}}.$$

The units for angular acceleration are usually rad/s^2 or rev/min^2.

Example   **A record has a small chip on its edge. If the record begins at rest and then goes to 45 revolutions per minute in 30 seconds, what is the angular acceleration of the chip?**

The record starts at rest, so the initial angular velocity is 0. The final angular velocity is 45 revolutions/minute. Thus, the angular acceleration is

$$\alpha = \frac{45 - 0}{\frac{1}{2}}$$

$$= 90 \text{ rev/min}^2.$$

Solve.

1. The record in the example was playing at 45 rev/min. A power surge lasting 2 seconds caused the record to speed up to 80 rev/min. What was the angular acceleration of the chip then?
1050 rev/min^2

2. When a car enters a curve in the road, the tires are turning at an angular velocity of 50 ft/s. At the end of the curve, the angular velocity of the tires is 60 ft/s. If the curve is an arc of a circle with radius 2000 feet and central angle $\theta = \frac{\pi}{4}$, and the car travels at a constant linear velocity of 40 mph, what is the angular acceleration?
0.37 ft/s^2

6-3

Enrichment

Periodic Phenomena

Periodic phenomena are common in everyday life. The first graph portrays the loudness of a foghorn as a function of time. The sound rises quickly to its loudest level, holds for about two seconds, drops off a little more quickly than it rose, then remains quiet for about four seconds before beginning a new cycle. The **period** of the cycle is eight seconds.

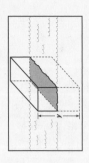

1. Give three examples of periodic phenomena, together with a typical period for each.

sample answers: the cycle of the moon (28 days), the swinging of a pendulum (one second), the cycle of the seasons (one year)

2. Sunrise is at 8 A.M. on December 21 in Function Junction and at 6 A.M. on June 21. Sketch a two-year graph of sunrise times in Function Junction.

State whether each function is periodic. If it is, give its period.

3.

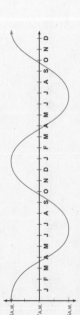

yes; 8

4.

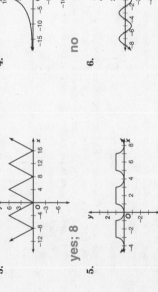

no

5.

yes; 4

6.

yes; 4

7. A student graphed a periodic function with a period of n. The student then translated the graph c units to the right and obtained the original graph. Describe the relationship between c and n. **c is a multiple of n.**

T63

Advanced Mathematical Concepts

6-4

Enrichment

Mass of a Floating Object

An object bobbing up and down in the water exhibits periodic motion. The greater the mass of the object (think of an ocean liner and a buoy), the longer the period of *oscillation* (up and down motion). The greater the horizontal cross-sectional area of the object, the shorter the period. If you know the period and the cross-sectional area, you can find the mass of the object.

Imagine a point on the waterline of a stationary floating object. Let y represent the vertical position of the point above or below the waterline when the object begins to oscillate. ($y = 0$ represents the waterline.) If we neglect air and water resistance, the equation of motion of the object is

$$y = A \sin\left(\sqrt{\frac{9800C}{M}}\, t\right),$$

where A is the amplitude of the oscillation, C is the horizontal cross-sectional area of the object in square meters, M is the mass of the object in kilograms, and t is the elapsed time since the beginning of the oscillation. The argument of the sine is measured in radians and y is measured in meters.

1. A 4-kg log has a cross-sectional area of 0.2 m². A point on the log has a maximum displacement of 0.4 m above or below the water line. Find the vertical position of the point 5 seconds after the log begins to bob.

≈ 0.26 below the water line

2. Find an expression for the period of an oscillating floating object.

$$p = 2\pi\sqrt{\frac{M}{9800C}}$$

3. Find the period of the log described in Exercise 1.

≈ 0.28 seconds

4. A buoy bobs up and down with a period of 0.6 seconds. The mean cross-sectional area of the buoy is 1.3 m². Use your expression for the period of an oscillating floating object to find the mass of the buoy.

≈ 116.2 kg

5. Write an equation of motion of the buoy described in Exercise 4 if the amplitude is 0.45 m. **$y = 0.45 \sin 10.47t$**

T64

Advanced Mathematical Concepts

6-5

NAME _____ DATE _____ PERIOD _____

Enrichment

Translating Graphs of Trigonometric Functions

In Lesson 3-2, you learned how changes in a polynomial function affect the graph of the function. If $a > 0$, the graph of $y \pm a = f(x)$ translates the graph of $f(x)$ downward or upward a units. The graph of $y = f(x \pm a)$ translates the graph of $f(x)$ left or right a units. These results apply to trigonometric functions as well.

Example 1 Graph $y = 3 \sin 2\theta$, $y = 3 \sin 2(\theta - 30°)$, and $y + 4 = 3 \sin 2\theta$ on the same coordinate axes.

Obtain the graph of $y = 3 \sin 2(\theta - 30°)$ by translating the graph of $y = 3 \sin 2\theta$ 30° to the right. Obtain the graph of $y + 4 = 3 \sin 2\theta$ by translating the graph of $y = 3 \sin 2\theta$ downward 4 units.

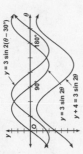

$y = 3 \sin 2(\theta - 30°)$
$y = 3 \sin 2\theta$
$y + 4 = 3 \sin 2\theta$

Example 2 Graph one cycle of $y = 6 \cos (5\theta + 80°) + 2$.

Step 1 Isolate the term involving the trigonometric function.
$y - 2 = 6 \cos (5\theta + 80°)$

Step 2 Factor out the coefficient of θ.
$y - 2 = 6 \cos 5(\theta + 16°)$

Step 3 Sketch $y = 6 \cos 5\theta$.

Step 4 Translate $y = 6 \cos 5\theta$ to obtain the graph of $y - 2 = 6 \cos 5(\theta + 16°)$.

$y = 6 \cos 5\theta$
$y - 2 = 6 \cos 5(\theta + 16°)$
$y - 2 = 6 \cos 5(\theta + 16°)$
$y = 6 \cos 5\theta$

Sketch these graphs on the same coordinate axes.

1. $y = 3 \sin 2(\theta + 45°)$

2. $y + 5 = 3 \sin 2(\theta + 90°)$

$y = 3 \sin 2(\theta + 45°)$
$y + 5 = 3 \sin 2(\theta + 90°)$

Graph one cycle of each curve on the same coordinate axes.

3. $y = 6 \cos (4\theta + 360°) + 3$

4. $y = 6 \cos 4\theta + 3$

$y = 6 \cos(4\theta + 360°) + 3$
$y = 6 \cos 4\theta + 3$

6-6

NAME _____ DATE _____ PERIOD _____

Enrichment

Approximating π

During the eighteenth century, the French scientist George de Buffon developed an experimental method for approximating π using probability. Buffon's method requires tossing a needle randomly onto an array of parallel and equidistant lines. If the needle intersects a line, it is a "hit." Otherwise, it is a "miss." The length of the needle must be less than or equal to the distance between the lines. For simplicity, we will demonstrate the method and its proof using a 2-inch needle and lines 2 inches apart.

hit

miss

needle

M

2 in.

1. Assume that the needle falls at an angle θ with the horizontal, and that the tip of the needle just touches a line. Find the distance d of the needle's midpoint M from the line. **sin θ**

2. Graph the function that relates θ and d for $0 \leq \theta \leq \frac{\pi}{2}$.

3. Suppose that the needle lands at an angle θ but a distance less than d. Is the toss a hit or a miss? **a hit**

4. Shade the portion of the graph containing points that represent hits. **Students should shade the lower portion of the graph.**

5. The area A under the curve you have drawn between $x = a$ and $x = b$ is given by $A = \cos a - \cos b$. Find the area of the shaded region of your graph. **1**

6. Draw a rectangle around the graph in Exercise 2 for $d = 0$ to 1 and $\theta = 0$ to $\frac{\pi}{2}$. The area of the rectangle is $1 \times \frac{\pi}{2} = \frac{\pi}{2}$.

The probability P of a hit is the area of the set of all "hit" points divided by the area of the set of all possible landing points. Complete the final fraction:

$P = \dfrac{\text{hit points}}{\text{all points}} = \dfrac{\text{shaded area}}{\text{total area}} = \dfrac{1}{\frac{\pi}{2}}$ $a = \dfrac{2}{\pi}$

7. Use the first and last expressions in the above equation to write π in terms of P. $\pi = \dfrac{2}{P}$

8. The Italian mathematician Lazzerini made 3408 needle tosses, scoring 2169 hits. Calculate Lazzerini's experimental value of π. **3.1424619**

NAME _____ DATE _____ PERIOD _____

6-7 Enrichment

Reading Mathematics: Understanding Graphs

Technically, a graph is a set of points where pairs of points are connected by a set of segments and/or arcs. If the graph is the graph of an equation, the set of points consists of those points whose coordinates satisfy the equation.

Practically speaking, to see a graph this way is as useless as seeing a word as a collection of letters. The full meaning of a graph and its value as a tool of understanding can be grasped only by viewing the graph as a whole. It is more useful to see a graph not just as a set of points, but as a picture of a function. The following suggestions, based on the idea of a graph as a picture, may help you reach a deeper understanding of the meaning of graphs.

a. **Read the equation of the graph as a title.** Get a sense of the behavior of the function by describing its characteristics to yourself in general terms. The graph shown depicts the function $y = 2 \sin x + \sin 2x$. In the region shown, the function increases, decreases, then increases again. It looks a bit like a sine curve but with steeper sides, sharper peaks and valleys, and a point of inflection at $x = \pi$.

b. **Focus on the details.** View them not as isolated or unrelated facts but as traits of the function that distinguish it from other functions. Think of the graph as a point that moves through the coordinate plane sketching a profile of the function. Use the function to guess the behavior of the graph beyond the region shown. The graph of $y = 2 \sin x + \sin 2x$ appears to exhibit point symmetry about the point of inflection $x = \pi$. It intersects the x-axis at 0, π, and 2π, and reaches a relative maximum of $y \approx 2.6$ at $x = \frac{\pi}{3}$ and a relative minimum of $y \approx -2.6$ at $x = \frac{5\pi}{3}$. Since the maximum value of $2 \sin x$ is 2 and the maximum value of $\sin 2x$ is 1, $y = 2 \sin x + \sin 2x$ will never exceed 3.

$y = 2 \sin x + \sin 2x$

Discuss the graph at the right. Use the above discussion as a model. You should discuss the graph's shape, critical points, and symmetry.

Sample answer: The graph depicts $y = x \sin \pi x$. The region shown has the shape of a W with a dip in the center peak. It reaches relative minima of $y \approx -1.5$ at about $x = \pm 1.5$ and of $y = 0$ at the origin. It reaches relative maxima of about 0.5 at about $x = \pm 0.5$. The graph also shows relative maxima of about 2.5 at about $x = \pm 2.5$. The graph appears to be symmetric about the y-axis.

$y = x \sin \pi x$

NAME _____ DATE _____ PERIOD _____

6-8 Enrichment

Algebraic Trigonometric Expressions

In Lesson 6-4, you learned how to use right triangles to find exact values of functions of inverse trigonometric functions. In calculus it is sometimes necessary to convert trigonometric expressions into algebraic ones. You can use the same method to do this.

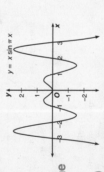

Example Write sin (arccos $4x$) as an algebraic expression in x.

Let $y = $ arccos $4x$ and let $z = $ side opposite $\angle y$.

$$(4x)^2 + z^2 = 1^2 \quad \textit{Pythagorean Theorem}$$
$$16x^2 + z^2 = 1$$
$$z^2 = 1 - 16x^2 \quad \textit{Take the square root of each side.}$$
$$z = \sqrt{1 - 16x^2}$$
$$\sin y = \frac{z}{1} \quad \textit{Definition of sine}$$
$$\sin y = \sqrt{1 - 16x^2}$$

Therefore, sin (arccos $4x$) $= \sqrt{1 - 16x^2}$.

Write each of the following as an algebraic expression in x.

1. cot (arccos $4x$)
$$\frac{4x}{\sqrt{1 - 16x^2}}$$

2. sin (arctan x)
$$\frac{x}{\sqrt{x^2 + 1}}$$

3. cos $\left(\text{arctan } \frac{x}{3}\right)$
$$\frac{3}{\sqrt{x^2 + 9}}$$

4. sin [arcsec $(x - 2)$]
$$\frac{\sqrt{x^2 - 4x + 3}}{x - 2}$$

5. cos $\left(\text{arcsin } \frac{x - h}{r}\right)$
$$\frac{\sqrt{r^2 - x^2 + 2xh - h^2}}{r}$$

7-1

Enrichment

The Physics of Soccer

Recall from Lesson 7-1 that the formula for the maximum height h of a projectile is $h = \dfrac{v_0^2 \sin^2 \theta}{2g}$, where θ is the measure of the angle of elevation in degrees, v_0 is the initial velocity in feet per second, and g is the acceleration due to gravity in feet per second squared.

Solve. Give answers to the nearest tenth.

1. A soccer player kicks a ball at an initial velocity of 60 ft/s and an angle of elevation of 40°. The acceleration due to gravity is 32 ft/s². Find the maximum height reached by the ball.

2. With what initial velocity must you kick a ball at an angle of 35° in order for it to reach a maximum height of 20 ft?

The distance d that a projected object travels is given by the formula $d = \dfrac{2v_0^2 \sin \theta \cos \theta}{g}$.

3. Find the distance traveled by the ball described in Exercise 1.

In order to kick a ball the greatest possible distance at a given initial velocity, a soccer player must maximize $d = \dfrac{2v_0^2 \sin \theta \cos \theta}{g}$. Since 2, v_0, and g are constants, this means the player must maximize $\sin \theta \cos \theta$.

sin 0°cos 0°	= sin 90°cos 90° = 0
sin 10°cos 10°	= sin 80°cos 80° = 0.1710
sin 20°cos 20°	= sin 70°cos 70° = 0.3214

4. Use the patterns in the table to hypothesize a value of θ for which $\sin \theta \cos \theta$ will be maximal. Use a calculator to check your hypothesis. At what angle should the player kick the ball to achieve the greatest distance?

7-2

Enrichment

Building from 1 = 1

By starting with the most fundamental identity of all, $1 = 1$, you can create new identities as complex as you would like them to be.

First, think of ways to write 1 using trigonometric identities. Some examples are the following.

$$1 = \cos A \sec A$$

$$1 = \csc^2 A - \cot^2 A$$

$$1 = \frac{\cos (A + 360°)}{\cos (360° - A)}$$

Choose two such expressions and write a new identity.

$$\cos A \sec A = \csc^2 A - \cot^2 A$$

Now multiply the terms of the identity by the terms of another identity of your choosing, preferably one that will allow some simplification upon multiplication.

$$\cos A \sec A = \csc^2 A - \cot^2 A$$
$$\times \qquad \frac{\sin A}{\cos A} = \tan A$$
$$\overline{\sin A \sec A = \tan A \csc^2 A - \cot A}$$

Beginning with 1 = 1, create two trigonometric identities.

1. _____

2. _____

Verify that each of the identities you created is an identity.

3. _____   4. _____

   _____   _____

   _____   _____

   _____   _____

   _____   _____

   _____   _____

Advanced Mathematical Concepts

7-3

Enrichment

Identities for the Products of Sines and Cosines

By adding the identities for the sines of the sum and difference of the measures of two angles, a new identity is obtained.

$$\sin (\alpha + \beta) = \sin \alpha \cos \beta + \cos \alpha \sin \beta$$
$$\sin (\alpha - \beta) = \sin \alpha \cos \beta - \cos \alpha \sin \beta$$

$$(\textbf{\textit{i}}) \ \sin (\alpha + \beta) + \sin (\alpha - \beta) = 2 \sin \alpha \cos \beta$$

This new identity is useful for expressing certain products as sums.

Example   **Write $\sin 3\theta \cos \theta$ as a sum.**

In the right side of identity ($\textbf{\textit{i}}$) let $\alpha = 3\theta$ and $\beta = \theta$ so that $2 \sin 3\theta \cos \theta = \sin (3\theta + \theta) + \sin (3\theta - \theta)$.
Thus, $\sin 3\theta \cos\theta = \frac{1}{2} \sin 4\theta + \frac{1}{2} \sin 2\theta$.

By subtracting the identities for $\sin (\alpha + \beta)$ and $\sin (\alpha - \beta)$, you obtain a similar identity for expressing a product as a difference.

$$(\textbf{\textit{ii}}) \ \sin (\alpha + \beta) - \sin (\alpha - \beta) = 2 \cos \alpha \sin \beta$$

Example   **Verify the identity $\frac{\cos 2x \sin x}{\sin 2x \cos x} = \frac{(\sin 3x - \sin x)^2}{\sin^2 3x - \sin^2 x}$.**

In the right sides of identities ($\textbf{\textit{i}}$) and ($\textbf{\textit{ii}}$) let $\alpha = 2x$ and $\beta = x$. Then write the following quotient.

$$\frac{2 \cos 2x \sin x}{2 \sin 2x \cos x} = \frac{\sin (2x + x) - \sin (2x - x)}{\sin (2x + x) + \sin (2x - x)}$$

By simplifying and multiplying by the conjugate, the identity is verified.

$$\frac{\cos 2x \sin x}{\sin 2x \cos x} = \frac{\sin 3x - \sin x}{\sin 3x + \sin x} \cdot \frac{\sin 3x - \sin x}{\sin 3x - \sin x}$$

$$= \frac{(\sin 3x - \sin x)^2}{\sin^2 3x - \sin^2 x}$$

Complete.

1. Use the identities for $\cos (\alpha + \beta)$ and $\cos (\alpha - \beta)$ to find identities for expressing the products $2 \cos \alpha \cos \beta$ and $2 \sin \alpha \sin \beta$ as a sum or difference.

2. Find the value of $\sin 105° \cos 75°$ by using the identity above.

7-4

Enrichment

Reading Mathematics: Using Examples

Most mathematics books, including this one, use examples to illustrate the material of each lesson. Examples are chosen by the authors to show how to apply the methods of the lesson and to point out places where possible errors can arise.

1. Explain the purpose of Example 1c in Lesson 7-4.

2. Explain the purpose of Example 3 in Lesson 7-4.

3. Explain the purpose of Example 4 in Lesson 7-4.

To make the best use of the examples in a lesson, try following this procedure:

a. When you come to an example, stop. Think about what you have just read. If you don't understand it, reread the previous section.

b. Read the example problem. Then instead of reading the solution, try solving the problem yourself.

c. After you have solved the problem or gone as far as you can go, study the solution given in the text. Compare your method and solution with those of the authors. If necessary, find out where you went wrong. If you don't understand the solution, reread the text or ask your teacher for help.

4. Explain the advantage of working an example yourself over simply reading the solution given in the text.

Enrichment

The Spectrum

In some ways, light behaves as though it were composed of waves. The wavelength of visible light ranges from about 4×10^{-5} cm for violet light to about 7×10^{-5} cm for red light.

As light passes through a medium, its velocity depends upon the wavelength of the light. The greater the wavelength, the greater the velocity. Since white light, including sunlight, is composed of light of varying wavelengths, waves will pass through the medium at an infinite number of different speeds. The index of refraction n of the medium is defined by $n = \frac{c}{v}$, where c is the velocity of light in a vacuum (3×10^{10} cm/s), and v is the velocity of light in the medium. As you can see, the index of refraction of a medium is not a constant. It depends on the wavelength and the velocity of light passing through it. (The index of refraction of diamond given in the lesson is an average.)

1. For all media, $n > 1$. Is the speed of light in a medium greater than or less than c? Explain.

2. A beam of violet light travels through water at a speed of 2.234×10^{10} cm/s. Find the index of refraction of water for violet light.

The diagram shows why a prism splits white light into a spectrum. Because they travel at different velocities in the prism, waves of light of different colors are refracted different amounts.

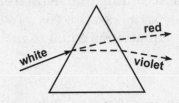

3. Beams of red and violet light strike crown glass at an angle of 20°. Use Snell's Law to find the difference between the angles of refraction of the two beams.

   violet light: $n = 1.531$ red light: $n = 1.513$

7-6

Enrichment

Slopes of Perpendicular Lines

The derivation of the normal form of a linear equation uses this familiar theorem, first stated in Lesson 1-6: Two nonvertical lines are perpendicular if and only if the slope of one is the negative reciprocal of the slope of the other.

You can use trigonometric identities to prove that if lines are perpendicular, then their slopes are negative reciprocals of each other.

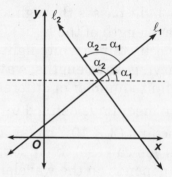

ℓ_1 and ℓ_2 are perpendicular lines.
α_1 and α_2 are the angles that ℓ_1 and ℓ_2, respectively, make with the horizontal.
Let m_1 = slope of ℓ_1
$\quad m_2$ = slope of ℓ_2

Complete the following exercises to prove that $m_1 = -\dfrac{1}{m_2}$.

1. Explain why $m_1 = \tan \alpha_1$ and $m_2 = \tan \alpha_2$.

2. According to the difference identity for the cosine function,
$\cos(\alpha_2 - \alpha_1) = \cos \alpha_2 \cos \alpha_1 + \sin \alpha_2 \sin \alpha_1$. Explain why the left side of the equation is equal to zero.

3. $\cos \alpha_2 \cos \alpha_1 + \sin \alpha_2 \sin \alpha_1 = 0$
$$\sin \alpha_2 \sin \alpha_1 = -\cos \alpha_2 \cos \alpha_1$$
$$\frac{\sin \alpha_1}{\cos \alpha_1} = -\frac{\cos \alpha_2}{\sin \alpha_2}$$

Complete using the tangent function. _____ = _____

Complete, using m_1 and m_2. _____ = _____

78

Advanced Mathematical Concepts

Enrichment

Deriving the Point-Line Distance

Line ℓ has the equation $Ax + By + C = 0$.
Answer these questions to derive the formula given
in Lesson 7-7 for the distance from $P(x_1, y_1)$ to ℓ .

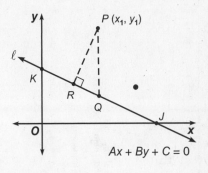

1. Use the equation of the line to find the
coordinates of J and K, the x- and y-intercepts
of ℓ .

2. $\overline{PQ}$ is a vertical segment from P to ℓ. Find the x-coordinate of Q.

3. Since Q is on ℓ, its coordinates must satisfy the equation of ℓ.
Use your answer to Exercise 2 to find the y-coordinate of Q.

4. Find PQ by finding the difference between the y-coordinates of P
and Q. Write your answer as a fraction.

5. Triangle KJO is a right triangle. Use your answers to Exercise 1
and the Pythagorean Theorem to find KJ. Simplify.

6. Since $\angle Q \cong \angle K$, $\triangle JKO \sim \triangle PQR$.

$$\frac{PR}{OJ} = \frac{PQ}{KJ}$$

Use your answers to Exercises 1, 4, and 5 to find PR, the distance
from P to ℓ. Simplify.

Answers (Lessons 7-1 and 7-2)

7-1 Enrichment

The Physics of Soccer

Recall from Lesson 7-1 that the formula for the maximum height h of a projectile is $h = \frac{v_0^2 \sin^2 \theta}{2g}$, where θ is the measure of the angle of elevation in degrees, v_0 is the initial velocity in feet per second, and g is the acceleration due to gravity in feet per second squared.

Solve. Give answers to the nearest tenth.

1. A soccer player kicks a ball at an initial velocity of 60 ft/s and an angle of elevation of 40°. The acceleration due to gravity is 32 ft/s². Find the maximum height reached by the ball.

   23.2 ft

2. With what initial velocity must you kick a ball at an angle of 35° in order for it to reach a maximum height of 20 ft?

   62.4 ft/s

The distance d that a projected object travels is given by the formula $d = \frac{2v_0^2 \sin \theta \cos \theta}{g}$.

3. Find the distance traveled by the ball described in Exercise 1.

   110.8 ft

In order to kick a ball the greatest possible distance at a given initial velocity, a soccer player must maximize $d = \frac{2v_0^2 \sin \theta \cos \theta}{g}$. Since 2, v_0, and g are constants, this means the player must maximize $\sin \theta \cos \theta$.

sin 0°cos 0°	= sin 90°cos 90° = 0
sin 10°cos 10°	= sin 80°cos 80° = 0.1710
sin 20°cos 20°	= sin 70°cos 70° = 0.3214

4. Use the patterns in the table to hypothesize a value of θ for which $\sin \theta \cos \theta$ will be maximal. Use a calculator to check your hypothesis. At what angle should the player kick the ball to achieve the greatest distance?

   45°

7-2 Enrichment

Building from 1 = 1

By starting with the most fundamental identity of all, $1 = 1$, you can create new identities as complex as you would like them to be.

First, think of ways to write 1 using trigonometric identities. Some examples are the following.

$$1 = \cos A \sec A$$
$$1 = \csc^2 A - \cot^2 A$$
$$1 = \frac{\cos (A + 360°)}{\cos (360° - A)}$$

Choose two such expressions and write a new identity.

$$\cos A \sec A = \csc^2 A - \cot^2 A$$

Now multiply the terms of the identity by the terms of another identity of your choosing, preferably one that will allow some simplification upon multiplication.

$$\begin{array}{r} \cos A \sec A = \csc^2 A - \cot^2 A \\ \times \quad \frac{\sin A}{\cos A} = \tan A \\ \hline \sin A \sec A = \tan A \csc^2 A - \cot A \end{array}$$

Beginning with 1 = 1, create two trigonometric identities. **Answers will vary.**

1. _____

2. _____

Verify that each of the identities you created is an identity.

3. _____

4. _____

7-3

NAME _____ DATE _____ PERIOD _____

Enrichment

Identities for the Products of Sines and Cosines

By adding the identities for the sines of the sum and difference of the measures of two angles, a new identity is obtained.

$$\sin(\alpha + \beta) = \sin\alpha\cos\beta + \cos\alpha\sin\beta$$
$$\sin(\alpha - \beta) = \sin\alpha\cos\beta - \cos\alpha\sin\beta$$
$$(i)\ \sin(\alpha + \beta) + \sin(\alpha - \beta) = 2\sin\alpha\cos\beta$$

This new identity is useful for expressing certain products as sums.

Example **Write $\sin 3\theta \cos\theta$ as a sum.**

In the right side of identity (i) let $\alpha = 3\theta$ and $\beta = \theta$ so that $2\sin 3\theta\cos\theta = \sin(3\theta + \theta) + \sin(3\theta - \theta)$.

Thus, $\sin 3\theta\cos\theta = \frac{1}{2}\sin 4\theta + \frac{1}{2}\sin 2\theta$.

By subtracting the identities for $\sin(\alpha + \beta)$ and $\sin(\alpha - \beta)$, you obtain a similar identity for expressing a product as a difference.

$(ii)\ \sin(\alpha + \beta) - \sin(\alpha - \beta) = 2\cos\alpha\sin\beta$

Example **Verify the identity $\dfrac{\cos 2x \sin x}{\sin 2x \cos x} = \dfrac{(\sin 3x - \sin x)^2}{\sin^2 3x - \sin^2 x}$.**

In the right sides of identities (i) and (ii) let $\alpha = 2x$ and $\beta = x$. Then write the following quotient.

$$\frac{2\cos 2x \sin x}{2\sin 2x \cos x} = \frac{\sin(2x + x) - \sin(2x - x)}{\sin(2x + x) + \sin(2x - x)}$$

By simplifying and multiplying by the conjugate, the identity is verified.

$$\frac{\cos 2x \sin x}{\sin 2x \cos x} = \frac{\sin 3x - \sin x}{\sin 3x + \sin x} \cdot \frac{\sin 3x - \sin x}{\sin 3x - \sin x}$$
$$= \frac{(\sin 3x - \sin x)^2}{\sin^2 3x - \sin^2 x}$$

Complete.

1. Use the identities for $\cos(\alpha + \beta)$ and $\cos(\alpha - \beta)$ to find identities for expressing the products $2\cos\alpha\cos\beta$ and $2\sin\alpha\sin\beta$ as a sum or difference.

$\cos(\alpha + \beta) = \cos\alpha\cos\beta - \sin\alpha\sin\beta$
$2\cos\alpha\cos\beta = \cos(\alpha + \beta) + \cos(\alpha - \beta)$
$\cos(\alpha - \beta) = \cos\alpha\cos\beta + \sin\alpha\sin\beta$
$2\sin\alpha\sin\beta = \cos(\alpha - \beta) - \cos(\alpha + \beta)$

2. Find the value of $\sin 105° \cos 75°$ by using the identity above.

$\sin 105° \cos 75° = \frac{1}{2}(\sin 180° + \sin 30°)$
$= \frac{1}{2}(0 + \frac{1}{2}) = \frac{1}{4}$ or 0.25

7-4

NAME _____ DATE _____ PERIOD _____

Enrichment

Reading Mathematics: Using Examples

Most mathematics books, including this one, use examples to illustrate the material of each lesson. Examples are chosen by the authors to show how to apply the methods of the lesson and to point out places where possible errors can arise.

1. Explain the purpose of Example 1c in Lesson 7-4.
   to illustrate how to use the double-angle identity for the tangent; to show how to find tan θ from information already known

2. Explain the purpose of Example 3 in Lesson 7-4.
   to illustrate how a double-angle identity can be applied to a real-world situation

3. Explain the purpose of Example 4 in Lesson 7-4.
   to illustrate the verification of a trigonometric identity involving a double-angle identity

To make the best use of the examples in a lesson, try following this procedure:

   a. When you come to an example, stop. Think about what you have just read. If you don't understand it, reread the previous section.

   b. Read the example problem. Then instead of reading the solution, try solving the problem yourself.

   c. After you have solved the problem or gone as far as you can go, study the solution given in the text. Compare your method and solution with those of the authors. If necessary, find out where you went wrong. If you don't understand the solution, reread the text or ask your teacher for help.

4. Explain the advantage of working an example yourself over simply reading the solution given in the text.
   Sample answer: This method checks your understanding of the material rather than your ability to follow the authors' logic. By allowing errors to arise in your solution, it helps you find areas of misunderstanding. Then it gives you a method for correcting your errors and checking your solution.

7-5

Enrichment

The Spectrum

In some ways, light behaves as though it were composed of waves. The wavelength of visible light ranges from about 4×10^{-5} cm for violet light to about 7×10^{-5} cm for red light.

As light passes through a medium, its velocity depends upon the wavelength of the light. The greater the wavelength, the greater the velocity. Since white light, including sunlight, is composed of light of varying wavelengths, waves will pass through the medium at an infinite number of different speeds. The index of refraction n of the medium is defined by $n = \frac{c}{v}$, where c is the velocity of light in a vacuum (3×10^{10} cm/s), and v is the velocity of light in the medium. As you can see, the index of refraction of a medium is not a constant. It depends on the wavelength and the velocity of light passing through it. (The index of refraction of diamond given in the lesson is an average.)

1. For all media, $n > 1$. Is the speed of light in a medium greater than or less than c? Explain.
less than; $v = \frac{c}{n}$. Since $n > 1$, $v < c$.

2. A beam of violet light travels through water at a speed of 2.234×10^{10} cm/s. Find the index of refraction of water for violet light.
1.343

The diagram shows why a prism splits white light into a spectrum. Because they travel at different velocities in the prism, waves of light of different colors are refracted different amounts.

3. Beams of red and violet light strike crown glass at an angle of 20°. Use Snell's Law to find the difference between the angles of refraction of the two beams.
violet light: $n = 1.531$ red light: $n = 1.513$
about 0.16°

7-6

Enrichment

Slopes of Perpendicular Lines

The derivation of the normal form of a linear equation uses this familiar theorem, first stated in Lesson 1-6: Two nonvertical lines are perpendicular if and only if the slope of one is the negative reciprocal of the slope of the other.

You can use trigonometric identities to prove that if lines are perpendicular, then their slopes are negative reciprocals of each other.

ℓ_1 and ℓ_2 are perpendicular lines.
α_1 and α_2 are the angles that ℓ_1 and ℓ_2, respectively, make with the horizontal.
Let m_1 = slope of ℓ_1
$\quad m_2$ = slope of ℓ_2

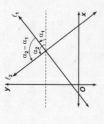

Complete the following exercises to prove that $m_1 = -\frac{1}{m_2}$.

1. Explain why $m_1 = \tan \alpha_1$ and $m_2 = \tan \alpha_2$.
$$\tan \alpha = \frac{\text{change in } y}{\text{change in } x} = m$$

2. According to the difference identity for the cosine function, $\cos (\alpha_2 - \alpha_1) = \cos \alpha_2 \cos \alpha_1 + \sin \alpha_2 \sin \alpha_1$. Explain why the left side of the equation is equal to zero.
$$\alpha_2 - \alpha_1 = 90° \text{ and } \cos 90° = 0.$$

3. $\cos \alpha_2 \cos \alpha_1 + \sin \alpha_2 \sin \alpha_1 = 0$
$$\sin \alpha_2 \sin \alpha_1 = -\cos \alpha_2 \cos \alpha_1$$
$$\frac{\sin \alpha_1}{\cos \alpha_1} = -\frac{\cos \alpha_2}{\sin \alpha_2}$$

Complete using the tangent function.
$$\tan \alpha_1 = -\frac{1}{\tan \alpha_2}$$

Complete, using m_1 and m_2.
$$m_1 = -\frac{1}{m_2}$$

NAME _____ DATE _____ PERIOD _____

7-7 Enrichment

Deriving the Point-Line Distance

Line ℓ has the equation $Ax + By + C = 0$.
Answer these questions to derive the formula given
in Lesson 7-7 for the distance from $P(x_1, y_1)$ to ℓ.

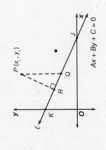

1. Use the equation of the line to find the
coordinates of J and K, the x- and y-intercepts
of ℓ.

$$J\left(-\frac{C}{A}, 0\right), K\left(0, -\frac{C}{B}\right)$$

2. $\overline{PQ}$ is a vertical segment from P to ℓ. Find the x-coordinate of Q.

$$x_1$$

3. Since Q is on ℓ, its coordinates must satisfy the equation of ℓ.
Use your answer to Exercise 2 to find the y-coordinate of Q.

$$-\frac{A}{B}x_1 - \frac{C}{B}$$

4. Find PQ by finding the difference between the y-coordinates of P
and Q. Write your answer as a fraction.

$$\left|\frac{Ax_1 + By_1 + C}{B}\right|$$

5. Triangle KJO is a right triangle. Use your answers to Exercise 1
and the Pythagorean Theorem to find KJ. Simplify.

$$\left|\frac{C\sqrt{A^2 + B^2}}{AB}\right|$$

6. Since $\angle Q \cong \angle K$, $\triangle JKO \sim \triangle PQR$.

$$\frac{PR}{OJ} = \frac{PQ}{KJ}$$

Use your answers to Exercises 1, 4, and 5 to find PR, the distance
from P to ℓ. Simplify.

$$PR = \frac{|Ax_1 + By_1 + C|}{\sqrt{A^2 + B^2}}$$

T79

Advanced Mathematical Concepts

8-1

Enrichment

More Than Two Forces Acting on an Object

Three or more forces may work on an object at one time. Each of these forces can be represented by a vector. To find the resultant vector that acts upon the object, you can add the individual vectors two at a time.

Example   A force of 80 N acts on an object at an angle of 70° at the same time that a force of 100 N acts at an angle of 150°. A third force of 120 N acts at an angle of 180°. Find the magnitude and direction of the resultant force acting on the object.

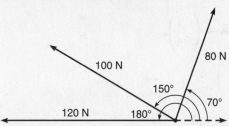

Add two vectors at a time. The order in which the vectors are added does not matter.

Add the 80-N vector and the 100-N vector first.

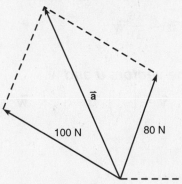

Now add the resulting vector to the 120-N vector.

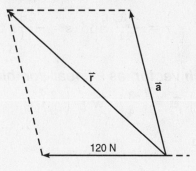

The resultant force is 219 N, with an amplitude of 145°.

Find the magnitude and amplitude of the resultant force acting on each object.

1. One force acts with 40 N at 50° on an object. A second force acts with 100 N at 110°. A third force acts with 10 N at 150°. Find the magnitude and amplitude of the resultant force.

2. One force acts with 75 N at 45°. A second force acts with 90 N at 90°. A third force acts with 120 N at 170°. Find the magnitude and amplitude of the resultant force.

8-2

Enrichment

Basis Vectors

The expression $\vec{v} = r\vec{u} + s\vec{w}$, the sum of two vectors each multiplied by scalars, is called a **linear combination** of the vectors $\vec{u}$ and $\vec{w}$.

Linear Combination Theorem in v_2	Every vector $\vec{v} \in v_2$ can be written as a linear combination of any two nonparallel vectors $\vec{u}$ and $\vec{w}$. The vectors $\vec{u}$ and $\vec{w}$ are said to form a basis for the vector space v_2 which contains all vectors having 1 column and 2 rows.

Example Write the vector $\vec{v} = \begin{pmatrix} -2 \\ 5 \end{pmatrix}$ as a linear combination of

the vectors $\vec{u} = \begin{pmatrix} 2 \\ 3 \end{pmatrix}$ and $\vec{w} = \begin{pmatrix} 1 \\ -4 \end{pmatrix}$.

$$\begin{pmatrix} -2 \\ 5 \end{pmatrix} = r\begin{pmatrix} 2 \\ 3 \end{pmatrix} + s\begin{pmatrix} 1 \\ -4 \end{pmatrix} = \begin{pmatrix} 2r + s \\ 3r - 4s \end{pmatrix}$$

$-2 = 2r + s$
$5 = 3r - 4s$

Solving the system of equations yields the solution

$r = -\dfrac{3}{11}$ and $s = -\dfrac{16}{11}$. So, $\vec{v} = -\dfrac{3}{11}\vec{u} - \dfrac{16}{11}\vec{w}$.

Write each vector as a linear combination of the vectors $\vec{u}$ and $\vec{w}$.

1. $\vec{v} = \begin{pmatrix} 1 \\ 5 \end{pmatrix}$, $\vec{u} = \begin{pmatrix} -3 \\ 4 \end{pmatrix}$, $\vec{w} = \begin{pmatrix} 2 \\ -2 \end{pmatrix}$
2. $\vec{v} = \begin{pmatrix} 1 \\ -1 \end{pmatrix}$, $\vec{u} = \begin{pmatrix} 2 \\ 3 \end{pmatrix}$, $\vec{w} = \begin{pmatrix} \frac{1}{4} \\ 1 \end{pmatrix}$

3. $\vec{v} = \begin{pmatrix} \frac{1}{2} \\ -1 \end{pmatrix}$, $\vec{u} = \begin{pmatrix} 0 \\ 4 \end{pmatrix}$, $\vec{w} = \begin{pmatrix} \frac{1}{2} \\ 1 \end{pmatrix}$
4. $\vec{v} = \begin{pmatrix} 2 \\ -7 \end{pmatrix}$, $\vec{u} = \begin{pmatrix} -1 \\ -3 \end{pmatrix}$, $\vec{w} = \begin{pmatrix} 4 \\ 2 \end{pmatrix}$

86

8-3

Enrichment

Basis Vectors in Three-Dimensional Space

The expression $\vec{v} = r\vec{u} + s\vec{w} + t\vec{z}$, the sum of two vectors each multiplied by scalars, is called a **linear combination** of the vectors $\vec{u}$, $\vec{w}$, and $\vec{z}$.

Every vector $\vec{v} \in v_3$ can be written as a linear combination of any three nonparallel vectors. The three nonparallel vectors are said to form a **basis** for v_3, which contains all vectors having 1 column and 3 rows.

Example   Write the vector $\vec{v} = \begin{pmatrix} -1 \\ -4 \\ 3 \end{pmatrix}$ as a linear combination of

the vectors $\vec{u} = \begin{pmatrix} 1 \\ 3 \\ 1 \end{pmatrix}$, $\vec{w} = \begin{pmatrix} 1 \\ -2 \\ 1 \end{pmatrix}$, and $\vec{z} = \begin{pmatrix} -1 \\ -1 \\ 1 \end{pmatrix}$.

$$\begin{pmatrix} -1 \\ -4 \\ 3 \end{pmatrix} = r\begin{pmatrix} 1 \\ 3 \\ 1 \end{pmatrix} + s\begin{pmatrix} 1 \\ -2 \\ 1 \end{pmatrix} + t\begin{pmatrix} -1 \\ -1 \\ 1 \end{pmatrix} = \begin{pmatrix} r + s - t \\ 3r - 2s - t \\ r + s + t \end{pmatrix}$$

$-1 = r + s - t$
$-4 = 3r - 2s - t$
$\ \ 3 = r + s + t$

Solving the system of equations yields the solution $r = 0$, $s = 1$, and $t = 2$. So, $\vec{v} = \vec{w} + 2\vec{z}$.

Write each vector as a linear combination of the vectors $\vec{u}$, $\vec{w}$, and $\vec{z}$.

1. $\vec{v} = \begin{pmatrix} -6 \\ -2 \\ 2 \end{pmatrix}$, $\vec{u} = \begin{pmatrix} 1 \\ 1 \\ 0 \end{pmatrix}$, $\vec{w} = \begin{pmatrix} 1 \\ 0 \\ 1 \end{pmatrix}$, and $\vec{z} = \begin{pmatrix} 0 \\ 1 \\ 1 \end{pmatrix}$

2. $\vec{v} = \begin{pmatrix} 5 \\ -2 \\ 0 \end{pmatrix}$, $\vec{u} = \begin{pmatrix} 1 \\ -2 \\ 3 \end{pmatrix}$, $\vec{w} = \begin{pmatrix} -1 \\ 0 \\ 1 \end{pmatrix}$, and $\vec{z} = \begin{pmatrix} 4 \\ 2 \\ -1 \end{pmatrix}$

3. $\vec{v} = \begin{pmatrix} 1 \\ -1 \\ 2 \end{pmatrix}$, $\vec{u} = \begin{pmatrix} 1 \\ 2 \\ -1 \end{pmatrix}$, $\vec{w} = \begin{pmatrix} 2 \\ 2 \\ 1 \end{pmatrix}$, and $\vec{z} = \begin{pmatrix} 1 \\ 0 \\ 1 \end{pmatrix}$

8-4

Enrichment

Vector Equations

Let $\vec{a}$, $\vec{b}$, and $\vec{c}$ be fixed vectors. The equation $f(x) = \vec{a} - 2x\vec{b} + x^2\vec{c}$ defines a vector function of x. For the values of x shown, the assigned vectors are given below.

x		-2	-1	0	1	2
$f(x)$	$\vec{a} + 4\vec{b} + 4\vec{c}$	$\vec{a} + 2\vec{b} + \vec{c}$	$\vec{a}$	$\vec{a} - 2\vec{b} + \vec{c}$	$\vec{a} - 4\vec{b} + 4\vec{c}$

If $\vec{a} = \langle 0, 1 \rangle$, $\vec{b} = \langle 1, 1 \rangle$, and $\vec{c} = \langle 2, -2 \rangle$, the resulting vectors for the values of x are as follows.

x	-2	-1	0	1	2
$f(x)$	$\langle 12, -3 \rangle$	$\langle 4, 1 \rangle$	$\langle 0, 1 \rangle$	$\langle 0, -3 \rangle$	$\langle 4, -11 \rangle$

For each of the following, complete the table of resulting vectors.

1. $f(x) = x^3\vec{a} - 2x^2\vec{b} + 3x\vec{c}$
   $\vec{a} = \langle 1, 1 \rangle$ $\vec{b} = \langle 2, 3 \rangle$ $\vec{c} = \langle 3, -1 \rangle$

x	$f(x)$
-1	
0	
1	
2	

2. $f(x) = 2x^2\vec{a} + 3x\vec{b} - 5\vec{c}$
   $\vec{a} = \langle 0, 1, 1 \rangle$ $\vec{b} = \langle 1, 0, 1 \rangle$ $\vec{c} = \langle 1, 1, 0 \rangle$

x	$f(x)$
-2	
-1	
0	
1	

3. $f(x) = x^2\vec{c} + 3x\vec{a} - 4\vec{b}$
   $\vec{a} = \langle 1, 1, 1 \rangle$ $\vec{b} = \langle 3, 2, 1 \rangle$ $\vec{c} = \langle 0, 1, 2 \rangle$

x	$f(x)$
0	
1	
2	
3	

4. $f(x) = x^3\vec{a} - x\vec{b} + 3\vec{c}$
   $\vec{a} = \langle 0, 1, -2 \rangle$ $\vec{b} = \langle 1, -2, 0 \rangle$ $\vec{c} = \langle -2, 0, 1 \rangle$

x	$f(x)$
-1	
0	
1	
3	

Advanced Mathematical Concepts

8-5

Enrichment

Linearly Dependent Vectors

The **zero vector** is $\langle 0, 0 \rangle$ in two dimensions, and $\langle 0, 0, 0 \rangle$ in three dimensions.

A set of vectors is called **linearly dependent** if and only if there exist scalars, not all zero, such that a linear combination of the vectors yields a zero vector.

Example   Are the vectors $\langle -1, 2, 1 \rangle$, $\langle 1, -1, 2 \rangle$, and $\langle 0, -2, -6 \rangle$ linearly dependent?

Solve $a\langle -1, 2, 1 \rangle + b\langle 1, -1, 2 \rangle + c\langle 0, -2, -6 \rangle = \langle 0, 0, 0 \rangle$.

$$-a + b = 0$$
$$2a - b - 2c = 0$$
$$a + 2b - 6c = 0$$

The above system does not have a unique solution. Any solution must satisfy the conditions that $a = b = 2c$.

Hence, one solution is $a = 1$, $b = 1$, and $c = \dfrac{1}{2}$.

$\langle -1, 2, 1 \rangle + \langle 1, -1, 2 \rangle + \dfrac{1}{2}\langle 0, -2, -6 \rangle = \langle 0, 0, 0 \rangle$, so the three vectors are linearly dependent.

Determine whether the given vectors are linearly dependent. Write yes or no. If the answer is yes, give a linear combination that yields a zero vector.

1. $\langle -2, 6 \rangle$, $\langle 1, -3 \rangle$

2. $\langle 3, 6 \rangle$, $\langle 2, 4 \rangle$

3. $\langle 1, 1, 1 \rangle$, $\langle -1, 0, 1 \rangle$, $\langle 1, -1, -1 \rangle$

4. $\langle 1, 1, 1 \rangle$, $\langle -1, 0, 1 \rangle$, $\langle -3, -2, -1 \rangle$

5. $\langle 2, -4, 6 \rangle$, $\langle 3, -1, 2 \rangle$, $\langle -6, 8, 10 \rangle$

6. $\langle 1, -2, 0 \rangle$, $\langle 2, 0, 3 \rangle$, $\left\langle -1, 1, \dfrac{9}{4} \right\rangle$

8-6

Enrichment

Using Parametric Equations to Find the Distance from a Point to a Plane

You can use parametric equations to help you find the distance from a point not on a plane to a given plane.

Example   **Find the distance from $P(-1, 1, 0)$ to the plane $x + 2y - z = 4$.**

Use the coefficients of the equation of the plane and the coordinates of the point to write the ratios below.

$$\frac{x + 1}{1} = \frac{y - 1}{2} = \frac{z - 0}{-1}$$

The denominators of these ratios represent a vector that is perpendicular to the plane, and passes through the given point.

Set t equal to each of the above ratios. Then, $t = \frac{x + 1}{1}$, $t = \frac{y - 1}{2}$, and $t = \frac{z - 0}{-1}$.

So, $x = t - 1$, $y = 2t + 1$, and $z = -t$ are parametric equations of the line.

Substitute these values into the equation of the plane.
$(t - 1) + 2(2t + 1) - (-t) = 4$
 Solve for t: $6t + 1 = 4$

$$t = \frac{1}{2}$$

This means that $t = \frac{1}{2}$ at the point of intersection of the vector and the plane.

The point of intersection is $\left(\frac{1}{2} - 1, 2\left(\frac{1}{2}\right) + 1, -\frac{1}{2}\right)$ or $\left(-\frac{1}{2}, 2, -\frac{1}{2}\right)$.

Use the distance formula:

$$d = \sqrt{\left(-1 - \left(-\frac{1}{2}\right)\right)^2 + (1 - 2)^2 + \left(0 - \left(-\frac{1}{2}\right)\right)^2} \approx 1.2 \text{ units}$$

Find the distance from the given point to the given plane. Round your answers to the nearest tenth.

1. from $(2, 0, -1)$ to $x - 2y + z = 3$ **2.** from $(1, 1, -1)$ to $2x + y - 3z = 5$

8-7

Enrichment

Coordinate Equations of Projectiles

The path of a projectile after it is launched is a parabola when graphed on a coordinate plane.

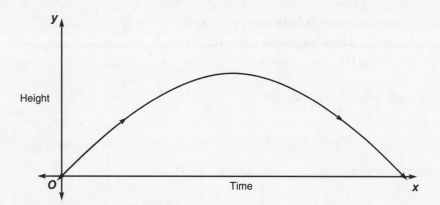

The path assumes that gravity is the only force acting on the projectile.

The equation of the path of a projectile on the coordinate plane is given by,

$$y = -\left(\frac{g}{2v_0{}^2 \cos^2\alpha}\right)x^2 + (\tan \alpha)x,$$

where g is the acceleration due to gravity, 9.8 m/s^2 or 32 ft/s^2, v_0 is the initial velocity, and α is the angle at which the projectile is fired.

Example   **Write the equation of a projectile fired at an angle of 10° to the horizontal with an initial velocity of 120 m/s.**

$$y = -\left(\frac{9.8}{2(120)^2 \cos^2 10°}\right)x^2 + (\tan 10°)x$$

$$y = -0.00035x^2 + 0.18x$$

Find the equation of the path of each projectile.

1. a projectile fired at 80° to the horizontal with an initial velocity of 200 ft/s

2. a projectile fired at 40° to the horizontal with an initial velocity of 150 m/s

8-8

Enrichment

Spherical Coordinates

There are many coordinate systems for locating a point in the two-dimensional plane. You have studied the two most common systems, rectangular coordinates and polar coordinates. The most commonly used three-dimensional coordinate systems are the extended rectangular system, with an added z-axis, and the *spherical coordinate* system, a modification of polar coordinates.

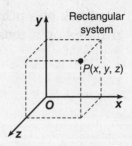

Note that the orientation of the axes shown is a different perspective than that used in your textbook.

Point $P(d, \theta, \phi)$ in three-dimensional space is located using three spherical coordinates:

d = distance from origin
θ = angle relative to x-axis
ϕ = angle relative to y-axis

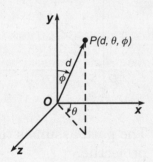

The figure at the right shows point Q with rectangular coordinates $(2, 5, 6)$.

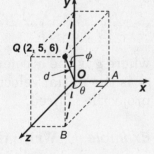

1. Find OA and AB.

2. Find OB by using the Pythagorean theorem.

3. Find QB.

4. Find d.

5. Use inverse trigonometric functions to find θ and ϕ to the nearest degree. Write the spherical coordinates of Q.

Find the spherical coordinates of the point with the given rectangular coordinates. Round distances to the nearest tenth and angles to the nearest degree.

6. $(4, 12, 3)$

7. $(-2, -3, -1)$

8. (a, b, c)

8-1

Enrichment

More Than Two Forces Acting on an Object

Three or more forces may work on an object at one time. Each of these forces can be represented by a vector. To find the resultant vector that acts upon the object, you can add the individual vectors two at a time.

Example A force of 80 N acts on an object at an angle of 70° at the same time that a force of 100 N acts at an angle of 150°. A third force of 120 N acts at an angle of 180°. Find the magnitude and direction of the resultant force acting on the object.

Add two vectors at a time. The order in which the vectors are added does not matter.

Add the 80-N vector and the 100-N vector first.

Now add the resulting vector to the 120-N vector.

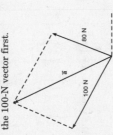

The resultant force is 219 N, with an amplitude of 145°.

Find the magnitude and amplitude of the resultant force acting on each object.

1. One force acts with 40 N at 50° on an object. A second force acts with 100 N at 110°. A third force acts with 10 N at 150°. Find the magnitude and amplitude of the resultant force. **131 N; 98°**

2. One force acts with 75 N at 45°. A second force acts with 90 N at 90°. A third force acts with 120 N at 170°. Find the magnitude and amplitude of the resultant force. **164 N; 112°**

8-2

Enrichment

Basis Vectors

The expression $\vec{v} = r\vec{u} + s\vec{w}$, the sum of two vectors each multiplied by scalars, is called a **linear combination** of the vectors $\vec{u}$ and $\vec{w}$.

Linear Combination Theorem in v_2	Every vector $\vec{v} \in v_2$ can be written as a linear combination of any two nonparallel vectors $\vec{u}$ and $\vec{w}$. The vectors $\vec{u}$ and $\vec{w}$ are said to form a basis for the vector space v_2 which contains all vectors having 1 column and 2 rows.

Example Write the vector $\vec{v} = \begin{pmatrix} -2 \\ 5 \end{pmatrix}$ as a linear combination of the vectors $\vec{u} = \begin{pmatrix} 2 \\ 3 \end{pmatrix}$ and $\vec{w} = \begin{pmatrix} 1 \\ -4 \end{pmatrix}$.

$$\begin{pmatrix} -2 \\ 5 \end{pmatrix} = r\begin{pmatrix} 2 \\ 3 \end{pmatrix} + s\begin{pmatrix} 1 \\ -4 \end{pmatrix} = \begin{pmatrix} 2r + s \\ 3r - 4s \end{pmatrix}$$

$$-2 = 2r + s$$
$$5 = 3r - 4s$$

Solving the system of equations yields the solution

$r = -\dfrac{3}{11}$ and $s = -\dfrac{16}{11}$. So, $\vec{v} = -\dfrac{3}{11}\vec{u} - \dfrac{16}{11}\vec{w}$.

Write each vector as a linear combination of the vectors $\vec{u}$ and $\vec{w}$.

1. $\vec{v} = \begin{pmatrix} 1 \\ 5 \end{pmatrix}$, $\vec{u} = \begin{pmatrix} -3 \\ 4 \end{pmatrix}$, $\vec{w} = \begin{pmatrix} 2 \\ -2 \end{pmatrix}$

$\vec{v} = 6\vec{u} + \dfrac{19}{2}\vec{w}$

2. $\vec{v} = \begin{pmatrix} 1 \\ -1 \end{pmatrix}$, $\vec{u} = \begin{pmatrix} 2 \\ 3 \end{pmatrix}$, $\vec{w} = \begin{pmatrix} \frac{1}{4} \\ 1 \end{pmatrix}$

$\vec{v} = \vec{u} - 4\vec{w}$

3. $\vec{v} = \begin{pmatrix} \frac{1}{2} \\ -1 \end{pmatrix}$, $\vec{u} = \begin{pmatrix} 0 \\ 4 \end{pmatrix}$, $\vec{w} = \begin{pmatrix} \frac{1}{2} \\ 1 \end{pmatrix}$

$\vec{v} = -\dfrac{1}{2}\vec{u} + \vec{w}$

4. $\vec{v} = \begin{pmatrix} 2 \\ -7 \end{pmatrix}$, $\vec{u} = \begin{pmatrix} -1 \\ -3 \end{pmatrix}$, $\vec{w} = \begin{pmatrix} 4 \\ 2 \end{pmatrix}$

$\vec{v} = \dfrac{16}{5}\vec{u} + \dfrac{13}{10}\vec{w}$

8-3 Enrichment

Basis Vectors in Three-Dimensional Space

The expression $\vec{v} = r\vec{u} + s\vec{w} + t\vec{z}$, the sum of two vectors each multiplied by scalars, is called a **linear combination** of the vectors $\vec{u}$, $\vec{w}$, and $\vec{z}$.

Every vector $\vec{v} \in v_3$ can be written as a linear combination of any three nonparallel vectors. The three nonparallel vectors are said to form a **basis** for v_3, which contains all vectors having 1 column and 3 rows.

Example Write the vector $\vec{v} = \begin{pmatrix} -1 \\ -4 \\ 3 \end{pmatrix}$ as a **linear combination of**

the vectors $\vec{u} = \begin{pmatrix} 1 \\ 3 \\ 1 \end{pmatrix}$, $\vec{w} = \begin{pmatrix} -1 \\ -2 \\ 1 \end{pmatrix}$, and $\vec{z} = \begin{pmatrix} -1 \\ -1 \\ 1 \end{pmatrix}$.

$$\begin{pmatrix} -1 \\ -4 \\ 3 \end{pmatrix} = r\begin{pmatrix} 1 \\ 3 \\ 1 \end{pmatrix} + s\begin{pmatrix} -1 \\ -2 \\ 1 \end{pmatrix} + t\begin{pmatrix} -1 \\ -1 \\ 1 \end{pmatrix} = \begin{pmatrix} r+s-t \\ 3r-2s-t \\ r+s+t \end{pmatrix}$$

$$-1 = r+s-t$$
$$-4 = 3r-2s-t$$
$$3 = r+s+t$$

Solving the system of equations yields the solution $r=0$, $s=1$, and $t=2$. So, $\vec{v} = \vec{w} + 2\vec{z}$.

Write each vector as a linear combination of the vectors $\vec{u}$, $\vec{w}$, and $\vec{z}$.

1. $\vec{v} = \begin{pmatrix} -6 \\ -2 \\ 1 \end{pmatrix}$, $\vec{u} = \begin{pmatrix} 1 \\ 1 \\ 1 \end{pmatrix}$, $\vec{w} = \begin{pmatrix} 1 \\ 0 \\ 1 \end{pmatrix}$, and $\vec{z} = \begin{pmatrix} 0 \\ 1 \\ 1 \end{pmatrix}$

$$\vec{v} = -5\vec{u} - \vec{w} + 3\vec{z}$$

2. $\vec{v} = \begin{pmatrix} 5 \\ -2 \\ 3 \end{pmatrix}$, $\vec{u} = \begin{pmatrix} 1 \\ -2 \\ 3 \end{pmatrix}$, $\vec{w} = \begin{pmatrix} -1 \\ 0 \\ 1 \end{pmatrix}$, and $\vec{z} = \begin{pmatrix} 4 \\ 2 \\ -1 \end{pmatrix}$

$$\vec{v} = \frac{8}{7}\vec{u} - \frac{23}{7}\vec{w} + \frac{1}{7}\vec{z}$$

3. $\vec{v} = \begin{pmatrix} -1 \\ -1 \\ 2 \end{pmatrix}$, $\vec{u} = \begin{pmatrix} 1 \\ 2 \\ -1 \end{pmatrix}$, $\vec{w} = \begin{pmatrix} 2 \\ 2 \\ 1 \end{pmatrix}$, and $\vec{z} = \begin{pmatrix} 1 \\ 0 \\ 1 \end{pmatrix}$

$$\vec{v} = -\frac{1}{2}\vec{u} + \frac{3}{2}\vec{z}$$

8-4 Enrichment

Vector Equations

Let $\vec{a}$, $\vec{b}$, and $\vec{c}$ be fixed vectors. The equation $f(x) = \vec{a} - 2x\vec{b} + x^2\vec{c}$ defines a vector function of x. For the values of x shown, the assigned vectors are given below.

x	-2	-1	0	1	2
f(x)	a+4b+4c	a+2b+c	a	a-2b+c	a-4b+4c

If $\vec{a} = \langle 0, 1 \rangle$, $\vec{b} = \langle 1, 1 \rangle$, and $\vec{c} = \langle 2, -2 \rangle$, the resulting vectors for the values of x are as follows.

x	-2	-1	0	1	2
f(x)	⟨12,-3⟩	⟨4,1⟩	⟨0,1⟩	⟨0,-3⟩	⟨4,-11⟩

For each of the following, complete the table of resulting vectors.

1. $f(x) = x^3\vec{a} - 2x^2\vec{b} + 3x\vec{c}$
$\vec{a} = \langle 1,1 \rangle$ $\vec{b} = \langle 2,3 \rangle$ $\vec{c} = \langle 3,-1 \rangle$

x	f(x)
-1	⟨-14,-4⟩
0	⟨0,0⟩
1	⟨6,-8⟩
2	⟨10,-22⟩

2. $f(x) = 2x^2\vec{a} + 3x\vec{b} - 5\vec{c}$
$\vec{a} = \langle 0,1,1 \rangle$ $\vec{b} = \langle 1,0,1 \rangle$ $\vec{c} = \langle 1,1,0 \rangle$

x	f(x)
-2	⟨-11,3,2⟩
-1	⟨-8,-3,-1⟩
0	⟨-5,-5,0⟩
1	⟨-2,-3,5⟩

3. $f(x) = x^2\vec{c} + 3x\vec{a} - 4\vec{b}$
$\vec{a} = \langle 1,1,1 \rangle$ $\vec{b} = \langle 3,2,1 \rangle$ $\vec{c} = \langle 0,1,2 \rangle$

x	f(x)
0	⟨-12,-8,-4⟩
1	⟨-9,-4,1⟩
2	⟨-6,2,10⟩
3	⟨-3,10,23⟩

4. $f(x) = x^3\vec{a} - x\vec{b} + 3\vec{c}$
$\vec{a} = \langle 0,1,-2 \rangle$ $\vec{b} = \langle 1,-2,0 \rangle$ $\vec{c} = \langle -2,0,1 \rangle$

x	f(x)
-1	⟨-5,-3,5⟩
0	⟨-6,0,3⟩
1	⟨-7,3,1⟩
3	⟨-9,33,-51⟩

8-5

NAME _____ DATE _____ PERIOD _____

Enrichment

Linearly Dependent Vectors

The **zero vector** is $\langle 0, 0 \rangle$ in two dimensions, and $\langle 0, 0, 0 \rangle$ in three dimensions.

A set of vectors is called **linearly dependent** if and only if there exist scalars, not all zero, such that a linear combination of the vectors yields a zero vector.

Example Are the vectors $\langle -1, 2, 1 \rangle$, $\langle 1, -1, 2 \rangle$, and $\langle 0, -2, -6 \rangle$ linearly dependent?

Solve $a\langle -1, 2, 1 \rangle + b\langle 1, -1, 2 \rangle + c\langle 0, -2, -6 \rangle = \langle 0, 0, 0 \rangle$.

$$-a + b = 0$$
$$2a - b - 2c = 0$$
$$a + 2b - 6c = 0$$

The above system does not have a unique solution. Any solution must satisfy the conditions that $a = b = 2c$.

Hence, one solution is $a = 1$, $b = 1$, and $c = \frac{1}{2}$.

$\langle -1, 2, 1 \rangle + \langle 1, -1, 2 \rangle + \frac{1}{2}\langle 0, -2, -6 \rangle = \langle 0, 0, 0 \rangle$, so the three vectors are linearly dependent.

Determine whether the given vectors are linearly dependent. Write yes or no. If the answer is yes, give a linear combination that yields a zero vector.

1. $\langle -2, 6 \rangle$, $\langle 1, -3 \rangle$
   yes; $\langle -2, 6 \rangle + 2\langle 1, -3 \rangle = \langle 0, 0 \rangle$

2. $\langle 3, 6 \rangle$, $\langle 2, 4 \rangle$
   yes; $2\langle 3, 6 \rangle - 3\langle 2, 4 \rangle = \langle 0, 0 \rangle$

3. $\langle 1, 1, 1 \rangle$, $\langle -1, 0, 1 \rangle$, $\langle 1, -1, -1 \rangle$
   no

4. $\langle 1, 1, 1 \rangle$, $\langle -1, 0, 1 \rangle$, $\langle -3, -2, -1 \rangle$
   yes; $2\langle 1, 1, 1 \rangle - \langle -1, 0, 1 \rangle + \langle -3, -2, -1 \rangle = \langle 0, 0, 0 \rangle$

5. $\langle 2, -4, 6 \rangle$, $\langle 3, -1, 2 \rangle$, $\langle -6, 8, 10 \rangle$
   no

6. $\langle 1, -2, 0 \rangle$, $\langle 2, 0, 3 \rangle$, $\langle -1, 1, \frac{9}{4} \rangle$
   no

8-6

NAME _____ DATE _____ PERIOD _____

Enrichment

Using Parametric Equations to Find the Distance from a Point to a Plane

You can use parametric equations to help you find the distance from a point not on a plane to a given plane.

Example Find the distance from $P(-1, 1, 0)$ to the plane $x + 2y - z = 4$.

Use the coefficients of the equation of the plane and the coordinates of the point to write the ratios below.

$$\frac{x+1}{1} = \frac{y-1}{2} = \frac{z-0}{-1}$$

The denominators of these ratios represent a vector that is perpendicular to the plane, and passes through the given point.

Set t equal to each of the above ratios. Then, $t = \frac{x+1}{1}$, $t = \frac{y-1}{2}$, and $t = \frac{z-0}{-1}$.

So, $x = t - 1$, $y = 2t + 1$, and $z = -t$ are parametric equations of the line.

Substitute these values into the equation of the plane.

$$(t - 1) + 2(2t + 1) - (-t) = 4$$

Solve for t: $6t + 1 = 4$

$$t = \frac{1}{2}$$

This means that $t = \frac{1}{2}$ at the point of intersection of the vector and the plane.

The point of intersection is $\left(\frac{1}{2} - 1, 2\left(\frac{1}{2}\right) + 1, -\frac{1}{2} \right)$ or $\left(-\frac{1}{2}, 2, -\frac{1}{2} \right)$.

Use the distance formula:

$$d = \sqrt{\left(-1 - \left(-\frac{1}{2}\right)\right)^2 + (1 - 2)^2 + \left(0 - \left(-\frac{1}{2}\right)\right)^2} \approx 1.2 \text{ units}$$

Find the distance from the given point to the given plane. Round your answers to the nearest tenth.

1. from $(2, 0, -1)$ to $x - 2y + z = 3$
   0.8 unit

2. from $(1, 1, -1)$ to $2x + y - 3z = 5$
   0.3 unit

Answers (Lessons 8-7 and 8-8)

8-7 Enrichment

Coordinate Equations of Projectiles

The path of a projectile after it is launched is a parabola when graphed on a coordinate plane.

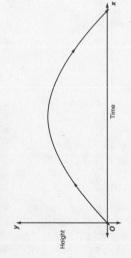

The path assumes that gravity is the only force acting on the projectile.

The equation of the path of a projectile on the coordinate plane is given by,

$$y = -\left(\frac{g}{2v_0^2 \cos^2 \alpha}\right)x^2 + (\tan \alpha)x,$$

where g is the acceleration due to gravity, 9.8 m/s² or 32 ft/s², v_0 is the initial velocity, and α is the angle at which the projectile is fired.

Example Write the equation of a projectile fired at an angle of 10° to the horizontal with an initial velocity of 120 m/s.

$$y = -\left(\frac{9.8}{2(120)^2 \cos^2 10°}\right)x^2 + (\tan 10°)x$$

$$y = -0.0003 5x^2 + 0.18x$$

Find the equation of the path of each projectile.

1. a projectile fired at 80° to the horizontal with an initial velocity of 200 ft/s

$$y = -0.013x^2 + 5.67x$$

2. a projectile fired at 40° to the horizontal with an initial velocity of 150 m/s

$$y = -0.00037x^2 + 0.84x$$

© Glencoe/McGraw-Hill   T91   Advanced Mathematical Concepts

8-8 Enrichment

Spherical Coordinates

There are many coordinate systems for locating a point in the two-dimensional plane. You have studied the two most common systems, rectangular coordinates and polar coordinates. The most commonly used three-dimensional coordinate systems are the extended rectangular system, with an added z-axis, and the *spherical coordinate system*, a modification of polar coordinates.

Note that the orientation of the axes shown is a different perspective than that used in your textbook.

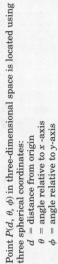

Point $P(d, \theta, \phi)$ in three-dimensional space is located using three spherical coordinates:

d = distance from origin
θ = angle relative to x-axis
ϕ = angle relative to y-axis

The figure at the right shows point Q with rectangular coordinates $(2, 5, 6)$.

1. Find OA and AB.

   2; 6

2. Find OB by using the Pythagorean theorem.

   $2\sqrt{10}$

3. Find QB.

   5

4. Find d.

   $\sqrt{65}$

5. Use inverse trigonometric functions to find θ and ϕ to the nearest degree. Write the spherical coordinates of Q.

   $(\sqrt{65}, 72°, 52°)$

Find the spherical coordinates of the point with the given rectangular coordinates. Round distances to the nearest tenth and angles to the nearest degree.

6. $(4, 12, 3)$

   $(13, 37°, 23°)$

7. $(-2, -3, -1)$

   $(3.7, -153°, 143°)$

8. (a, b, c)

   $\left(\sqrt{a^2 + b^2 + c^2},\ \arctan\left(\frac{c}{a}\right),\ \arccos\left(\frac{b}{\sqrt{a^2 + b^2 + c^2}}\right)\right)$

© Glencoe/McGraw-Hill   T92   Advanced Mathematical Concepts

9-1

Enrichment

Distance on the Earth's Surface

As you learned in Lesson 9-1, lines of longitude on Earth's surface intersect at the North and South Poles. A line of longitude that passes completely around Earth is called a **great circle**. All great circles have the same circumference, found by calculating the circumference of a circle with Earth's radius, 3963.2 miles. (Since Earth is slightly flattened at the poles, it is not precisely spherical. The difference is so small, however, that for most purposes it can be ignored.)

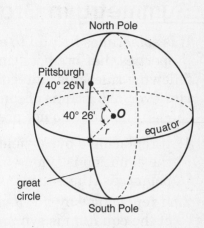

1. Find the circumference of a great circle.

On a great circle, position is measured in degrees north or south of the equator. Pittsburgh's position of 40° 26' N means that radii from Earth's center to Pittsburgh and to the point of intersection of the equator and Pittsburgh's longitude line form an angle of 40° 26'. (See the figure above.)

2. Find the length of one degree of arc on a longitude line.

3. Charleston, South Carolina (32° 46' N), and Guayaquil, Ecuador (2° 9' S), both lie on Pittsburgh's longitude line. Find the distance from Pittsburgh to each of the other cities.

Because circles of latitude are drawn parallel to the equator, their radii and circumferences grow steadily shorter as they approach the poles. The length of one degree of arc on a circle of latitude depends on how far north or south of the equator the circle is located. The figure at the right shows a circle of latitude of radius r located θ degrees north of the equator. Because the radii of the equator and the circle of latitude are parallel, $m\angle NEO = \theta$. Therefore, $\cos \theta = \dfrac{r}{R}$, which gives $r = R \cos \theta$, where R represents the radius of Earth.

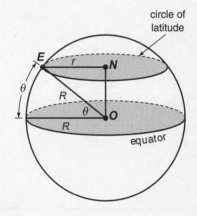

4. Find the radius and circumference of a circle of latitude located 70° north of the equator.

5. Find the length of one degree of arc on the circle described in Exercise 4.

6. Bangor, Maine, and Salem, Oregon, are both located at latitude 44° 50' N. Their respective longitudes are 68° 46' and 123° 2' west of Greenwich. Find the distance from Bangor to Salem.

9-2

Enrichment

Symmetry in Graphs of Polar Equations

It is sometimes helpful to analyze polar equations for certain
properties that predict symmetry in the graph of the equation. The
following rules guarantee the existence of symmetry in the graph.
However, the graphs of some polar equations exhibit symmetry even
though the rules do not predict it.

1. If replacing θ by $-\theta$ yields the same equation, then the graph of
   the equation is symmetric with respect to the line containing the
   polar axis (the x-axis in the rectangular coordinate system).

2. If replacing θ by $\pi - \theta$ yields the same equation, then the graph
   of the equation is symmetric with respect to the line

   $\theta = \dfrac{\pi}{2}$ (the y-axis in the rectangular coordinate system).

3. If replacing r by $-r$ yields the same equation, then the graph
   of the equation is symmetric with respect to the pole.

Example   **Identify the symmetry of and graph $r = 3 + 3 \sin \theta$.**
Since $\sin (\pi - \theta) = \sin \theta$, by rule 2 the graph is symmetric
with respect to the line $\theta = \dfrac{\pi}{2}$. Therefore, it is only necessary
to plot points in the first and fourth quadrants.

θ	$3 + 3 \sin \theta$	(r, θ)
$-\dfrac{\pi}{2}$	0	$\left(0, -\dfrac{\pi}{2}\right)$
$-\dfrac{\pi}{3}$	0.4	$\left(0.4, -\dfrac{\pi}{3}\right)$
$-\dfrac{\pi}{6}$	1.5	$\left(1.5, -\dfrac{\pi}{6}\right)$
0	3.0	$(3.0, 0)$
$\dfrac{\pi}{6}$	4.5	$\left(4.5, \dfrac{\pi}{6}\right)$
$\dfrac{\pi}{3}$	5.6	$\left(5.6, \dfrac{\pi}{3}\right)$
$\dfrac{\pi}{2}$	6.0	$\left(6.0, \dfrac{\pi}{2}\right)$

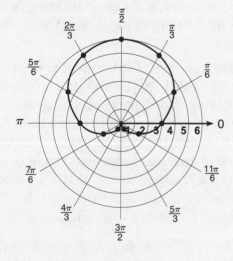

The points in the second and third quadrants are found by using
symmetry.

Identify the symmetry of and graph each polar equation on polar grid paper.

1. $r = 2 + 3 \cos \theta$

2. $r^2 = 4 \sin 2\theta$

9-3

Enrichment

Polar Roses

The polar equation $r = a \sin n\theta$ graphs as a rose.
When $n = 1$, the rose is a circle — a flower with one leaf.

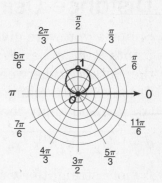

Sketch the graphs of these roses.

1. $r = 2 \sin 2\theta$

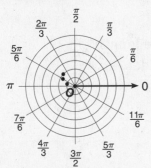

2. $r = -2 \sin 3\theta$

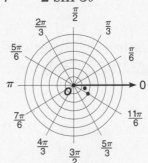

3. $r = -2 \sin 4\theta$

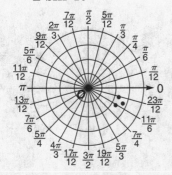

4. $r = 2 \sin 5\theta$

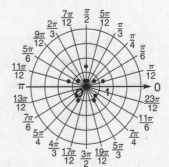

5. The graph of the equation $r = a \sin n\theta$ is a rose. Use your results from Exercises 1–4 to complete these conjectures.

  a. The distance across a petal is __?__ units.

  b. If n is an odd integer, the number of leaves is __?__.

  c. If n is an even integer, the number of leaves is __?__.

6. Write $r = 2 \sin 2\theta$ in rectangular form.

7. The total area A of the three leaves in the three-leaved rose $r = a \sin 3\theta$ is given by $A = \dfrac{1}{4} a^2\pi$. For a four-leaved rose, the area is $A = \dfrac{1}{2}a^2\pi$.

  a. Find the area of a four-leaved rose with $a = 6$.
  b. Write the equation of a three-leaved rose with area 36π.

9-4

Enrichment

Distance Using Polar Coordinates

Suppose you were given the polar coordinates of two points $P_1(r_1, \alpha_1)$ and $P_2(r_2, \alpha_2)$ and were asked to find the distance d between the points. One way would be to convert to rectangular coordinates (x_1, y_1) and (x_2, y_2), and apply the distance formula

$$d = \sqrt{(x_2 - x_1)^2 + (y_2 - y_1)^2}.$$

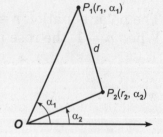

A more straightforward method makes use of the Law of Cosines.

1. In the above figure, the distance d between P_1 and P_2 is the length of one side of $\triangle OP_1P_2$. Find the lengths of the other two sides.

2. Determine the measure of $\angle P_1OP_2$.

3. Write an expression for d^2 using the Law of Cosines.

4. Write a formula for the distance d between the points $P_1(r_1, \alpha_1)$ and $P_2(r_2, \alpha_2)$.

5. Find the distance between the points $(3, 45°)$ and $(5, 25°)$. Round your answer to three decimal places.

6. Find the distance between the points $\left(2, \dfrac{\pi}{2}\right)$ and $\left(4, \dfrac{\pi}{8}\right)$. Round your answer to three decimal places.

7. The distance from the point $(5, 80°)$ to the point $(r, 20°)$ is $\sqrt{21}$. Find r.

9-5

Enrichment

Cycle Quadruples

Four nonnegative integers are arranged in cyclic order to make a "cyclic quadruple." In the example, this quadruple is 23, 8, 14, and 32.

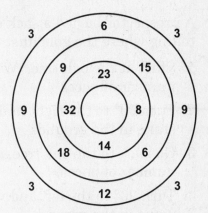

The next cyclic quadruple is formed from the absolute values of the four differences of adjacent integers:

$|23 - 8| = 15$ $|8 - 14| = 6$ $|14 - 32| = 18$ $|32 - 23| = 9$

By continuing in this manner, you will eventually get four equal integers. In the example, the equal integers appear in three steps.

Solve each problem.

1. Start with the quadruple 25, 17, 55, 47. In how many steps do the equal integers appear?

2. Some interesting things happen when one or more of the original numbers is 0. Draw a diagram showing a beginning quadruple of three zeros and one nonnegative integer. Predict how many steps it will take to reach 4 equal integers. Also, predict what that integer will be. Complete the diagram to check your predictions.

3. Start with four integers, two of them zero. If the zeros are opposite one another, how many steps does it take for the zeros to disappear?

4. Start with two equal integers and two zeros. The zeros are next to one another. How many steps does it take for the zeros to disappear?

5. Start with two nonequal integers and two zeros. The zeros are next to one another. How many steps does it take for the zeros to disappear?

6. Start with three equal integers and one zero. How many steps does it take for the zero to disappear?

7. Describe the remaining cases with one zero and tell how many steps it takes for the zero to disappear.

9-6

Enrichment

A Complex Treasure Hunt

A prospector buried a sack of gold dust. He then wrote instructions telling where the gold dust could be found:

1. Start at the oak tree. Walk to the mineral spring counting the number of paces.

2. Turn 90° to the right and walk an equal number of paces. Place a stake in the ground.

3. Go back to the oak tree. Walk to the red rock counting the number of paces.

4. Turn 90° to the left and walk an equal number of paces. Place a stake in the ground.

5. Find the spot halfway between the stakes. There you will find the gold.

Years later, an expert in complex numbers found the instructions in a rusty tin can. Some additional instructions told how to get to the general area where the oak tree, the mineral spring, and the red rock could be found. The expert hurried to the area and readily located the spring and the rock. Unfortunately, hundreds of oak trees had sprung up since the prospector's day, and it was impossible to know which one was referred to in the instructions. Nevertheless, through prudent application of complex numbers, the expert found the gold. Especially helpful in the quest were the following facts.

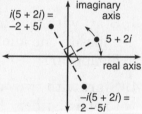

- The distance between the graphs of two complex numbers can be represented by the absolute value of the difference between the numbers.

- Multiplication by i rotates the graph of a complex number 90° counterclockwise. Multiplication by $-i$ rotates it 90° clockwise.

The expert drew a map on the complex plane, letting $S(-1 + 0i)$ be the spring and $R(1 + 0i)$ be the rock. Since the location of the oak tree was unknown, the expert represented it by $T(a + bi)$.

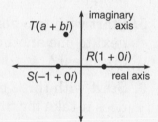

1. Find the distance from the oak tree to the spring. Express the distance as a complex number.

2. Write the complex number whose graph would be a 90° counterclockwise rotation of your answer to Exercise 1. This is where the first stake should be placed.

3. Repeat Exercises 1 and 2 for the distance from the tree to the rock. Where should the second stake be placed?

4. The gold is halfway between the stakes. Find the coordinates of the location.

102 *Advanced Mathematical Concepts*

9-7

Enrichment

Complex Conjugates

In Lesson 9-5, you learned that complex numbers in the form $a + bi$ and $a - bi$ are called conjugates. You can show that two numbers are conjugates by finding the appropriate values of a and b.

1. Show that the solutions of $x^2 + 2x + 3 = 0$ are conjugates.

2. Show that the solutions of $Ax^2 + Bx + C = 0$ are conjugates when $B^2 - 4AC < 0$.

The conjugate of the complex number z is represented by $\bar{z}$.

3. $z = a + bi$. Use $\bar{z}$ to find the reciprocal of z.

4. $z = r(\cos \theta + i \sin \theta)$. Find $\bar{z}$. Express your answer in polar form.

Use your answer to Exercise 3 to solve Exercises 4 and 5.

5. Find $z \cdot \bar{z}$.

6. Find $z \div \bar{z}$. $(z \neq 0)$

9-8 Enrichment

Algebraic Numbers

A complex number is said to be **algebraic** if it is a zero of a
polynomial with integer coefficients. For example, if p and q
are integers with no common factors and $q \neq 0$, then $\frac{p}{q}$ is a zero
of $qx - p$. This shows that every rational number is algebraic. Some
irrational numbers can be shown to be algebraic.

Example   **Show that $1 + \sqrt{3}$ is algebraic.**

Let $x = 1 + \sqrt{3}$. Then
$$x - 1 = \sqrt{3}$$
$$(x - 1)^2 = (\sqrt{3})^2$$
$$x^2 - 2x + 1 = 3$$
$$x^2 - 2x - 2 = 0$$

Thus, $1 + \sqrt{3}$ is a zero of $x^2 - 2x - 2$, so $1 + \sqrt{3}$ is an
algebraic number.

If a complex number is not algebraic, it is said to be **trancendental**.
The best-known transcendental numbers are π and e. Proving that
these numbers are not algebraic was a difficult task. It was not
until 1873 that the French mathematician Charles Hermite was
able to show that e is transcendental. It wasn't until 1882 that
C. L. F. Lindemann of Munich showed that π is also transcendental.

*Show that each complex number is algebraic by finding a
polynomial with integer coefficients of which the given
number is a zero.*

1. $\sqrt{2}$

2. i

3. $2 - i$

4. $\sqrt[3]{3}$

5. $4 - \sqrt[4]{2}i$

6. $\sqrt{3} + i$

7. $\sqrt{1 + \sqrt[3]{5}}$

8. $\sqrt[3]{2 - \sqrt{3}}$

          104   *Advanced Mathematical Concepts*

9-1 Enrichment

Distance on the Earth's Surface

As you learned in Lesson 9-1, lines of longitude on Earth's surface intersect at the North and South Poles. A line of longitude that passes completely around Earth is called a **great circle**. All great circles have the same circumference, found by calculating the circumference of a circle with Earth's radius, 3963.2 miles. (Since Earth is slightly flattened at the poles, it is not precisely spherical. The difference is so small, however, that for most purposes it can be ignored.)

1. Find the circumference of a great circle.
24,901.5 miles

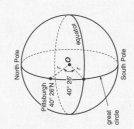

On a great circle, position is measured in degrees north or south of the equator. Pittsburgh's position of 40° 26′ N means that radii from Earth's center to Pittsburgh and to the point of intersection of the equator and Pittsburgh's longitude line form an angle of 40° 26′. (See the figure above.)

2. Find the length of one degree of arc on a longitude line.
69.2 miles

3. Charleston, South Carolina (32° 46′ N), and Guayaquil, Ecuador (2° 9′ S), both lie on Pittsburgh's longitude line. Find the distance from Pittsburgh to each of the other cities.
530.3 miles; 2945.5 miles

Because circles of latitude are drawn parallel to the equator, their radii and circumferences grow steadily shorter as they approach the poles. The length of one degree of arc on a circle of latitude depends on how far north or south of the equator the circle is located. The figure at the right shows a circle of latitude of radius r located θ degrees north of the equator. Because the radii of the equator and the circle of latitude are parallel, $m\angle NEO = \theta$. Therefore, $\cos \theta = \dfrac{r}{R}$, which gives $r = R \cos \theta$, where R represents the radius of Earth.

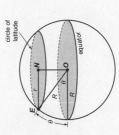

4. Find the radius and circumference of a circle of latitude located 70° north of the equator. **1355.5 miles; 8516.8 miles**

5. Find the length of one degree of arc on the circle described in Exercise 4. **23.7 miles**

6. Bangor, Maine, and Salem, Oregon, are both located at latitude 44° 50′ N. Their respective longitudes are 68° 46′ and 123° 2′ west of Greenwich. Find the distance from Bangor to Salem.
2662.0 miles

9-2 Enrichment

Symmetry in Graphs of Polar Equations

It is sometimes helpful to analyze polar equations for certain properties that predict symmetry in the graph of the equation. The following rules guarantee the existence of symmetry in the graph. However, the graphs of some polar equations exhibit symmetry even though the rules do not predict it.

1. If replacing θ by $-\theta$ yields the same equation, then the graph of the equation is symmetric with respect to the line containing the polar axis (the x-axis in the rectangular coordinate system).

2. If replacing θ by $\pi - \theta$ yields the same equation, then the graph of the equation is symmetric with respect to the line $\theta = \dfrac{\pi}{2}$ (the y-axis in the rectangular coordinate system).

3. If replacing r by $-r$ yields the same equation, then the graph of the equation is symmetric with respect to the pole.

Example Identify the symmetry of and graph $r = 3 + 3 \sin \theta$.

Since $\sin (\pi - \theta) = \sin \theta$, by rule 2 the graph is symmetric with respect to the line $\theta = \dfrac{\pi}{2}$. Therefore, it is only necessary to plot points in the first and fourth quadrants.

θ	$3 + 3 \sin \theta$	(r, θ)
$-\dfrac{\pi}{2}$	0	$\left(0, -\dfrac{\pi}{2}\right)$
$-\dfrac{\pi}{3}$	0.4	$\left(0.4, -\dfrac{\pi}{3}\right)$
$-\dfrac{\pi}{6}$	1.5	$\left(1.5, -\dfrac{\pi}{6}\right)$
0	3.0	$(3.0, 0)$
$\dfrac{\pi}{6}$	4.5	$\left(4.5, \dfrac{\pi}{6}\right)$
$\dfrac{\pi}{3}$	5.6	$\left(5.6, \dfrac{\pi}{3}\right)$
$\dfrac{\pi}{2}$	6.0	$\left(6.0, \dfrac{\pi}{2}\right)$

The points in the second and third quadrants are found by using symmetry.

See students' graphs.

Identify the symmetry of and graph each polar equation on polar grid paper.

1. $r = 2 + 3 \cos \theta$
Symmetric with respect to polar axis

2. $r^2 = 4 \sin 2\theta$
Symmetric with respect to the pole

9-3

Enrichment

Polar Roses

The polar equation $r = a \sin n\theta$ graphs as a rose.
When $n = 1$, the rose is a circle — a flower with one leaf.

Sketch the graphs of these roses.

1. $r = 2 \sin 2\theta$

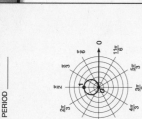

2. $r = -2 \sin 3\theta$

3. $r = -2 \sin 4\theta$

4. $r = 2 \sin 5\theta$

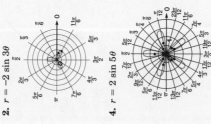

5. The graph of the equation $r = a \sin n\theta$ is a rose. Use your results from Exercises 1–4 to complete these conjectures.

a. The distance across a petal is __?__ units. $|a|$

b. If n is an odd integer, the number of leaves is __?__. n

c. If n is an even integer, the number of leaves is __?__. $2n$

6. Write $r = 2 \sin 2\theta$ in rectangular form. $(x^2 + y^2)^2 = 16x^2y^2$

7. The total area A of the three leaves in the three-leaved rose
$r = a \sin 3\theta$ is given by $A = \frac{1}{4} a^2\pi$. For a four-leaved rose, the
area is $A = \frac{1}{2} a^2\pi$.

a. Find the area of a four-leaved rose with $a = 6$. 18π

b. Write the equation of a three-leaved rose with area 36π.
Sample answer: $r = 12 \sin 3\theta$

9-4

Enrichment

Distance Using Polar Coordinates

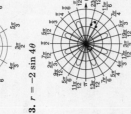

Suppose you were given the polar coordinates of two
points $P_1(r_1, \alpha_1)$ and $P_2(r_2, \alpha_2)$ and were asked to find
the distance d between the points. One way would be
to convert to rectangular coordinates (x_1, y_1) and
(x_2, y_2), and apply the distance formula

$$d = \sqrt{(x_2 - x_1)^2 + (y_2 - y_1)^2}.$$

A more straightforward method makes use of the Law
of Cosines.

1. In the above figure, the distance d between P_1 and P_2 is the length
of one side of $\triangle OP_1P_2$. Find the lengths of the other two sides.

r_1 and r_2

2. Determine the measure of $\angle P_1OP_2$.

$\alpha_1 - \alpha_2$

3. Write an expression for d^2 using the Law of Cosines.

$d^2 = r_1^2 + r_2^2 - 2r_1r_2 \cos(\alpha_1 - \alpha_2)$

4. Write a formula for the distance d between the points
$P_1(r_1, \alpha_1)$ and $P_2(r_2, \alpha_2)$.

$d = \sqrt{r_1^2 + r_2^2 - 2r_1r_2 \cos(\alpha_1 - \alpha_2)}$

5. Find the distance between the points $(3, 45°)$ and $(5, 25°)$. Round
your answer to three decimal places.
2.410

6. Find the distance between the points $\left(2, \frac{\pi}{2}\right)$ and $\left(4, \frac{\pi}{8}\right)$. Round
your answer to three decimal places.
3.725

7. The distance from the point $(5, 80°)$ to the point $(r, 20°)$ is $\sqrt{21}$.
Find r.
1 or 4

NAME _____ DATE _____ PERIOD _____

9-5 Enrichment

Cycle Quadruples

Four nonnegative integers are arranged in cyclic order to make a "cyclic quadruple." In the example, this quadruple is 23, 8, 14, and 32.

The next cyclic quadruple is formed from the absolute values of the four differences of adjacent integers:

$|23 - 8| = 15$ $|8 - 14| = 6$ $|14 - 32| = 18$ $|32 - 23| = 9$

By continuing in this manner, you will eventually get four equal integers. In the example, the equal integers appear in three steps.

Solve each problem.

1. Start with the quadruple 25, 17, 55, 47. In how many steps do the equal integers appear? **4 steps**

2. Some interesting things happen when one or more of the original numbers is 0. Draw a diagram showing a beginning quadruple of three zeros and one nonnegative integer. Predict how many steps it will take to reach 4 equal integers. Also, predict what that integer will be. Complete the diagram to check your predictions. **3 steps; a**

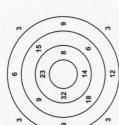 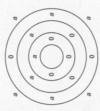

3. Start with four integers, two of them zero, opposite one another, how many steps does it take for the zeros to disappear? **1 step**

4. Start with two equal integers and two zeros, next to one another. How many steps does it take for the zeros to disappear? **2 steps**

5. Start with two nonequal integers and two zeros, next to one another. How many steps does it take for the zeros to disappear? **3 steps**

6. Start with three equal integers and one zero. How many steps does it take for the zero to disappear? **3 steps**

7. Describe the remaining cases with one zero and tell how many steps it takes for the zero to disappear.

(1) **all integers different; 1 step**
(2) **opposite nonzero integers equal, but different from third integer; 1 step**
(3) **two adjacent integers equal, but different from third integer; 2 steps**

© Glencoe/McGraw-Hill   T101   *Advanced Mathematical Concepts*

NAME _____ DATE _____ PERIOD _____

9-6 Enrichment

A Complex Treasure Hunt

A prospector buried a sack of gold dust. He then wrote instructions telling where the gold dust could be found:

1. Start at the oak tree. Walk to the mineral spring counting the number of paces.

2. Turn 90° to the right and walk an equal number of paces. Place a stake in the ground.

3. Go back to the oak tree. Walk to the red rock counting the number of paces.

4. Turn 90° to the left and walk an equal number of paces. Place a stake in the ground.

5. Find the spot halfway between the stakes. There you will find the gold.

Years later, an expert in complex numbers found the instructions in a rusty tin can. Some additional instructions told how to get to the general area where the oak tree, the mineral spring, and the red rock could be found. The expert hurried to the area and readily located the spring and the rock. Unfortunately, hundreds of oak trees had sprung up since the prospector's day, and it was impossible to know which one was referred to in the instructions. Nevertheless, through prudent application of complex numbers, the expert found the gold. Especially helpful in the quest were the following facts.

- The distance between the graphs of two complex numbers can be represented by the absolute value of the difference between the numbers.

- Multiplication by i rotates the graph of a complex number 90° counterclockwise. Multiplication by $-i$ rotates it 90° clockwise.

The expert drew a map on the complex plane, letting $S(-1 + 0i)$ be the spring and $R(1 + 0i)$ be the rock. Since the location of the oak tree was unknown, the expert represented it by $T(a + bi)$.

1. Find the distance from the oak tree to the spring. Express it as a complex number.
$$|(a + 1) + bi|$$

2. Write the complex number whose graph would be a 90° counterclockwise rotation of your answer to Exercise 1. This is where the first stake should be placed. $-b + (a + 1)i$

3. Repeat Exercises 1 and 2 for the distance from the tree to the rock. Where should the second stake be placed? $b - (a - 1)i$

4. The gold is halfway between the stakes. Find the coordinates of the location. $(0 + i)$, **the point on the imaginary axis 1 unit from the origin**

© Glencoe/McGraw-Hill   T102   *Advanced Mathematical Concepts*

9-7

NAME _____ DATE _____ PERIOD _____

Enrichment

Complex Conjugates

In Lesson 9-5, you learned that complex numbers in the form $a + bi$ and $a - bi$ are called conjugates. You can show that two numbers are conjugates by finding the appropriate values of a and b.

1. Show that the solutions of $x^2 + 2x + 3 = 0$ are conjugates.
The solutions are $-1 + i\sqrt{2}$ and $-1 - i\sqrt{2}$, so $a = -1$ and $b = \sqrt{2}$.

2. Show that the solutions of $Ax^2 + Bx + C = 0$ are conjugates when $B^2 - 4AC < 0$.
By the quadratic formula, the solutions are
$$-\frac{B}{2A} + i\frac{\sqrt{B^2 - 4AC}}{2A} \text{ and } -\frac{B}{2A} - i\frac{\sqrt{B^2 - 4AC}}{2A},$$
$$\text{so } a = -\frac{B}{2A} \text{ and } b = \frac{\sqrt{B^2 - 4AC}}{2A}.$$

The conjugate of the complex number z is represented by $\bar{z}$.

3. $z = a + bi$. Use $\bar{z}$ to find the reciprocal of z.
$$\frac{a}{a^2 + b^2} - i\frac{b}{a^2 + b^2} = \frac{\bar{z}}{|z|^2}$$

4. $z = r(\cos\theta + i\sin\theta)$. Find $\bar{z}$. Express your answer in polar form.
$$r[\cos(-\theta) + i\sin(-\theta)]$$

Use your answer to Exercise 3 to solve Exercises 4 and 5.

5. Find $z \cdot \bar{z}$.
$$r^2 = |z|^2$$

6. Find $z \div \bar{z}$. $(z \neq 0)$
$$\cos 2\theta + i\sin 2\theta = \frac{z^2}{|z|^2}$$

9-8

NAME _____ DATE _____ PERIOD _____

Enrichment

Algebraic Numbers

A complex number is said to be **algebraic** if it is a zero of a polynomial with integer coefficients. For example, if p and q are integers with no common factors and $q \neq 0$, then $\frac{p}{q}$ is a zero of $qx - p$. This shows that every rational number is algebraic. Some irrational numbers can be shown to be algebraic.

Example **Show that $1 + \sqrt{3}$ is algebraic.**

Let $x = 1 + \sqrt{3}$. Then
$$x - 1 = \sqrt{3}$$
$$(x - 1)^2 = (\sqrt{3})^2$$
$$x^2 - 2x + 1 = 3$$
$$x^2 - 2x - 2 = 0$$

Thus, $1 + \sqrt{3}$ is a zero of $x^2 - 2x - 2$, so $1 + \sqrt{3}$ is an algebraic number.

If a complex number is not algebraic, it is said to be **transcendental.** The best-known transcendental numbers are π and e. Proving that these numbers are not algebraic was a difficult task. It was not until 1873 that the French mathematician Charles Hermite was able to show that e is transcendental. It wasn't until 1882 that C. L. F. Lindemann of Munich showed that π is also transcendental.

Show that each complex number is algebraic by finding a polynomial with integer coefficients of which the given number is a zero.

1. $\sqrt{\sqrt{2} - 2}$
$x^2 - 2$

2. i
$x^2 + 1$

3. $2 - i$
$x^2 - 4x + 5$

4. $\sqrt[3]{3}$
$x^3 - 3$

5. $4 - \sqrt[4]{2i}$
$x^4 - 16x^3 + 96x^2 - 256x - 254$

6. $\sqrt{3} + i$
$x^4 - 4x^2 + 16$

7. $\sqrt{1 + \sqrt[3]{5}}$
$x^6 - 3x^4 + 3x^2 - 6$

8. $\sqrt[3]{2} - \sqrt{3}$
$x^6 - 4x^3 + 1$

10-1 Enrichment

Mathematics and History: Hypatia

Hypatia (A.D. 370–415) is the earliest woman mathematician whose life is well documented. Born in Alexandria, Egypt, she was widely known for her keen intellect and extraordinary mathematical ability. Students from Europe, Asia, and Africa flocked to the university at Alexandria to attend her lectures on mathematics, astronomy, philosophy, and mechanics.

Hypatia wrote several major treatises in mathematics. Perhaps the most significant of these was her commentary on the *Arithmetica* of Diophantus, a mathematician who lived and worked in Alexandria in the third century. In her commentary, Hypatia offered several observations about the *Arithmetica's* Diophantine problems— problems for which one was required to find only the rational solutions. It is believed that many of these observations were subsequently incorporated into the original manuscript of the *Arithmetica*.

In modern mathematics, the solutions of a **Diophantine equation** are restricted to integers. In the exercises, you will explore some questions involving simple Diophantine equations.

For each equation, find three solutions that consist of an ordered pair of integers.

1. $2x - y = 7$

2. $x + 3y = 5$

3. $6x - 5y = -8$

4. $-11x - 4y = 6$

5. Refer to your answers to Exercises 1–4. Suppose that the integer pair (x_1, y_1) is a solution of $Ax - By = C$. Describe how to find other integer pairs that are solutions of the equation.

6. Explain why the equation $3x + 6y = 7$ has no solutions that are integer pairs.

7. *True* or *false*: Any line on the coordinate plane must pass through at least one point whose coordinates are integers. Explain.

10-2

Enrichment

Spheres

The set of all points in three-dimensional space that are a fixed distance r (the **radius**), from a fixed point C (the **center**), is called a **sphere**. The equation below is an algebraic representation of the sphere shown at the right.

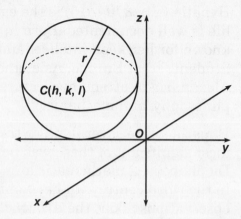

$$(x - h)^2 + (y - k)^2 + (z - l)^2 = r^2$$

A line segment containing the center of a sphere and having its endpoints on the sphere is called a **diameter** of the sphere. The endpoints of a diameter are called **poles** of the sphere. A **great circle** of a sphere is the intersection of the sphere and a plane containing the center of the sphere.

1. If $x^2 + y^2 - 4y + z^2 + 2z - 4 = 0$ is an equation of a sphere and $(1, 4, -3)$ is one pole of the sphere, find the coordinates of the opposite pole.

2. **a.** On the coordinate system at the right, sketch the sphere described by the equation $x^2 + y^2 + z^2 = 9$.

   b. Is $P(2, -2, -2)$ inside, outside, or on the sphere?

   c. Describe a way to tell if a point with coordinates $P(a, b, c)$ is inside, outside, or on the sphere with equation $x^2 + y^2 + z^2 = r^2$.

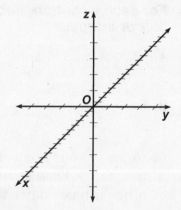

3. If $x^2 + y^2 + z^2 - 4x + 6y - 2z - 2 = 0$ is an equation of a sphere, find the circumference of a great circle, and the surface area and volume of the sphere.

4. The equation $x^2 + y^2 = 4$ represents a set of points in three-dimensional space. Describe that set of points in your own words. Illustrate with a sketch on the coordinate system at the right.

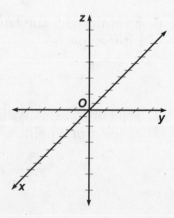

10-3

Enrichment

Superellipses

The circle and the ellipse are members of an interesting family of curves that were first studied by the French physicist and mathematician Gabriel Lamé (1795-1870). The general equation for the family is

$$\left|\frac{x}{a}\right|^n + \left|\frac{y}{b}\right|^n = 1, \text{ with } a \neq 0, b \neq 0, \text{ and } n > 0.$$

For even values of n greater than 2, the curves are called **superellipses**.

1. Consider two curves that are *not* superellipses. Graph each equation on the grid at the right. State the type of curve produced each time.

   a. $\left|\frac{x}{2}\right|^2 + \left|\frac{y}{2}\right|^2 = 1$

   b. $\left|\frac{x}{3}\right|^2 + \left|\frac{y}{2}\right|^2 = 1$

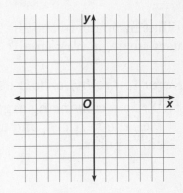

2. In each of the following cases you are given values of a, b, and n to use in the general equation. Write the resulting equation. Then graph. Sketch each graph on the grid at the right.

   a. $a = 2, b = 3, n = 4$

   b. $a = 2, b = 3, n = 6$

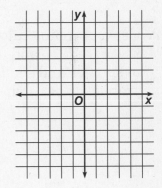

   c. $a = 2, b = 3, n = 8$

3. What shape will the graph of $\left|\frac{x}{2}\right|^n + \left|\frac{y}{3}\right|^n = 1$ approximate for greater and greater even, whole-number values of n?

10-4

Enrichment

Moving Foci

Recall that the equation of a hyperbola with center
at the origin and horizontal transverse axis has the

equation $\frac{x^2}{a^2} - \frac{y^2}{b^2} = 1$. The foci are at $(-c, 0)$ and

$(c, 0)$, where $c^2 = a^2 + b^2$, the vertices are at $(-a, 0)$
and $(a, 0)$, and the asymptotes have equations

$y = \pm\frac{b}{a}x$. Such a hyperbola is shown at the right.

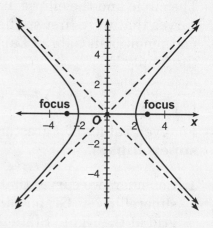

What happens to the shape of the graph as c grows
very large or very small?

Refer to the hyperbola described above.

1. Write a convincing argument to show that as c approaches 0, the
foci, the vertices, and the center of the hyperbola become the
same point.

2. Use a graphing calculator or computer to graph $x^2 - y^2 = 1$,
$x^2 - y^2 = 0.1$, and $x^2 - y^2 = 0.01$. (Such hyperbolas correspond
to smaller and smaller values of c.) Describe the changes in the
graphs. What shape do the graphs approach as c approaches 0?

3. Suppose a is held fixed and c approaches infinity. How does the
graph of the hyperbola change?

4. Suppose b is held fixed and c approaches infinity. How does the
graph of the hyperbola change?

10-5 Enrichment

Tilted Parabolas

The diagram at the right shows a fixed point $F(1, 1)$ and a line d whose equation is $y = -x - 2$. If $P(x, y)$ satisfies the condition that $PD = PF$, then P is on a parabola. Our objective is to find an equation for the tilted parabola; which is the locus of all points that are the same distance from $(1,1)$ and the line $y = -x - 2$.

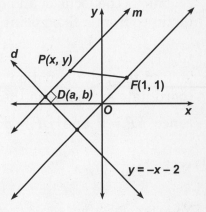

To do this, first find an equation for the line m through $P(x, y)$ and perpendicular to line d at $D(a, b)$. Using this equation and the equation for line d, find the coordinates (a, b) of point D in terms of x and y. Then use $(PD)^2 = (PF)^2$ to find an equation for the parabola.

Refer to the discussion above.

1. Find an equation for line m.

2. Use the equations for lines m and d to show that the coordinates of point D are $D(a, b) = D\left(\dfrac{x - y - 2}{2}, \dfrac{y - x - 2}{2}\right)$.

3. Use the coordinates of F, P, and D, along with $(PD)^2 = (PF)^2$ to find an equation of the parabola with focus F and directrix d.

4. a. Every parabola has an axis of symmetry. Find an equation for the axis of symmetry of the parabola described above. Justify your answer.

b. Use your answer from part **a** to find the coordinates of the vertex of the parabola. Justify your answer.

10-6

Enrichment

Polar Graphs of Conics

A conic is the locus of all points such that the ratio e of the distance from a fixed point F and a fixed line d is constant.

$$\frac{FP}{DP} = e$$

To find the polar equation of the conic, use a polar coordinate system with the origin at the focus.

Since $FP = r$ and $DP = p + r \cos \theta$, $\frac{r}{p + r \cos \theta} = e$.

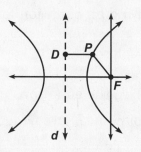

Now solve for r.

$$r = \frac{ep}{1 - e \cos \theta}$$

You can classify a conic section by its eccentricity.

| $e = 1$: parabola | $0 < e < 1$: ellipse | $e > 1$: hyperbola |
| | $e = 0$: circle | |

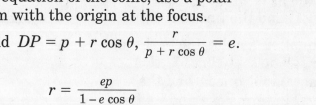

Graph each relation and identify the conic.

1. $r = \dfrac{4}{1 - \cos \theta}$

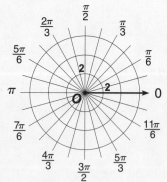

2. $r = \dfrac{4}{2 - \cos \theta}$

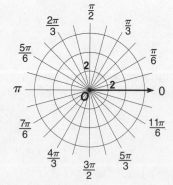

3. $r = \dfrac{4}{2 + \sin \theta}$

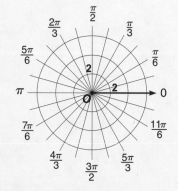

4. $r = \dfrac{4}{1 + 2 \sin \theta}$

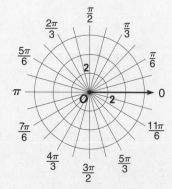

10-7 Enrichment

Graphing with Addition of *y*-Coordinates

Equations of parabolas, ellipses, and hyperbolas that are "tipped" with respect to the *x*- and *y*-axes are more difficult to graph than the equations you have been studying.

Often, however, you can use the graphs of two simpler equations to graph a more complicated equation. For example, the graph of the ellipse in the diagram at the right is obtained by adding the *y*-coordinate of each point on the circle and the *y*-coordinate of the corresponding point of the line.

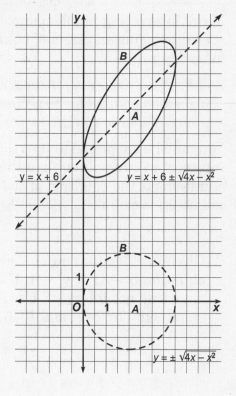

Graph each equation. State the type of curve for each graph.

1. $y = 6 - x \pm \sqrt{4 - x^2}$

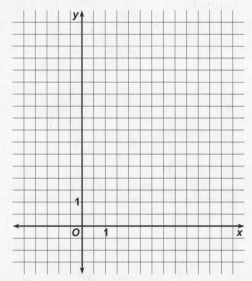

2. $y = x \pm \sqrt{x}$

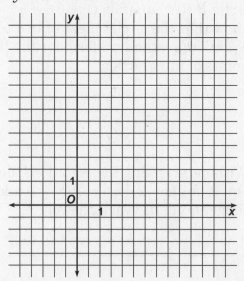

Use a separate sheet of graph paper to graph these equations. State the type of curve for each graph.

3. $y = 2x \pm \sqrt{7 + 6x - x^2}$

4. $y = -2x \pm \sqrt{-2x}$

Advanced Mathematical Concepts

10-8 Enrichment

Intersections of Circles

Many interesting problems involving circles can be solved by using a system of equations. Consider the following problem.

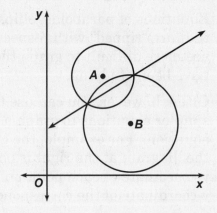

Find an equation for the straight line that contains the two points of intersection of two intersecting circles whose equations are given.

You may be surprised to find that if the given circles intersect in two points, then the difference of their equations is the equation of the line containing the intersection points.

1. Circle A has equation $x^2 + y^2 = 1$ and circle B has equation $(x - 3)^2 + y^2 = 1$. Use a sketch to show that the circles do not intersect. Use an algebraic argument to show that circles A and B do not intersect.

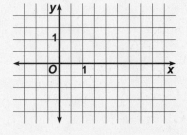

2. Circle A has equation $(x - 2)^2 + (y + 1)^2 = 16$ and circle B has equation $(x + 3)^2 + y^2 = 9$. Use a sketch to show that the circles meet in two points. Then find an equation in standard form for the line containing the points of intersection.

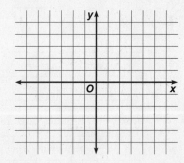

3. Without graphing the equations, decide if the circles with equations $(x - 2)^2 + (y - 2)^2 = 8$ and $(x - 3)^2 + (y - 4)^2 = 4$ are tangent. Justify your answer.

10-1 Enrichment

Mathematics and History: Hypatia

Hypatia (A.D. 370–415) is the earliest woman mathematician whose life is well documented. Born in Alexandria, Egypt, she was widely known for her keen intellect and extraordinary mathematical ability. Students from Europe, Asia, and Africa flocked to the university at Alexandria to attend her lectures on mathematics, astronomy, philosophy, and mechanics.

Hypatia wrote several major treatises in mathematics. Perhaps the most significant of these was her commentary on the *Arithmetica* of Diophantus, a mathematician who lived and worked in Alexandria in the third century. In her commentary, Hypatia offered several observations about the *Arithmetica*'s Diophantine problems— problems for which one was required to find only the rational solutions. It is believed that many of these observations were subsequently incorporated into the original manuscript of the *Arithmetica*.

In modern mathematics, the solutions of a **Diophantine equation** are restricted to integers. In the exercises, you will explore some questions involving simple Diophantine equations.

For each equation, find three solutions that consist of an ordered pair of integers.

1. $2x - y = 7$

$(1, -5), (0, -7), (-1, -9)$

2. $x + 3y = 5$

$(2, 1), (5, 0), (8, -1)$

3. $6x - 5y = -8$

$(2, 4), (-3, -2), (-8, -8)$

4. $-11x - 4y = 6$

$(2, -7), (-2, 4), (-6, 15)$

5. Refer to your answers to Exercises 1–4. Suppose that the integer pair (x_1, y_1) is a solution of $Ax - By = C$. Describe how to find other integer pairs that are solutions of the equation.

Other integer pairs are of the form $(x_1 + n \cdot B, y_1 - n \cdot A)$, where n is any nonzero integer.

6. Explain why the equation $3x + 6y = 7$ has no solutions that are integer pairs.

Rewrite $3x + 6y = 7$ as $3(x + 2y) = 7$. If x and y are integers 7 would have to be an integral multiple of 3.

7. *True or false:* Any line on the coordinate plane must pass through at least one point whose coordinates are integers. Explain.

False; An equation like $3x + 6y = 7$ has no integer-pair solutions, so the graph of such an equation is a line that passes through no point whose coordinates are integers.

10-2 Enrichment

Spheres

The set of all points in three-dimensional space that are a fixed distance r (the **radius**), from a fixed point C (the **center**), is called a **sphere**. The equation below is an algebraic representation of the sphere shown at the right.

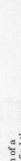

$$(x - h)^2 + (y - k)^2 + (z - l)^2 = r^2$$

A line segment containing the center of a sphere and having its endpoints on the sphere is called a **diameter** of the sphere. The endpoints of a diameter are called **poles** of the sphere. A **great circle** of a sphere is the intersection of the sphere and a plane containing the center of the sphere.

1. If $x^2 + y^2 + z^2 + 2z - 4 = 0$ is an equation of a sphere and $(1, 4, -3)$ is one pole of the sphere, find the coordinates of the opposite pole.

$(-1, 0, 1)$

2. a. On the coordinate system at the right, sketch the sphere described by the equation $x^2 + y^2 + z^2 = 9$.

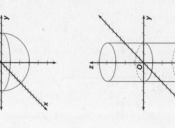

b. Is $P(2, -2, -2)$ inside, outside, or on the sphere?

outside

c. Describe a way to tell if a point with coordinates $P(a, b, c)$ is inside, outside, or on the sphere with equation $x^2 + y^2 + z^2 = r^2$.

$a^2 + b^2 + c^2 < r^2$: **inside the sphere**
$a^2 + b^2 + c^2 = r^2$: **on the sphere**
$a^2 + b^2 + c^2 > r^2$: **outside the sphere**

3. If $x^2 + y^2 + z^2 - 4x + 6y - 2z - 2 = 0$ is an equation of a sphere, find the circumference of a great circle, and the surface area and volume of the sphere.

8π units; 64π square units; $\dfrac{256\pi}{3}$ cubic units

4. The equation $x^2 + y^2 = 4$ represents a set of points in three-dimensional space. Describe that set of points in your own words. Illustrate with a sketch on the coordinate system at the right.

a cylinder

10-4 Enrichment

Moving Foci

Recall that the equation of a hyperbola with center at the origin and horizontal transverse axis has the equation $\frac{x^2}{a^2} - \frac{y^2}{b^2} = 1$. The foci are at $(-c, 0)$ and $(c, 0)$, where $c^2 = a^2 + b^2$, the vertices are at $(-a, 0)$ and $(a, 0)$, and the asymptotes have equations $y = \pm \frac{b}{a} x$. Such a hyperbola is shown at the right.

What happens to the shape of the graph as c grows very large or very small?

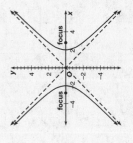

Refer to the hyperbola described above.

1. Write a convincing argument to show that as c approaches 0, the foci, the vertices, and the center of the hyperbola become the same point.
Since $0 < a < c$, as c approaches 0, a approaches 0. So the x-coordinates of the foci and vertices approach 0, which is the x-coordinate of the center. Since the y-coordinates are equal, the points become the same.

2. Use a graphing calculator or computer to graph $x^2 - y^2 = 1$, $x^2 - y^2 = 0.1$, and $x^2 - y^2 = 0.01$. (Such hyperbolas correspond to smaller and smaller values of c.) Describe the changes in the graphs. What shape do the graphs approach as c approaches 0?
The asymptotes remain the same, but the branches become sharper near the vertices. The graphs approach the lines $y = x$ and $y = -x$.

3. Suppose a is held fixed and c approaches infinity. How does the graph of the hyperbola change?
The vertices remain at $(\pm a, 0)$, but the branches become shallower, or flatter. The graphs approach the vertical lines $x = -a$ and $x = a$.

4. Suppose b is held fixed and c approaches infinity. How does the graph of the hyperbola change?
The vertices recede to infinity and the branches each come closer and closer to themselves. As c approaches infinity, the graphs tend to disappear.

10-3 Enrichment

Superellipses

The circle and the ellipse are members of an interesting family of curves that were first studied by the French physicist and mathematician Gabriel Lamé (1795-1870). The general equation for the family is

$$\left|\frac{x}{a}\right|^n + \left|\frac{y}{b}\right|^n = 1, \text{ with } a \neq 0, b \neq 0, \text{ and } n > 0.$$

For even values of n greater than 2, the curves are called **superellipses**.

1. Consider two curves that are *not* superellipses. Graph each equation on the grid at the right. State the type of curve produced each time.

a. $\left|\frac{x}{2}\right|^2 + \left|\frac{y}{2}\right|^2 = 1$ **circle**

b. $\left|\frac{x}{3}\right|^2 + \left|\frac{y}{2}\right|^2 = 1$ **ellipse**

2. In each of the following cases you are given values of a, b, and n to use in the general equation. Write the resulting equation. Then graph. Sketch each graph on the grid at the right.

a. $a = 2, b = 3, n = 4$ $\left|\frac{x}{2}\right|^4 + \left|\frac{y}{3}\right|^4 = 1$

b. $a = 2, b = 3, n = 6$ $\left|\frac{x}{2}\right|^6 + \left|\frac{y}{3}\right|^6 = 1$

c. $a = 2, b = 3, n = 8$ $\left|\frac{x}{2}\right|^8 + \left|\frac{y}{3}\right|^8 = 1$

3. What shape will the graph of $\left|\frac{x}{2}\right|^n + \left|\frac{y}{3}\right|^n = 1$ approximate for greater and greater even, whole-number values of n?
a rectangle that is 6 units long and 4 units wide, centered at the origin

Answers (Lessons 10-5 and 10-6)

10-5 Enrichment

Tilted Parabolas

The diagram at the right shows a fixed point $F(1, 1)$ and a line d whose equation is $y = -x - 2$. If $P(x, y)$ satisfies the condition that $PD = PF$, then P is on a parabola. Our objective is to find an equation for the tilted parabola; which is the locus of all points that are the same distance from $(1,1)$ and the line $y = -x - 2$.

To do this, first find an equation for the line m through $P(x, y)$ and perpendicular to line d at $D(a, b)$. Using this equation and the equation for line d, find the coordinates (a, b) of point D in terms of x and y. Then use $(PD)^2 = (PF)^2$ to find an equation for the parabola.

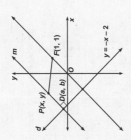

Refer to the discussion above.

1. Find an equation for line m.

$$x - y + (b - a) = 0$$

2. Use the equations for lines m and d to show that the coordinates of point D are $D(a, b) = D\left(\dfrac{x - y - 2}{2}, \dfrac{y - x - 2}{2}\right)$.

From the equation for line m,
$-a + b = -x + y$. **From the equation for d,**
$a + b = -2$. **Subtract to get** $a = \dfrac{x - y - 2}{2}$.
Add to get $b = \dfrac{y - x - 2}{2}$.

3. Use the coordinates of F, P, and D, along with $(PD)^2 = (PF)^2$ to find an equation of the parabola with focus F and directrix d.

$$x^2 - 2xy + y^2 - 8x - 8y = 0$$

4. a. Every parabola has an axis of symmetry. Find an equation for the axis of symmetry of the parabola described above. Justify your answer.

$y = x$, **since** $y = x$ **contains** $F(1,1)$ **and is perpendicular to** d.

b. Use your answer from part **a** to find the coordinates of the vertex of the parabola. Justify your answer.

$(0,0)$, **since** $(0,0)$ **is midway between point** F **and line** d.

10-6 Enrichment

Polar Graphs of Conics

A conic is the locus of all points such that the ratio e of the distance from a fixed point F and a fixed line d is constant.

$$\frac{FP}{DP} = e$$

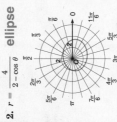

To find the polar equation of the conic, use a polar coordinate system with the origin at the focus.

Since $FP = r$ and $DP = p + r\cos\theta$, $\dfrac{r}{p + r\cos\theta} = e$.

Now solve for r. $r = \dfrac{ep}{1 - e\cos\theta}$

You can classify a conic section by its eccentricity.

$e = 1$: parabola $0 < e < 1$: ellipse
$e = 0$: circle $e > 1$: hyperbola

Graph each relation and identify the conic.

1. $r = \dfrac{4}{1 - \cos\theta}$ **parabola**

2. $r = \dfrac{4}{2 - \cos\theta}$ **ellipse**

3. $r = \dfrac{4}{2 + \sin\theta}$ **ellipse**

4. $r = \dfrac{4}{1 + 2\sin\theta}$ **hyperbola**

10-7

Enrichment

Graphing with Addition of y-Coordinates

Equations of parabolas, ellipses, and hyperbolas that are "tipped" with respect to the x- and y-axes are more difficult to graph than the equations you have been studying.

Often, however, you can use the graphs of two simpler equations to graph a more complicated equation. For example, the graph of the ellipse in the diagram at the right is obtained by adding the y-coordinate of each point on the circle and the y-coordinate of the corresponding point of the line.

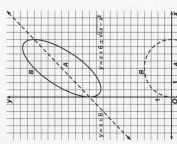

$y = x + 6 \pm \sqrt{4x - x^2}$

A

$y = x + 6$

$y = \pm\sqrt{4x - x^2}$

Graph each equation. State the type of curve for each graph.

1. $y = 6 - x \pm \sqrt{4 - x^2}$ **ellipse**

$y = 6 - x \pm \sqrt{4 - x^2}$

$y = 6 - x$

$y = \pm \sqrt{4 - x^2}$

2. $y = x \pm \sqrt{x}$ **parabola**

$y = x \pm \sqrt{x}$

$y = x$

$y = \pm\sqrt{x}$

Use a separate sheet of graph paper to graph these equations. State the type of curve for each graph.

3. $y = 2x \pm \sqrt{7 + 6x - x^2}$ **ellipse;**
See students' graphs.

4. $y = -2x \pm \sqrt{-2x}$ **parabola;**
See students' graphs.

10-8

Enrichment

Intersections of Circles

Many interesting problems involving circles can be solved by using a system of equations. Consider the following problem.

Find an equation for the straight line that contains the two points of intersection of two intersecting circles whose equations are given.

You may be surprised to find that if the given circles intersect in two points, then the difference of their equations is the equation of the line containing the intersection points.

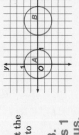

1. Circle A has equation $x^2 + y^2 = 1$ and circle B has equation $(x - 3)^2 + y^2 = 1$. Use a sketch to show that the circles do not intersect. Use an algebraic argument to show that circles A and B do not intersect.

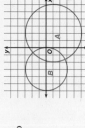

The distance between the centers is 3. Since the sum of the radii is 2, there is 1 unit of space between the circles. Thus, the circles do not intersect.

2. Circle A has equation $(x - 2)^2 + (y + 1)^2 = 16$ and circle B has equation $(x + 3)^2 + y^2 = 9$. Use a sketch to show that the circles meet in two points. Then find an equation in standard form for the line containing the points of intersection.

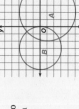

$10x - 2y + 11 = 0$

3. Without graphing the equations, decide if the circles with equations $(x - 2)^2 + (y - 2)^2 = 8$ and $(x - 3)^2 + (y - 4)^2 = 4$ are tangent. Justify your answer.

The distance between the centers is $\sqrt{5} \approx 2.24$. Since the sum of the radii is $2 + 2\sqrt{2} \approx 4.83$, the circles overlap and meet in two points; they are not tangent.

11-1

Enrichment

Look for Cases

Many problems can be partitioned into a few cases. The cases are classifications within the problem that are exclusive one to another but which taken together comprise all the possibilities in the problem. Divisions into cases are made where the characteristics of the problem are most critical.

Example   **If $a > b$ and $\dfrac{1}{a} > \dfrac{1}{b}$, what must be true of a and b?**

One of the critical characteristics of inequalities is that changing the signs of the left and right sides requires changing the sense of the inequality. This suggests classifying a and b according to signs. Since neither a nor b can equal zero in the second inequality and $a > b$, the cases are:

  (i) a and b are both positive.
  (ii) a and b are both negative.
  (iii) a is positive and b is negative.

An important characteristic of reciprocals is that 1 and –1 are their own reciprocals. Therefore, within each of the above cases consider examples of these three subclassifications:

  (A) a and b are both greater than 1 (or < -1).
  (B) a and b are both fractions whose absolute values are less than one.
  (C) a is greater than 1 (or -1) and b is less than 1 (or -1).

For case (i), consider these examples.

(A) $3 > 2 \rightarrow \dfrac{1}{3} < \dfrac{1}{2}$ (B) $\dfrac{1}{4} > \dfrac{1}{5} \rightarrow 4 < 5$ (C) $\dfrac{3}{2} > \dfrac{3}{4} \rightarrow \dfrac{2}{3} < \dfrac{4}{3}$

For case (ii), consider these examples.

(A) $-2 > -3 \rightarrow -\dfrac{1}{2} < -\dfrac{1}{3}$ (B) $-\dfrac{1}{5} > -\dfrac{1}{4} \rightarrow -5 < -4$

(C) $-\dfrac{3}{4} > -\dfrac{3}{2} \rightarrow -\dfrac{4}{3} < -\dfrac{2}{3}$

For case (iii), consider these examples.

(A) $2 > -3 \rightarrow \dfrac{1}{2} > -\dfrac{1}{3}$ (B) $\dfrac{1}{5} > -\dfrac{1}{4} \rightarrow 5 > -4$ (C) $\dfrac{3}{4} > -\dfrac{3}{2} \rightarrow \dfrac{4}{3} > -\dfrac{2}{3}$

Notice that the second given inequality, $\dfrac{1}{a} > \dfrac{1}{b}$, only holds true in case (iii). We conclude that a must be positive and b negative to satisfy both given inequalities.

Complete.

1. Find the positive values of b such that $b^{x_1} > b^{x_2}$ whenever $x_1 < x_2$.

2. Solve $\dfrac{x}{x+1} > 0$.

3. Find the domain of $f(x) = \sqrt{3 - |x - 2|}$.

11-2

Enrichment

Finding Solutions of $x^y = y^x$

Perhaps you have noticed that if x and y are interchanged in equations such as $x = y$ and $xy = 1$, the resulting equation is equivalent to the original equation. The same is true of the equation $x^y = y^x$. However, finding solutions of $x^y = y^x$ and drawing its graph is not a simple process.

Solve each problem. Assume that x and y are positive real numbers

1. If $a > 0$, will (a, a) be a solution of $x^y = y^x$? Justify your answer.

2. If $c > 0$, $d > 0$, and (c, d) is a solution of $x^y = y^x$, will (d, c) also be a solution? Justify your answer.

3. Use 2 as a value for y in $x^y = y^x$. The equation becomes $x^2 = 2^x$.
   a. Find equations for two functions, $f(x)$ and $g(x)$ that you could graph to find the solutions of $x^2 = 2^x$. Then graph the functions on a separate sheet of graph paper.

   b. Use the graph you drew for part **a** to state two solutions for $x^2 = 2^x$. Then use these solutions to state two solutions for $x^y = y^x$.

4. In this exercise, a graphing calculator will be very helpful. Use the technique from Exercise 3 to complete the tables below. Then graph $x^y = y^x$ for positive values of x and y. If there are asymptotes, show them in your diagram using dotted lines. Note that in the table, some values of y call for one value of x, others call for two.

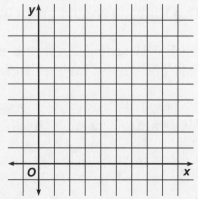

x	y
	$\frac{1}{2}$
	$\frac{3}{4}$
	1
	2
	2
	3
	3

x	y
	4
	4
	5
	5
	8
	8

11-3

Enrichment

Approximations for π and e

The following expression can be used to approximate e. If greater and greater values of n are used, the value of the expression approximates e more and more closely.

$$\left(1 + \frac{1}{n}\right)^n$$

Another way to approximate e is to use this infinite sum. The greater the value of n, the closer the approximation.

$$e = 1 + 1 + \frac{1}{2} + \frac{1}{2 \cdot 3} + \frac{1}{2 \cdot 3 \cdot 4} + \ldots + \frac{1}{2 \cdot 3 \cdot 4 \cdot \ldots \cdot n} + \ldots$$

In a similar manner, π can be approximated using an infinite product discovered by the English mathematician John Wallis (1616-1703).

$$\frac{\pi}{2} = \frac{2}{1} \cdot \frac{2}{3} \cdot \frac{4}{3} \cdot \frac{4}{5} \cdot \frac{6}{5} \cdot \frac{6}{7} \ldots \frac{2n}{2n - 1} \cdot \frac{2n}{2n + 1} \ldots$$

Solve each problem.

1. Use a calculator with an e^x key to find e to 7 decimal places.

2. Use the expression $\left(1 + \frac{1}{n}\right)^n$ to approximate e to 3 decimal places. Use 5, 100, 500, and 7000 as values of n.

3. Use the infinite sum to approximate e to 3 decimal places. Use the whole numbers from 3 through 6 as values of n.

4. Which approximation method approaches the value of e more quickly?

5. Use a calculator with a π key to find π to 7 decimal places.

6. Use the infinite product to approximate π to 3 decimal places. Use the whole numbers from 3 through 6 as values of n.

7. Does the infinite product give good approximations for π quickly?

8. Show that $\pi^4 + \pi^5$ is equal to e^6 to 4 decimal places.

9. Which is larger, e^π or π^e?

10. The expression $x^{\frac{1}{x}}$ reaches a maximum value at $x = e$. Use this fact to prove the inequality you found in Exercise 9.

11-4

Enrichment

Musical Relationships

The frequencies of notes in a musical scale that are one octave apart are related by an exponential equation. For the eight C notes on a piano, the equation is $C_n = C_1 2^{n-1}$, where C_n represents the frequency of note C_n.

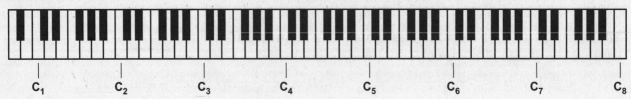

C_1 C_2 C_3 C_4 C_5 C_6 C_7 C_8

1. Find the relationship between C_1 and C_2.
2. Find the relationship between C_1 and C_4.

The frequencies of consecutive notes are related by a common ratio r. The general equation is $f_n = f_1 r^{n-1}$.

3. If the frequency of middle C is 261.6 cycles per second and the frequency of the next higher C is 523.2 cycles per second, find the common ratio r. (Hint: The two Cs are 12 notes apart.) Write the answer as a radical expression.

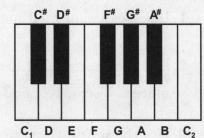

C♯ D♯   F♯ G♯ A♯

C_1 D E F G A B C_2

4. Substitute decimal values for r and f_1 to find a specific equation for f_n.

5. Find the frequency of F♯ above middle C.

6. The frets on a guitar are spaced so that the sound made by pressing a string against one fret has about 1.0595 times the wavelength of the sound made by using the next fret. The general equation is $w_n = w_0 (1.0595)^n$. Describe the arrangement of the frets on a guitar.

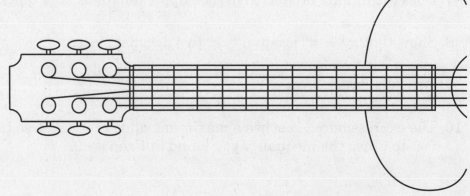

11-5

Enrichment

The Slide Rule

Before the invention of electronic calculators, computations were often performed on a slide rule. A slide rule is based on the idea of logarithms. It has two movable rods labeled with C and D scales. Each of the scales is logarithmic.

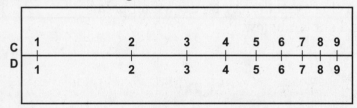

To multiply 2×3 on a slide rule, move the C rod to the right as shown below. You can find 2×3 by adding log 2 to log 3, and the slide rule adds the lengths for you. The distance you get is 0.778, or the logarithm of 6.

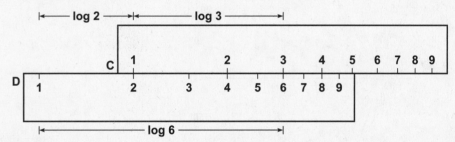

Follow the steps to make a slide rule.

1. Use graph paper that has small squares, such as 10 squares to the inch. Using the scales shown at the right, plot the curve $y = \log x$ for $x = 1$, 1.5, and the whole numbers from 2 through 10. Make an obvious heavy dot for each point plotted.

2. You will need two strips of cardboard. A 5-by-7 index card, cut in half the long way, will work fine. Turn the graph you made in Exercise 1 sideways and use it to mark a logarithmic scale on each of the two strips. The figure shows the mark for 2 being drawn.

3. Explain how to use a slide rule to divide 8 by 2.

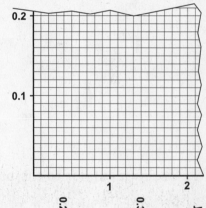

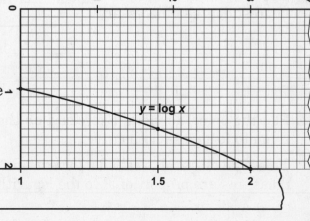

11-6

Enrichment

Spirals

Consider an angle in standard position with its vertex at a point O and its initial side on a polar axis. Remember that point P on the terminal side of the angle can be named by (r, θ), where r is the directed distance of the point from O and θ is the measure of the angle. As you learned, graphs in this system may be drawn on polar coordinate paper such as the kind shown below.

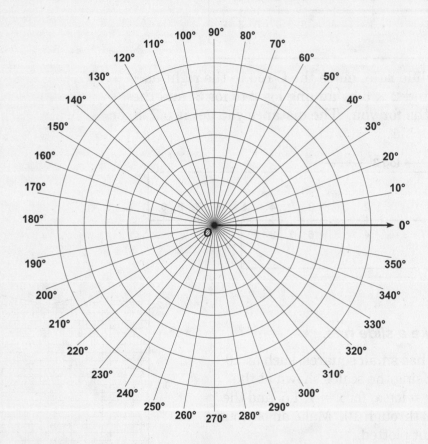

1. Use a calculator to complete the table for $\log_2 r = \dfrac{\theta}{120}$. (To find $\log_2 a$ on a calculator, press [LOG] a [÷] [LOG] 2). Round θ to the nearest degree if necessary.

r		1	2	3	4	5	6	7	8
θ									

2. Plot the points found in Exercise 1 on the grid above and connect them to form a smooth curve.

This type of spiral is called a *logarithmic spiral* because the angle measures are proportional to the logarithms of the radii.

11-7

Enrichment

Hyperbolic Functions

The *hyperbolic functions* are a family of functions of great importance in calculus and higher-level mathematics. Because they are defined in terms of the hyperbola, their name is derived from that word. These functions have an interesting relationship to the number e and to the trigonometric functions, uniting those seemingly unrelated subjects with the conic sections.

The hyperbolic functions can be written in terms of e.

Hyperbolic sine of x: $\sinh x = \dfrac{e^x - e^{-x}}{2}$

Hyperbolic cosine of x: $\cosh x = \dfrac{e^x + e^{-x}}{2}$

Hyperbolic tangent of x: $\tanh x = \dfrac{\sinh x}{\cosh x} = \dfrac{e^x - e^{-x}}{e^x + e^{-x}}$

Identities involving hyperbolic functions exhibit strong resemblances to trigonometric identities.

Example   **Show that $\sinh 2x = 2 \sinh x \cosh x$.**

$\sinh 2x = \dfrac{e^{2x} - e^{-2x}}{2}$ $\leftarrow$ Replace x in the definition above by $2x$.

$= 2\left(\dfrac{e^{2x} - e^{-2x}}{4}\right)$

$= 2\left(\dfrac{(e^x)^2 - (e^{-x})^2}{4}\right)$ $\leftarrow$ difference of two squares

$= 2\left(\dfrac{e^x - e^{-x}}{2}\right)\left(\dfrac{e^x + e^{-x}}{2}\right)$

$= 2 \sinh x \cosh x$

1. Find $\cosh^2 x - \sinh^2 x$.

Prove each identity.

2. $\sinh(-x) = -\sinh x$

3. $\sinh(x + y) = \sinh x \cosh y + \cosh x \sinh y$

NAME _____ DATE _____ PERIOD _____

11-1 Enrichment

Look for Cases

Many problems can be partitioned into a few cases. The cases are classifications within the problem that are exclusive one to another but which taken together comprise all the possibilities in the problem. Divisions into cases are made where the characteristics of the problem are most critical.

Example If $a > b$ and $\dfrac{1}{a} > \dfrac{1}{b}$, what must be true of a and b?

One of the critical characteristics of inequalities is that changing the signs of the left and right sides requires changing the sense of the inequality. This suggests classifying a and b according to signs. Since neither a nor b can equal zero in the second inequality and $a > b$, the cases are:

(i) a and b are both positive.
(ii) a and b are both negative.
(iii) a is positive and b is negative.

An important characteristic of reciprocals is that 1 and −1 are their own reciprocals. Therefore, within each of the above cases consider examples of these three subclassifications:

(A) a and b are both greater than 1 (or < -1).
(B) a and b are both fractions whose absolute values are less than one.
(C) a is greater than 1 (or −1) and b is less than 1 (or −1).

For case (i), consider these examples.

(A) $3 > 2 \rightarrow \dfrac{1}{3} < \dfrac{1}{2}$ (B) $\dfrac{1}{4} > \dfrac{1}{5} \rightarrow 4 < 5$ (C) $\dfrac{3}{2} > \dfrac{3}{4} \rightarrow \dfrac{2}{3} < \dfrac{4}{3}$

For case (ii), consider these examples.

(A) $-2 > -3 \rightarrow -\dfrac{1}{2} < -\dfrac{1}{3}$ (B) $-\dfrac{1}{5} > -\dfrac{1}{4} \rightarrow -5 < -4$

(C) $-\dfrac{3}{4} > -\dfrac{3}{2} \rightarrow -\dfrac{4}{3} < -\dfrac{2}{3}$

For case (iii), consider these examples.

(A) $2 > -3 \rightarrow \dfrac{1}{2} > -\dfrac{1}{3}$ (B) $\dfrac{1}{5} > -\dfrac{1}{4} \rightarrow 5 > -4$ (C) $\dfrac{3}{4} > -\dfrac{3}{2} \rightarrow \dfrac{4}{3} > -\dfrac{2}{3}$

Notice that the second given inequality, $\dfrac{1}{a} > \dfrac{1}{b}$, only holds true in case (iii). We conclude that a must be positive and b negative to satisfy both given inequalities.

Complete.

1. Find the positive values of b such that $b^{x_1} > b^{x_2}$ whenever $x_1 < x_2$.
   $0 < b < 1$

2. Solve $\dfrac{x}{x+1} > 0$. **$x > 0$ or $x < -1$**

3. Find the domain of $f(x) = \sqrt{3 - |x - 2|}$. **$\{x \mid -1 \le x \le 5\}$**

NAME _____ DATE _____ PERIOD _____

11-2 Enrichment

Finding Solutions of $x^y = y^x$

Perhaps you have noticed that if x and y are interchanged in equations such as $x = y$ and $xy = 1$, the resulting equation is equivalent to the original equation. The same is true of the equation $x^y = y^x$. However, finding solutions of $x^y = y^x$ and drawing its graph is not a simple process.

Solve each problem. Assume that x and y are positive real numbers.

1. If $a > 0$, will (a, a) be a solution of $x^y = y^x$? Justify your answer.
   Yes, since $a^a = a^a$ must be true by the reflexive prop. of equality.

2. If $c > 0$, $d > 0$, and (c, d) is a solution of $x^y = y^x$, will (d, c) also be a solution? Justify your answer.
   Yes; replacing x with d, y with c gives $d^c = c^d$; but if (c, d) is a solution, $c^d = d^c$. So, by the symmetric property of equality, $d^c = c^d$ is true.

3. Use 2 as a value for y in $x^y = y^x$. The equation becomes $x^2 = 2^x$.
   a. Find equations for two functions, $f(x)$ and $g(x)$ that you could graph to find the solutions of $x^2 = 2^x$. Then graph the functions on a separate sheet of graph paper.
   $f(x) = x^2$, $g(x) = 2^x = 2^x$ See students' graphs.
   b. Use the graph you drew for part **a** to state two solutions for $x^2 = 2^x$. Then use these solutions to state two solutions for $x^y = y^x$.
   Sample answer: 2 or 4; (2, 2), (4, 2)

4. In this exercise, a graphing calculator will be very helpful. Use the technique from Exercise 3 to complete the tables below. Then graph $x^y = y^x$ for positive values of x and y. If there are asymptotes, show them in your diagram using dotted lines. Note that in the table, some values of y call for one value of x, others call for two.

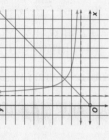

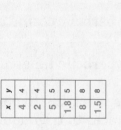

x	y
$\frac{1}{2}$	$\frac{1}{2}$
$\frac{3}{4}$	$\frac{3}{4}$
1	1
2	2
4	2
3	3
2.5	3

x	y
4	4
2	4
5	5
1.8	5
8	8
1.5	8

11-3 Enrichment

Approximations for π and e

The following expression can be used to approximate e. If greater and greater values of n are used, the value of the expression approximates e more and more closely.

$$\left(1 + \frac{1}{n}\right)^n$$

Another way to approximate e is to use this infinite sum. The greater the value of n, the closer the approximation.

$$e = 1 + 1 + \frac{1}{2} + \frac{1}{2 \cdot 3} + \frac{1}{2 \cdot 3 \cdot 4} + \dots + \frac{1}{2 \cdot 3 \cdot 4 \cdot \dots \cdot n} + \dots$$

In a similar manner, π can be approximated using an infinite product discovered by the English mathematician John Wallis (1616-1703).

$$\frac{\pi}{2} = \frac{2}{1} \cdot \frac{2}{3} \cdot \frac{4}{3} \cdot \frac{4}{5} \cdot \frac{6}{5} \cdot \frac{6}{7} \cdots \frac{2n}{2n-1} \cdot \frac{2n}{2n+1} \cdots$$

Solve each problem.

1. Use a calculator with an e^x key to find e to 7 decimal places.
   2.7182818

2. Use the expression $\left(1 + \frac{1}{n}\right)^n$ to approximate e to 3 decimal places. Use 5, 100, 500, and 7000 as values of n.
   2.488, 2.705, 2.716, 2.718

3. Use the infinite sum to approximate e to 3 decimal places. Use the whole numbers from 3 through 6 as values of n.
   2.667, 2.708, 2.717, 2.718

4. Which approximation method approaches the value of e more quickly?
   the infinite sum

5. Use a calculator with a π key to find π to 7 decimal places.
   3.1415927

6. Use the infinite product to approximate π to 3 decimal places. Use the whole numbers from 3 through 6 as values of n.
   2.926, 2.972, 3.002, 3.023

7. Does the infinite product give good approximations for π quickly?
   no

8. Show that $\pi^4 + \pi^5$ is equal to e^6 to 4 decimal places.
   To 4 decimal places, they both equal 403.4288.

9. Which is larger, e^π or π^e?
   $e^\pi > \pi^e$

10. The expression $x^{\frac{1}{x}}$ reaches a maximum value at $x = e$. Use this fact to prove the inequality you found in Exercise 9.
    $e^{\frac{1}{e}} > \pi^{\frac{1}{\pi}} ; \left(e^{\frac{1}{e}}\right)^{\pi e} > \left(\pi^{\frac{1}{\pi}}\right)^{\pi e} ; e^\pi > \pi^e$

11-4 Enrichment

Musical Relationships

The frequencies of notes in a musical scale that are one octave apart are related by an exponential equation. For the eight C notes on a piano, the equation is $C_n = C_1 2^{n-1}$, where C_n represents the frequency of note C_n.

1. Find the relationship between C_1 and C_2.
   $C_2 = 2C_1$

2. Find the relationship between C_1 and C_4.
   $C_4 = 8C_1$

The frequencies of consecutive notes are related by a common ratio r. The general equation is $f_n = f_1 r^{n-1}$.

3. If the frequency of middle C is 261.6 cycles per second and the frequency of the next higher C is 523.2 cycles per second, find the common ratio r. (Hint: The two Cs are 12 notes apart.) Write the answer as a radical expression.
   $r = \sqrt[12]{2}$

4. Substitute decimal values for r and f_1 to find a specific equation for f_n.
   $f_n = 261.6\,(1.05946)^{n-1}$

5. Find the frequency of F$^\#$ above middle C.
   $f_7 = 261.6\,(1.05946)^6 \approx 369.95$

6. The frets on a guitar are spaced so that the sound made by pressing a string against one fret has about 1.0595 times the wavelength of the sound made by using the next fret. The general equation is $u_n = u_0\,(1.0595)^n$. Describe the arrangement of the frets on a guitar.
   The frets are spaced in a logarithmic scale.

11-5 Enrichment

The Slide Rule

Before the invention of electronic calculators, computations were often performed on a slide rule. A slide rule is based on the idea of logarithms. It has two movable rods labeled with C and D scales. Each of the scales is logarithmic.

To multiply 2×3 on a slide rule, move the C rod to the right as shown below. You can find 2×3 by adding $\log 2$ to $\log 3$, and the slide rule adds the lengths for you. The distance you get is 0.778, or the logarithm of 6.

1-2 See students' work.

Follow the steps to make a slide rule.

1. Use graph paper that has small squares, such as 10 squares to the inch. Using the scales shown at the right, plot the curve $y = \log x$ for $x = 1$, 1.5, and the whole numbers from 2 through 10. Make an obvious heavy dot for each point plotted.

2. You will need two strips of cardboard. A 5-by-7 index card, cut in half the long way, will work fine. Turn the graph you made in Exercise 1 sideways and use it to mark a logarithmic scale on each of the two strips. The figure shows the mark for 2 being drawn.

3. Explain how to use a slide rule to divide **8 by 2. Line up the 2 on the C scale with the 8 on the D scale. The quotient is the number on the D scale below the 1 on the C scale.**

T125 *Advanced Mathematical Concepts*

11-6 Enrichment

Spirals

Consider an angle in standard position with its vertex at a point O and its initial side on a polar axis. Remember that point P on the terminal side of the angle can be named by (r, θ), where r is the directed distance of the point from O and θ is the measure of the angle. As you learned, graphs in this system may be drawn on polar coordinate paper such as the kind shown below.

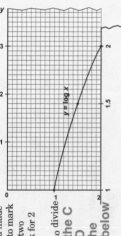
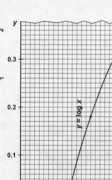

1. Use a calculator to complete the table for $\log_2 r = \frac{\theta}{120}$. (To find $\log_2 a$ on a calculator, press $\boxed{\text{LOG}}\ a\ \boxed{+}\ \boxed{\text{LOG}}\ 2$). Round θ to the nearest degree if necessary.

r	1	2	3	4	5	6	7	8
θ	0°	120°	190°	240°	279°	310°	337°	360°

2. Plot the points found in Exercise 1 on the grid above and connect them to form a smooth curve. **See graph above.**

This type of spiral is called a *logarithmic spiral* because the angle measures are proportional to the logarithms of the radii.

T126 *Advanced Mathematical Concepts*

NAME _____ DATE _____ PERIOD _____

11-7 Enrichment

Hyperbolic Functions

The *hyperbolic functions* are a family of functions of great importance in calculus and higher-level mathematics. Because they are defined in terms of the hyperbola, their name is derived from that word. These functions have an interesting relationship to the number e and to the trigonometric functions, uniting those seemingly unrelated subjects with the conic sections.

The hyperbolic functions can be written in terms of e.

Hyperbolic sine of x: $\sinh x = \dfrac{e^x - e^{-x}}{2}$

Hyperbolic cosine of x: $\cosh x = \dfrac{e^x + e^{-x}}{2}$

Hyperbolic tangent of x: $\tanh x = \dfrac{\sinh x}{\cosh x} = \dfrac{e^x - e^{-x}}{e^x + e^{-x}}$

Identities involving hyperbolic functions exhibit strong resemblances to trigonometric identities.

Example   **Show that $\sinh 2x = 2 \sinh x \cosh x$.**

$$\sinh\ 2x = \frac{e^{2x} - e^{-2x}}{2} \qquad \leftarrow \ \text{Replace } x \text{ in the definition above by } 2x.$$

$$= 2\left(\frac{e^{2x} - e^{-2x}}{4}\right)$$

$$= 2\left(\frac{(e^x)^2 - (e^{-x})^2}{4}\right) \qquad \leftarrow \ \text{difference of two squares}$$

$$= 2\left(\frac{e^x - e^{-x}}{2}\right)\left(\frac{e^x + e^{-x}}{2}\right)$$

$$= 2 \sinh x \cosh x$$

1. Find $\cosh^2 x - \sinh^2 x$.   **1**

Prove each identity.

2. $\sinh(-x) = -\sinh x$

$\sinh(-x) = \dfrac{e^{-x} - e^x}{2} = \dfrac{-(e^x - e^{-x})}{2} = -\left(\dfrac{e^x - e^{-x}}{2}\right) = -\sinh x$

3. $\sinh(x + y) = \sinh x \cosh y + \cosh x \sinh y$

$\sinh(x + y) = \dfrac{e^{x+y} - e^{-(x+y)}}{2}$

$= \dfrac{e^{x+y} - e^{-(x+y)}}{4} + \dfrac{e^{x+y} - e^{-(x+y)}}{4}$

$= \dfrac{e^x - e^{-x}}{2} \cdot \dfrac{e^y + e^{-y}}{2} + \dfrac{e^x + e^{-x}}{2} \cdot \dfrac{e^y - e^{-y}}{2}$

$= \sinh x \cosh y + \cosh x \sinh y$

12-1

Enrichment

Quadratic Formulas for Sequences

An ordinary arithmetic sequence is formed using a rule such as $bn + c$. The first term is c, b is called the common difference, and n takes on the values 0, 1, 2, 3, and so on. The value of term $n + 1$ equals $b(n + 1) + c$ or $bn + b + c$. So, the value of a term is a function of the term number.

Some sequences use quadratic functions. A method called *finite differences* can be used to find the values of the terms. Notice what happens when you subtract twice as shown in this table.

n	$an^2 + bn + c$
0	c
1	$a + b + c$
2	$4a + 2b + c$
3	$9a + 3b + c$
4	$16a + 4b + c$

$a + b$ $3a + b$ $5a + b$ $7a + b$ $2a$ $2a$ $2a$

A sequence that yields a common difference after two subtractions can be generated by a quadratic expression. For example, the sequence 1, 5, 12, 22, 35, . . . gives a common difference of 3 after two subtractions. Using the table above, you write and solve three equations to find the general rule. The equations are $1 = c$, $5 = a + b + c$, and $12 = 4a + 2b + c$.

Solve each problem.

1. Refer to the sequence in the example above. Solve the system of equations for a, b, and c and then find the quadratic expression for the sequence. Then write the next three terms.

2. The number of line segments connecting n points forms the sequence 0, 0, 1, 3, 6, 10, . . . , in which n is the number of points and the term value is the number of line segments. What is the common difference after the second subtraction? Find a quadratic expression for the term value.

3. The maximum number of regions formed by n chords in a circle forms the sequence 1, 2, 4, 7, 11, 16, . . . (A chord is a line segment joining any two points on a circle.) Draw circles to illustrate the first four terms of the sequence. Then find a quadratic expression for the term value.

12-2

Enrichment

Sequences as Functions

A **geometric sequence** can be defined as a function whose domain is the set of positive integers.

$$n = \quad 1 \quad\quad 2 \quad\quad 3 \quad\quad 4 \quad\quad \ldots$$
$$\downarrow \quad\quad \downarrow \quad\quad \downarrow \quad\quad \downarrow \quad\quad \downarrow$$
$$f(n) = \quad ar^{1-1} \quad ar^{2-1} \quad ar^{3-1} \quad ar^{4-1} \quad \ldots$$

In the exercises, you will have the opportunity to explore geometric sequences from a function and graphing point of view.

Graph each geometric sequence for n = 1, 2, 3 and 4.

1. $f(n) = 2^n$

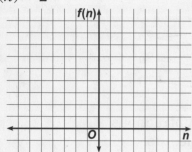

2. $f(n) = (0.5)^n$

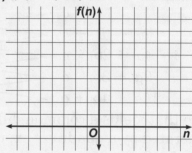

3. $f(n) = (-2)^n$

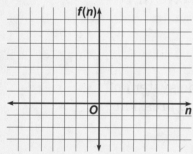

4. $f(n) = (-0.5)^n$

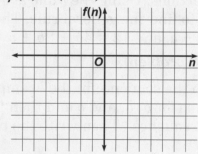

5. Describe how the graph of a geometric sequence depends on the common ratio.

6. Let $f(n) = 2^n$, where n is a positive integer.

   a. Show graphically that for any M the graph of $f(n)$ rises above and stays above the horizontal line $y = M$.

   b. Show algebraically that for any M, there is a positive integer N such that $2^n > M$ for all $n > N$.

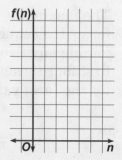

12-3

Enrichment

Solving Equations Using Sequences

You can use sequences to solve many equations. For example, consider $x^2 + x - 1 = 0$. You can proceed as follows.

$$x^2 + x - 1 = 0$$

$$x(x + 1) = 1$$

$$x = \frac{1}{1 + x}$$

Next, define the sequence: $a_1 = 0$ and $a_n = \frac{1}{1 + a_{n-1}}$.

The limit of the sequence is a solution to the original equation.

1. Let $a_1 = 0$ and $a_n = \frac{1}{1 + a_{n-1}}$.

   a. Write the first five terms of the sequence. Do not simplify.

   b. Write decimals for the first five terms of the sequence.

   c. Use a calculator to compute a_6, a_7, a_8, and a_9. Compare a_9 with the positive solution of $x^2 + x - 1 = 0$ found by using the quadratic formula.

2. Use the method described above to find a root of $3x^2 - 2x - 3 = 0$.

3. Write a BASIC program using the procedure outlined above to find a root of the equation $3x^2 - 2x - 3 = 0$. In the program,

   let $a_1 = 0$ and $a_n = \frac{3}{3a_{n-1} - 2}$. Run the program. Compare the

   time it takes to run the program to the time it takes to evaluate the terms of the sequence by using a calculator.

12-4

Enrichment

Alternating Series

The series below is called an alternating series.

$$1 - 1 + 1 - 1 + \cdots$$

The reason is that the signs of the terms alternate. An interesting question is whether the series converges. In the exercises, you will have an opportunity to explore this series and others like it.

1. Consider $1 - 1 + 1 - 1 + \cdots$.

   a. Write an argument that suggests that the sum is 1.

   b. Write an argument that suggests that the sum is 0.

   c. Write an argument that suggests that there is no sum.
   (*Hint*: Consider the sequence of partial sums.)

If the series formed by taking the absolute values of the terms of a given series is convergent, then the given series is said to be **absolutely convergent**. It can be shown that any absolutely convergent series is convergent.

2. Make up an alternating series, other than a geometric series with negative common ratio, that has a sum. Justify your answer.

12-5

Enrichment

Street Networks: Finding All Possible Routes

A section of a city is laid out in square blocks. Going north from the intersection of 1st Avenue and 1st Street, the avenues are 1st, 2nd, 3rd, and so on. Going east, the streets are numbered in the same way.

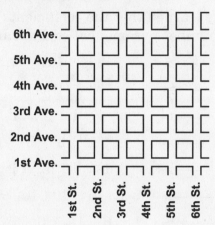

Factorials can be used to find the number, $r(e, n)$, of different routes between two intersections.

$$r(e, n) = \frac{[(e - 1) + (n - 1)]!}{(e - 1)! \, (n - 1)!}$$

The number of streets going east is e; the number of avenues going north is n.

The following problems examine the possible routes from one location to another. Assume that you never use a route that is unnecessarily long. Assume that $e \geq 1$ and $n \geq 1$.

Solve each problem.

1. List all the possible routes from 1st Street and 1st Avenue to 4th Street and 3rd Avenue. Use ordered pairs to show the routes, with street numbers first and avenue numbers second. Each route must start at (1, 1) and end at (4, 3).

2. Use the formula to compute the number of routes from (1, 1) to (4, 3). There are 4 streets going east and 3 avenues going north.

3. Find the number of routes from 1st Street and 1st Avenue to 7th Street and 6th Avenue.

       Advanced Mathematical Concepts

12-6

Enrichment

Patterns in Pascal's Triangle

You have learned that the coefficients in the expansion of $(x + y)^n$ yield a number pyramid called **Pascal's triangle**.

Row 1 ⟶ 1
Row 2 ⟶ 1 1
Row 3 ⟶ 1 2 1
Row 4 ⟶ 1 3 3 1
Row 5 ⟶ 1 4 6 4 1
Row 6 ⟶ 1 5 10 10 5 1
Row 7 ⟶ 1 6 15 20 15 6 1

As many rows can be added to the bottom of the pyramid as you need.

This activity explores some of the interesting properties of this famous number pyramid.

1. Pick a row of Pascal's triangle.
   a. What is the sum of all the numbers in all the rows above the row you picked?

   b. What is the sum of all the numbers in the row you picked?

   c. How are your answers for parts **a** and **b** related?

   d. Repeat parts **a** through **c** for at least three more rows of Pascal's triangle. What generalization seems to be true?

   e. See if you can prove your generalization.

2. Pick any row of Pascal's triangle that comes after the first.
   a. Starting at the left end of the row, find the sum of the odd numbered terms.

   b. In the same row, find the sum of the even numbered terms.

   c. How do the sums in parts a and b compare?

   d. Repeat parts **a** through **c** for at least three other rows of Pascal's triangle. What generalization seems to be true?

12-7 Enrichment

Power Series

A **power series** is a series of the form

$$a_0 + a_1x + a_2x^2 + a_3x^3 + \cdots$$

where each a_i is a real number. Many functions can be represented by power series. For instance, the function $f(x) = e^x$ can be represented by the series

$$e^x = 1 + x + \frac{x^2}{2!} + \frac{x^3}{3!} + \cdots .$$

Use a graphing calculator or computer to graph the functions in Exercises 1–4.

1. $f_2(x) = 1 + x$

2. $f_3(x) = 1 + x + \frac{x^2}{2!}$

3. $f_4(x) = 1 + x + \frac{x^2}{2!} + \frac{x^3}{3!}$

4. $f_5(x) = 1 + x + \frac{x^2}{2!} + \frac{x^3}{3!} + \frac{x^4}{4!}$

5. Write a statement that relates the sequence of graphs suggested by Exercies 1–4 and the function $y = e^x$.

6. The series $1 + x^2 + x^4 + x^6 + \cdots$ is a power series for which each $a_i = 1$. The series is also a geometric series with first term 1 and common ratio x^2.

 a. Find the function that this power series represents.

 b. For what values of x does the series give the values of the function in part **a**?

7. Find a power series representation for the function $f(x) = \dfrac{3}{1 + x^2}$.

12-8

Enrichment

Depreciation

To run a business, a company purchases assets such as equipment or buildings. For tax purposes, the company distributes the cost of these assets as a business expense over the course of a number of years. Since assets depreciate (lose some of their market value) as they get older, companies must be able to figure the depreciation expense they are allowed to take when they file their income taxes.

Depreciation expense is a function of these three values:
1. **asset cost**, or the amount the company paid for the asset;
2. **estimated useful life**, or the number of years the company can expect to use the asset;
3. **residual or trade-in value**, or the expected cash value of the asset at the end of its useful life.

In any given year, the **book value** of an asset is equal to the asset cost minus the accumulated depreciation. This value represents the unused amount of asset cost that the company may depreciate in future years. The useful life of the asset is over once its book value is equal to its residual value.

There are several methods of determining the amount of depreciation in a given year. In the **declining-balance method**, the depreciation expense allowed each year is equal to the book value of the asset at the beginning of the year times the depreciation rate. Since the depreciation expense for any year is dependent upon the depreciation expense for the previous year, the process of determining the depreciation expense for a year is an iteration.

The table below shows the first two iterates of the depreciation schedule for a $2500 computer with a residual value of $500 if the depreciation rate is 40%.

End of Year	Asset Cost	Depreciation Expense	Book Value at End of Year
1	$2500	$1000 (40% of $2500)	$1500 ($2500 - $1000)
2	$2500	$600 (40% of $1500)	$900 ($1500 - $600)

1. Find the next two iterates for the depreciation expense function.

2. Find the next two iterates for the end-of-year book value function.

3. Explain the depreciation expense for year 5.

12-9

Enrichment

Conjectures and Mathematical Induction

Frequently, the pattern in a set of numbers is not immediately evident. Once you make a conjecture about a pattern, you can use mathematical induction to prove your conjecture.

1. a. Graph $f(x) = x^2$ and $g(x) = 2^x$ on the axes shown at the right.

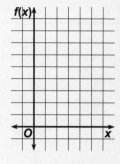

   b. Write a conjecture that compares n^2 and 2^n, where n is a positive integer.

   c. Use mathematical induction to prove your response from part b.

2. Refer to the diagrams at the right.

   a. How many dots would there be in the fourth diagram S_4 in the sequence?

S_1 S_2 S_3

   b. Describe a method that you can use to determine the number of dots in the fifth diagram S_5 based on the number of dots in the fourth diagram, S_4. Verify your answer by constructing the fifth diagram.

   c. Find a formula that can be used to compute the number of dots in the nth diagram of this sequence. Use mathematical induction to prove your formula is correct.

12-1 Enrichment

Quadratic Formulas for Sequences

An ordinary arithmetic sequence is formed using a rule such as $bn + c$. The first term is c, b is called the common difference, and n takes on the values 0, 1, 2, 3, and so on. The value of term $n + 1$ equals $b(n + 1) + c$ or $bn + b + c$. So, the value of a term is a function of the term number.

Some sequences use quadratic functions. A method called *finite differences* can be used to find the values of the terms. Notice what happens when you subtract twice as shown in this table.

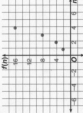

n	$an^2 + bn + c$		
0	c		
1	$a + b + c$	$a + b$	
2	$4a + 2b + c$	$3a + b$	$2a$
3	$9a + 3b + c$	$5a + b$	$2a$
4	$16a + 4b + c$	$7a + b$	$2a$

A sequence that yields a common difference after two subtractions can be generated by a quadratic expression. For example, the sequence 1, 5, 12, 22, 35, . . . gives a common difference of 3 after two subtractions. Using the table above, you write and solve three equations to find the general rule. The equations are $1 = c$, $5 = a + b + c$, and $12 = 4a + 2b + c$.

Solve each problem.

1. Refer to the sequence in the example above. Solve the system of equations for a, b, and c and then find the quadratic expression for the sequence. Then write the next three terms.

   $\frac{3}{2}n^2 + \frac{5}{2}n + 1;$ **51, 70, 92**

2. The number of line segments connecting n points forms the sequence 0, 0, 1, 3, 6, 10, . . . , in which n is the number of points and the term value is the number of line segments. What is the common difference after the second subtraction? Find a quadratic expression for the term value.

   $1; \frac{1}{2}n^2 - \frac{1}{2}n$

3. The maximum number of regions formed by n chords in a circle forms the sequence 1, 2, 4, 7, 11, 16, . . . (A chord is a line segment joining any two points on a circle.) Draw circles to illustrate the first four terms of the sequence. Then find a quadratic expression for the term value.

   $\frac{1}{2}n^2 + \frac{1}{2}n + 1$

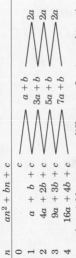

T133 *Advanced Mathematical Concepts*

12-2 Enrichment

Sequences as Functions

A **geometric sequence** can be defined as a function whose domain is the set of positive integers.

$$n = \quad 1 \quad 2 \quad 3 \quad 4$$
$$f(n) = \quad ar^{1-1} \quad ar^{2-1} \quad ar^{3-1} \quad ar^{4-1} \quad \ldots$$

In the exercises, you will have the opportunity to explore geometric sequences from a function and graphing point of view.

Graph each geometric sequence for $n = 1, 2, 3$ and 4.

1. $f(n) = 2^n$

2. $f(n) = (0.5)^n$

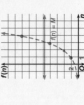

3. $f(n) = (-2)^n$

4. $f(n) = (-0.5)^n$

5. Describe how the graph of a geometric sequence depends on the common ratio.

   $r > 1$: **graph rises to the right.**

   $r < -1$: **graph rises and falls and high and low points move away from the n-axis.**

   $0 < r < 1$: **graph falls to the right.**

   $-1 < r < 0$: **graph rises and falls and high and low points approach the n-axis.**

6. Let $f(n) = 2^n$, where n is a positive integer.

   a. Show graphically that for any M the graph of $f(n)$ rises above and stays above the horizontal line $y = M$.

   b. Show algebraically that for any M, there is a positive integer N such that $2^n > M$ for all $n > N$.

   Choose a positive integer $N > \log_2 M$. Then $2^N > 2^{\log_2 M} = M$.

T134 *Advanced Mathematical Concepts*

12-3 Enrichment

Solving Equations Using Sequences

You can use sequences to solve many equations. For example, consider $x^2 + x - 1 = 0$. You can proceed as follows.

$$x^2 + x - 1 = 0$$
$$x(x + 1) = 1$$
$$x = \frac{1}{1 + x}$$

Next, define the sequence: $a_1 = 0$ and $a_n = \frac{1}{1 + a_{n-1}}$.

The limit of the sequence is a solution to the original equation.

1. Let $a_1 = 0$ and $a_n = \frac{1}{1 + a_{n-1}}$.

a. Write the first five terms of the sequence. Do not simplify.

$$0, 1, \frac{1}{1+1}, \frac{1}{1+\frac{1}{1+1}}, \frac{1}{1+\frac{1}{1+\frac{1}{1+1}}}$$

b. Write decimals for the first five terms of the sequence.
0, 1, 0.5, 0.6667, 0.6

c. Use a calculator to compute a_6, a_7, a_8, and a_9. Compare a_9 with the positive solution of $x^2 + x - 1 = 0$ found by using the quadratic formula.
0.625, 0.6154, 0.6190, 0.6176; solution by quadratic formula: 0.6180

2. Use the method described above to find a root of $3x^2 - 2x - 3 = 0$. **−0.7208**

3. Write a BASIC program using the procedure outlined above to find a root of the equation $3x^2 - 2x - 3 = 0$. In the program,

let $a_1 = 0$ and $a_n = \frac{3}{3a_{n-1} - 2}$. Run the program. Compare the

time it takes to run the program to the time it takes to evaluate the terms of the sequence by using a calculator.

```
10 DIM A[100]
20 A[1] = 0
30 FOR I = 2 TO 100
40 A[I] = 3/(3*A[I − 1] − 2)
50 NEXT I
60 PRINT A[100]
```

12-4 Enrichment

Alternating Series

The series below is called an alternating series.

$$1 - 1 + 1 - 1 + \cdots$$

The reason is that the signs of the terms alternate. An interesting question is whether the series converges. In the exercises, you will have an opportunity to explore this series and others like it.

1. Consider $1 - 1 + 1 - 1 + \cdots$.

a. Write an argument that suggests that the sum is 1.
$$1 - 1 + 1 - 1 + \cdots = 1 + (-1 + 1) + (-1 + 1) + \cdots$$
$$= 1 + 0 + 0 + \cdots$$
$$= 1$$

b. Write an argument that suggests that the sum is 0.
$$1 - 1 + 1 - 1 + \cdots = (1 - 1) + (1 - 1) + (1 - 1) + \cdots$$
$$= 0 + 0 + 0 + \cdots$$
$$= 0$$

c. Write an argument that suggests that there is no sum. (*Hint:* Consider the sequence of partial sums.)
Let S_n be the nth partial sum. Then
$$S_n = \begin{cases} 1 \text{ if } n \text{ is odd.} \\ 0 \text{ if } n \text{ is even.} \end{cases}$$
Since 1, 0, 1, 0, ... has no limit, the original series has no sum.

If the series formed by taking the absolute values of the terms of a given series is convergent, then the given series is said to be **absolutely convergent**. It can be shown that any absolutely convergent series is convergent.

2. Make up an alternating series, other than a geometric series with negative common ratio, that has a sum. Justify your answer. **Sample answer:**
$$\frac{1}{1} - \frac{1}{4} + \frac{1}{9} - \frac{1}{16} + \cdots \text{ is convergent because}$$
the absolute value of each term is less than or equal to the corresponding term in a p-series with $p = 2$.

12-5 Enrichment

NAME _____ DATE _____ PERIOD _____

Street Networks: Finding All Possible Routes

A section of a city is laid out in square blocks. Going north from the intersection of 1st Avenue and 1st Street, the avenues are 1st, 2nd, 3rd, and so on. Going east, the streets are numbered in the same way.

Factorials can be used to find the number, $r(e, n)$, of different routes between two intersections.

$$r(e, n) = \frac{[(e-1) + (n-1)]!}{(e-1)!\,(n-1)!}$$

The number of streets going east is e; the number of avenues going north is n.

The following problems examine the possible routes from one location to another. Assume that you never use a route that is unnecessarily long. Assume that $e \geq 1$ and $n \geq 1$.

Solve each problem.

1. List all the possible routes from 1st Street and 1st Avenue to 4th Street and 3rd Avenue. Use ordered pairs to show the routes, with street numbers first and avenue numbers second. Each route must start at (1, 1) and end at (4, 3).

(1, 1) → (2, 1) → (3, 1) → (4, 1) → (4, 2) → (4, 3)
(1, 1) → (2, 1) → (3, 1) → (4, 1) → (4, 2) → (4, 3)
(1, 1) → (2, 1) → (3, 1) → (3, 2) → (3, 3) → (4, 3)
(1, 1) → (2, 1) → (3, 1) → (3, 2) → (4, 2) → (4, 3)
(1, 1) → (2, 1) → (2, 2) → (2, 3) → (3, 3) → (4, 3)
(1, 1) → (2, 1) → (2, 2) → (3, 2) → (4, 2) → (4, 3)
(1, 1) → (2, 1) → (2, 2) → (3, 2) → (3, 3) → (4, 3)
(1, 1) → (1, 2) → (2, 2) → (2, 3) → (3, 3) → (4, 3)
(1, 1) → (1, 2) → (2, 2) → (3, 2) → (4, 2) → (4, 3)
(1, 1) → (1, 2) → (2, 2) → (3, 2) → (3, 3) → (4, 3)
(1, 1) → (1, 2) → (2, 2) → (2, 3) → (3, 3) → (4, 3)
(1, 1) → (1, 2) → (1, 3) → (2, 3) → (3, 3) → (4, 3)

2. Use the formula to compute the number of routes from (1, 1) to (4, 3). There are 4 streets going east and 3 avenues going north.

$$\frac{(3 + 2)!}{3!\,2!} = 10$$

3. Find the number of routes from 1st Street and 1st Avenue to 7th Street and 6th Avenue.

$$\frac{(6 + 5)!}{6!\,5!} = 462$$

12-6 Enrichment

NAME _____ DATE _____ PERIOD _____

Patterns in Pascal's Triangle

You have learned that the coefficients in the expansion of $(x + y)^n$ yield a number pyramid called **Pascal's triangle.**

Row 1 → 1 1
Row 2 → 1 1
Row 3 → 1 2 1
Row 4 → 1 3 3 1
Row 5 → 1 4 6 4 1
Row 6 → 1 5 10 10 5 1
Row 7 → 1 6 15 20 15 6 1

As many rows can be added to the bottom of the pyramid as you need.

This activity explores some of the interesting properties of this famous number pyramid.

1. Pick a row of Pascal's triangle.
   a. What is the sum of all the numbers in all the rows above the row you picked? **See students' work.**
   b. What is the sum of all the numbers in the row you picked? **See students' work.**
   c. How are your answers for parts a and b related? **The answer for part b is 1 more than the answer for part a.**
   d. Repeat parts a through c for at least three more rows of Pascal's triangle. What generalization seems to be true? **It appears that the sum of the numbers in any row is 1 more than the sum of the numbers in all of the rows above it.**
   e. See if you can prove your generalization. **Sum of numbers in row $n = 2^{n-1}$. The sum of the numbers in the rows above row n is $2^0 + 2^1 + 2^2 + \ldots + 2^{n-2}$, which, by the formula for sum of a geometric series, is $2^{n-1} - 1$.**

2. Pick any row of Pascal's triangle that comes after the first.
   a. Starting at the left end of the row, find the sum of the odd numbered terms. **See students' work.**
   b. In the same row, find the sum of the even numbered terms. **See students' work.**
   c. How do the sums in parts a and b compare? **The sums are equal.**
   d. Repeat parts a through c for at least three other rows of Pascal's triangle. What generalization seems to be true? **In any row of Pascal's triangle after the first, the sum of the odd numbered terms is equal to the sum of the even numbered terms.**

12-7 Enrichment

Power Series

A **power series** is a series of the form

$$a_0 + a_1 x + a_2 x^2 + a_3 x^3 + \cdots$$

where each a_i is a real number. Many functions can be represented by power series. For instance, the function $f(x) = e^x$ can be represented by the series

$$e^x = 1 + x + \frac{x^2}{2!} + \frac{x^3}{3!} + \cdots.$$

Check students' graphs.
Use a graphing calculator or computer to graph the functions in Exercises 1–4.

1. $f_2(x) = 1 + x$

2. $f_3(x) = 1 + x + \frac{x^2}{2!}$

3. $f_4(x) = 1 + x + \frac{x^2}{2!} + \frac{x^3}{3!}$

4. $f_5(x) = 1 + x + \frac{x^2}{2!} + \frac{x^3}{3!} + \frac{x^4}{4!}$

5. Write a statement that relates the sequence of graphs suggested by Exercises 1–4 and the function $y = e^x$.

The functions defined by the partial sums converge to $y = e^x$. That is, as n increases, the graphs of f_n come into closer coincidence with the graph of $y = e^x$ for more and more values of x.

6. The series $1 + x^2 + x^4 + x^6 + \cdots$ is a power series for which each $a_i = 1$. The series is also a geometric series with first term 1 and common ratio x^2.

   a. Find the function that this power series represents. $y = \dfrac{1}{1 - x^2}$

   b. For what values of x does the series give the values of the function in part **a**? $-1 < x < 1$

7. Find a power series representation for the function $f(x) = \dfrac{3}{1 + x^2}$.

   $3 - 3x^2 + 3x^4 - 3x^6 + \cdots$

12-8 Enrichment

Depreciation

To run a business, a company purchases assets such as equipment or buildings. For tax purposes, the company distributes the cost of these assets as a business expense over the course of a number of years. Since assets depreciate (lose some of their market value) as they get older, companies must be able to figure the depreciation expense they are allowed to take when they file their income taxes.

Depreciation expense is a function of these three values:
1. **asset cost**, or the amount the company paid for the asset;
2. **estimated useful life**, or the number of years the company can expect to use the asset;
3. **residual or trade-in value**, or the expected cash value of the asset at the end of its useful life.

In any given year, the **book value** of an asset is equal to the asset cost minus the accumulated depreciation. This value represents the unused amount of asset cost that the company may depreciate in future years. The useful life of the asset is over once its book value is equal to its residual value.

There are several methods of determining the amount of depreciation in a given year. In the **declining-balance method**, the depreciation expense allowed each year is equal to the book value of the asset at the beginning of the year times the depreciation rate. Since the depreciation expense for any year is dependent upon the depreciation expense for the previous year, the process of determining the depreciation expense for a year is an iteration.

The table below shows the first two iterates of the depreciation schedule for a $2500 computer with a residual value of $500 if the depreciation rate is 40%.

End of Year	Asset Cost	Depreciation Expense	Book Value at End of Year
1	$2500	$1000 (40% of $2500)	$1500 ($2500 - $1000)
2	$2500	$600 (40% of $1500)	$900 ($1500 - $600)

1. Find the next two iterates for the depreciation expense function.
   $360; $40 (only $40 remains of the asset cost before the residual value is reached)

2. Find the next two iterates for the end-of-year book value function.
   $540; $500

3. Explain the depreciation expense for year 5.
   There is no depreciation expense because the book value equals the residual value.

NAME _____ DATE _____ PERIOD _____

12-9

Enrichment

Conjectures and Mathematical Induction

Frequently, the pattern in a set of numbers is not immediately evident. Once you make a conjecture about a pattern, you can use mathematical induction to prove your conjecture.

1. **a.** Graph $f(x) = x^2$ and $g(x) = 2^x$ on the axes shown at the right.

   b. Write a conjecture that compares n^2 and 2^n, where n is a positive integer. **If $n > 4$, $n^2 < 2^n$.**

   c. Use mathematical induction to prove your response from part b.

   $n = 5$: $5^2 = 25 < 2^5$
   $5^2 = 25 < 32 = 2^5$

   Assume the statement is true for $n = k$. Prove it is true for $n = k + 1$.

   $(k+1)^2 = k^2 + 2k + 1 < k^2 + (k-1)k + 1$ since $2 < k - 1$
   $< k^2 + 2^k + 1 - k$ since $k^2 < 2^k$
   $< 2^k + 2^k$ since $1 - k < 0$
   $= 2^{k+1}$

   So the statement is true for $n > 4$.

2. Refer to the diagrams at the right.

S_1 S_2 S_3

   a. How many dots would there be in the fourth diagram S_4 in the sequence?
   16

   b. Describe a method that you can use to determine the number of dots in the fifth diagram S_5 based on the number of dots in the fourth diagram, S_4. Verify your answer by constructing the fifth diagram.

   Add 5 to the number of dots in S_4. S_5 would have $16 + 5$ or 21 dots.

   c. Find a formula that can be used to compute the number of dots in the nth diagram of this sequence. Use mathematical induction to prove your formula is correct. $S_n = 5_n - 4$

   Verify that S_n is true for $n = 1$.
   $S_1 = 5(1) - 4$ or 1. Assume S_n is true for $n = k$. Prove it is true for $n = k + 1$.

   $S_{k+1} = S_k + 5$
   $S_{k+1} = 5(k+1) - 4$
   $= 5k + 5 - 4$
   $= (5k - 4) + 5$
   $= S_k + 5$

13-1

Enrichment

Permutation and Combination Algebra

Expressions involving $P(n, r)$ and $C(n, r)$, the symbols for permutations and combinations, can sometimes be simplified or used in equations as though they were algebraic expressions. You can solve problems involving such expressions by applying the definitions of $P(n, r)$ and $C(n, r)$.

Example **Simplify $C(n, n-1)$.**

By the definition of $C(n, r)$, $C(n, n-1) = \dfrac{n!}{(n-[n-1])!(n-1)!}$

$$= \dfrac{n!}{(n-n+1)!(n-1)!}$$

$$= \dfrac{n!}{1!(n-1)!}$$

$$= \dfrac{n!}{(n-1)!}$$

$$= n$$

Simplify.

1. $P(n, n-1)$

2. $C(n, n)$

3. $C(n, 1)$

4. $P(n, n)$

5. $C(n+1, n)$

6. $C(n+1, n-1)$

Solve for n.

7. $P(n, 5) = 7\, P(n, 4)$

8. $C(n, n-2) = 6$

9. $C(n+2, 4) = 6\, C(n, 2)$

10. $P(n, 5) = 9\, P(n-1, 4)$

13-2

Enrichment

Approximating Factorials

James Stirling (1692-1770) was a teacher, a friend of Sir Isaac
Newton, and a mathematician who made important contributions to
calculus. Today he is best remembered as the creator of a formula for
approximating factorials.

Stirling's Formula	$n! \approx \sqrt{2n\pi}\left(\dfrac{n}{e}\right)^n$, where e is the irrational number 2.7182818....

1. Stirling proved that the ratio $\dfrac{n!}{\sqrt{2n\pi}\left(\dfrac{n}{e}\right)^n}$ is less than $\dfrac{12n}{12n-1}$.

As n increases, will the approximations obtained using Stirling's
formula become more accurate or less accurate? Explain.

2. Complete the chart.

n	$n!$	$\sqrt{2n\pi}\left(\dfrac{n}{e}\right)^n$	$\dfrac{n!}{\sqrt{2n\pi}\left(\dfrac{n}{e}\right)^n}$
10			
20			
30			
40			
50			
60			

148

13-3

Enrichment

Geometric Probability

If a dart, thrown at random, hits the triangular
board shown at the right, what is the chance
that is will hit the shaded region? This chance,
also called a probability, can be determined by
analyzing the area of the board. This ratio
indicates what fraction of the tosses should hit
in the shaded region.

$$\frac{\text{area of shaded region}}{\text{area of triangular board}} = \frac{\frac{1}{2}(4)(6)}{\frac{1}{2}(8)(6)}$$

$$= \frac{12}{24} \text{ or } \frac{1}{2}$$

In general, if S is a subregion of some region R, then the probability
$P(S)$ that a point, chosen at random, belongs to subregion S is given
by the following.

$$P(S) = \frac{\text{area of subregion } S}{\text{area of region } R}$$

***Find the probability that a point, chosen at random, belongs to the shaded
subregions of the following regions.***

1.

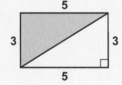

2.

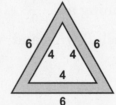

3.

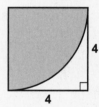

*The dart board shown at the right has 5 concentric
circles whose centers are also the center of the square
board. Each side of the board is 38 cm, and the radii of
the circles are 2 cm, 5 cm, 8 cm, 11 cm, and 14 cm. A
dart hitting within one of the circular regions scores the
number of points indicated on the board, while a hit
anywhere else scores 0 points. If a dart, thrown at
random, hits the board, find the probability of scoring the
indicated number of points. Write your answer in terms
of* π.

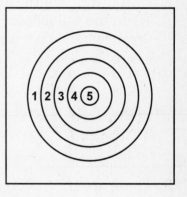

4. 0 points

5. 1 point

6. 2 points

7. 3 points

8. 4 points

9. 5 points

13-4

Enrichment

Probability and Tic-Tac-Toe

What would be the chances of winning at tic-tac-toe if it were turned into a game of pure chance? To find out, the nine cells of the tic-tac-toe board are numbered from 1 to 9 and chips (also numbered from 1 to 9) are put into a bag. Player A draws a chip at random and enters an X in the corresponding cell. Player B does the same and enters an O.

To solve the problem, assume that both players draw all their chips without looking and all X and O entries are made at the same time. There are four possible outcomes: a draw, A wins, B wins, and either A or B can win.

There are 16 arrangements that result in a draw. Reflections and rotations must be counted as shown below.

```
O X O      X O X      O O X
X O X      O O X      X X O
X O X      X X O      O X X
  4          4          8
```

There are 36 arrangements in which either player may win because both players have winning triples.

```
X X X    X X X    X O X    X X X    X X X    X X O
O O O    X O X    X X X    X X O    O O O    X X X
X O X    O O O    O O O    O O O    X X O    O O O
  4        4        4        8        8        8
```

In these 36 cases, A's chances of winning are $\frac{13}{40}$.

1. Find the 12 arrangements in which B wins and A cannot.

2. Below are 12 of the arrangements in which A wins and B cannot. Write the numbers to show the reflections and rotations for each arrangement. What is the total number?

```
O X O    X O X    X X X    X X X    X O O    X O X
X X X    O X O    X O O    O X O    X X X    X X O
O X O    X O X    X O O    O X O    O O X    O O X

X X O    X X X    X X X    X X X    X O O    X X O
O X X    O X O    X O O    X O O    X X X    O X O
O O X    O O X    O X O    O O X    O X O    X O X
```

3. There are $\frac{9!}{5!4!}$ different
and equally probable
distributions. Complete
the chart to find the
probability for a draw
or for A or B to win.

Draw: $\frac{16}{126}$		=
		_____
A wins:	$+ \ \frac{13}{40}\left(\frac{36}{126}\right)$	=
_____		_____
B wins:	$+$	=
_____	_____	_____

Advanced Mathematical Concepts

13-5

Enrichment

Probability in Genetics

The Austrian monk and botanist Gregor Mendel discovered the basic laws of genetics during the nineteenth century. Through experiments with pea plants, Mendel found that cells in living organisms contain pairs of units that control traits in the offspring of the organism. We now call these units *genes*. If the genes in a cell are identical, the trait is *pure*. If they are different, the trait is *hybrid*. A trait like *tallness* which masks other traits, preventing them from showing up in offspring, is *dominant*. Otherwise, it is *recessive*. A combination of a dominant gene and a recessive gene will always produce a hybrid displaying the dominant trait.

Example   **Two hybrid tall pea plants are crossed. What is the probability that the offspring will be short?**

Punnett squares are used to analyze gene combinations. Use capital letters to represent dominant genes and lower-case letters to represent recessive genes.

	T	t
T	TT	Tt
t	Tt	tt

T = tall t = short

The table shows the four equally possible outcomes. One of the outcomes, TT, is a pure tall plant. Two of the outcomes, Tt and Tt, are hybrid tall plants. Only one of the outcomes, tt, is a short plant. Therefore, the probability that an offspring will be short is $\frac{1}{4}$.

Use Punnett squares to solve.

1. A pure dominant yellow pea plant (Y) is crossed with a pure recessive white pea plant (w).

   a. What are the possible outcomes?

   b. Find the probability that an offspring will be yellow.

2. A hybrid tall pea plant is crossed with a short plant. Find the probability that an offspring will be short.

3. Brown eyes are dominant over blue eyes in humans. What is the probability that a woman with blue eyes and a man with hybrid brown eyes will have a child with blue eyes?

4. What is the probability that the offspring of a hybrid-tall, hybrid-yellow pea plant and a hybrid-tall white plant will be short white?

13-6

Enrichment

Combinations and Pascal's Triangle

Pascal's triangle is a special array of numbers invented by Blaise
Pascal (1623-1662). The values in Pascal's triangle can be found
using the combinations shown below.

1. Evaluate the expression in each cell of the triangle

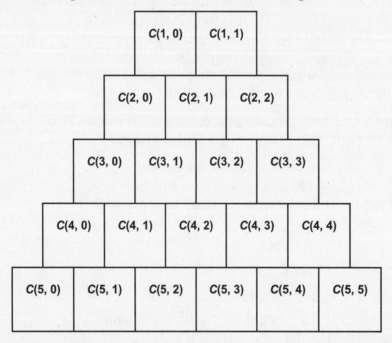

2. The pattern shows the relationship between $C(n, r)$ and Pascal's triangle.
In general, it is true that $C(n, r) + C(n, r + 1) = C(n + 1, r + 1)$.
Complete the proof of this property. In each step, the denominator has
been given.

$$C(n, r) + C(n, r + 1) = \frac{}{r!(n - r)!} + \frac{}{(r + 1)!(n - r - 1)!}$$

$$= \frac{}{r!(n - r)!(r + 1)} + \frac{}{(r + 1)!(n - r - 1)!(n - r)}$$

$$= \frac{}{(r + 1)!(n - r)!} + \frac{}{(r + 1)!(n - r)!}$$

$$= \frac{}{(r + 1)!(n - r)!}$$

$$= \frac{}{(r + 1)!(n - r)!}$$

$$= \frac{}{(r + 1)!(n - r)!}$$

$$= \frac{}{(r + 1)![(n + 1) - (r + 1)]!}$$

$$= C(n + 1, r + 1)$$

13-1 Enrichment

Permutation and Combination Algebra

Expressions involving $P(n, r)$ and $C(n, r)$, the symbols for permutations and combinations, can sometimes be simplified or used in equations as though they were algebraic expressions. You can solve problems involving such expressions by applying the definitions of $P(n, r)$ and $C(n, r)$.

Example **Simplify** $C(n, n-1)$.

By the definition of $C(n, r)$, $C(n, n-1) = \dfrac{n!}{(n-[n-1])!(n-1)!}$

$$= \dfrac{n!}{(n-n+1)!(n-1)!}$$

$$= \dfrac{n!}{1!(n-1)!}$$

$$= \dfrac{n!}{(n-1)!}$$

$$= n$$

Simplify.

1. $P(n, n-1)$ $n!$

2. $C(n, n)$ 1

3. $C(n, 1)$ n

4. $P(n, n)$ $n!$

5. $C(n+1, n)$ $n+1$

6. $C(n+1, n-1)$ $\dfrac{(n+1)n}{2}$

Solve for n.

7. $P(n, 5) = 7\, P(n, 4)$ 11

8. $C(n, n-2) = 6$ 4

9. $C(n+2, 4) = 6\, C(n, 2)$ 7

10. $P(n, 5) = 9\, P(n-1, 4)$ 9

13-2 Enrichment

Approximating Factorials

James Stirling (1692-1770) was a teacher, a friend of Sir Isaac Newton, and a mathematician who made important contributions to calculus. Today he is best remembered as the creator of a formula for approximating factorials.

| Stirling's Formula | $n! \approx \sqrt{2n\pi}\left(\dfrac{n}{e}\right)^n$, where e is the irrational number 2.7182818.... |

1. Stirling proved that the ratio $\dfrac{n!}{\sqrt{2n\pi}\left(\frac{n}{e}\right)^n}$ is less than $\dfrac{12n}{12n-1}$.

As n increases, will the approximations obtained using Stirling's formula become more accurate or less accurate? Explain.

More accurate; the fraction $\dfrac{12n}{12n-1}$ is always greater than 1.

As n grows larger, however, $12n$ gets closer to $12n-1$.

The fraction $\dfrac{12n}{12n-1}$ gets smaller and closer to 1.

2. Complete the chart.

n	$n!$	$\sqrt{2n\pi}\left(\dfrac{n}{e}\right)^n$	$\dfrac{n!}{\sqrt{2n\pi}\left(\frac{n}{e}\right)^n}$
10	3.6288×10^6	3.5987×10^6	1.008
20	2.4329×10^{18}	2.4228×10^{18}	1.004
30	2.6525×10^{32}	2.6452×10^{32}	1.003
40	8.1592×10^{47}	8.1422×10^{47}	1.002
50	3.0414×10^{64}	3.0363×10^{64}	1.002
60	8.3210×10^{81}	8.3094×10^{81}	1.001

13-3

Enrichment

Geometric Probability

If a dart, thrown at random, hits the triangular board shown at the right, what is the chance that is will hit the shaded region? This chance, also called a probability, can be determined by analyzing the area of the board. This ratio indicates what fraction of the tosses should hit in the shaded region.

$$\frac{\text{area of shaded region}}{\text{area of triangular board}} = \frac{\frac{1}{2}(4)(6)}{\frac{1}{2}(8)(6)}$$

$$= \frac{12}{24} \text{ or } \frac{1}{2}$$

In general, if S is a subregion of some region R, then the probability $P(S)$ that a point, chosen at random, belongs to subregion S is given by the following. $P(S) = \frac{\text{area of subregion } S}{\text{area of region } R}$

Find the probability that a point, chosen at random, belongs to the shaded subregions of the following regions.

1. $\dfrac{1}{2}$

2. $\dfrac{5}{9}$

The dart board shown at the right has 5 concentric circles whose centers are also the center of the square board. Each side of the board is 38 cm, and the radii of the circles are 2 cm, 5 cm, 8 cm, 11 cm, and 14 cm. A dart hitting within one of the circular regions scores the number of points indicated on the board, while a hit anywhere else scores 0 points. If a dart, thrown at random, hits the board, find the probability of scoring the indicated number of points. Write your answer in terms of π.

4. 0 points $\dfrac{361 - 49\pi}{361}$

5. 1 point $\dfrac{75\pi}{1444}$

6. 2 points $\dfrac{3\pi}{76}$

7. 3 points $\dfrac{39\pi}{1444}$

8. 4 points $\dfrac{21\pi}{1444}$

9. 5 points $\dfrac{\pi}{361}$

T149

Advanced Mathematical Concepts

13-4

Enrichment

Probability and Tic-Tac-Toe

What would be the chances of winning at tic-tac-toe if it were turned into a game of pure chance? To find out, the nine cells of the tic-tac-toe board are numbered from 1 to 9 and chips (also numbered from 1 to 9) are put into a bag. Player A draws a chip at random and enters an X in the corresponding cell. Player B does the same and enters an O.

To solve the problem, assume that both players draw all their chips without looking and all X and O entries are made at the same time. There are four possible outcomes: a draw, A wins, B wins, and either A or B can win.

There are 16 arrangements that result in a draw. Reflections and rotations must be counted as shown below.

```
o x o    o x o
x o x    x o x
o x o    o x o
  4        4
```

```
x x o    x x o
o o x    x o o
x o x    o o x
  4        8
```

```
x x x    x x x    x x o
o o x    x o o    o o x
x x o    o x x    x x o
  4        4        8
```

There are 36 arrangements in which either player may win because both players have winning triples.

```
x x x    x x x    x x x    x x x
o o x    x o x    x o o    o o o
x o x    o o o    o o o    x x o
  4        4        4        8
```

```
x x o    x o x    x x x    x x o
x o o    x o o    o o o    o x o
o o x    o x x    x x o    x o x
  4        4        8        8
```

In these 36 cases, A's chances of winning are $\dfrac{13}{40}$.

1. Find the 12 arrangements in which B wins and A cannot.

```
o o x   o x o
x o x   o x o
x x o   x x o   4
```

2. Below are 12 of the arrangements in which A wins and B cannot. Write the numbers to show the reflections and rotations for each arrangement. What is the total number? **62**

```
o x x x   1   x x x x   x o o 4   x o x
x x x 1   x x o 1   x x o 4   x x x 4   x x o 4
o x o x   x o o   o x o 0   o x o 0   o o x

o x x 4   x x x 4   o x x x   x o o   x x o 8
o o x 4   x o o 8   x x o 8   x x x 8   o x o 8
o o x 4   o o x   o x o 0   o x x 8   x o x
```

3. There are $\dfrac{9!}{5!4!}$ different and equally probable distributions. Complete the chart to find the probability for a draw or for A or B to win.

Draw:	$\dfrac{16}{126}$	$= \dfrac{8}{63}$
A wins:	$\dfrac{62}{126} + \dfrac{13}{40}\left(\dfrac{36}{126}\right)$	$= \dfrac{737}{1260}$
B wins:	$\dfrac{12}{126} + \dfrac{27}{40}\left(\dfrac{36}{126}\right)$	$= \dfrac{121}{420}$

T150

Advanced Mathematical Concepts

13-5

NAME _____ DATE _____ PERIOD _____

Enrichment

Probability in Genetics

The Austrian monk and botanist Gregor Mendel discovered the basic laws of genetics during the nineteenth century. Through experiments with pea plants, Mendel found that cells in living organisms contain pairs of units that control traits in the offspring of the organism. We now call these units *genes*. If the genes in a cell are identical, the trait is *pure*. If they are different, the trait is *hybrid*. A trait like *tallness* which masks other traits, preventing them from showing up in offspring, is *dominant*. Otherwise, it is *recessive*. A combination of a dominant gene and a recessive gene will always produce a hybrid displaying the dominant trait.

Example   **Two hybrid tall pea plants are crossed. What is the probability that the offspring will be short?**

Punnett squares are used to analyze gene combinations. Use capital letters to represent dominant genes and lower-case letters to represent recessive genes.

	T	t
T	TT	Tt
t	Tt	tt

T = tall   t = short

The table shows the four equally possible outcomes. One of the outcomes, TT, is a pure tall plant. Two of the outcomes, Tt and Tt, are hybrid tall plants. Only one of the outcomes, tt, is a short plant. Therefore, the probability that an offspring will be short is $\frac{1}{4}$.

Use Punnett squares to solve.

1. A pure dominant yellow pea plant (Y) is crossed with a pure recessive white pea plant (w).

   a. What are the possible outcomes? **Yw, Yw, Yw, Yw**

   b. Find the probability that an offspring will be yellow. **1**

2. A hybrid tall pea plant is crossed with a short plant. Find the probability that an offspring will be short. **$\frac{1}{2}$**

3. Brown eyes are dominant over blue eyes in humans. What is the probability that a woman with blue eyes and a man with hybrid brown eyes will have a child with blue eyes? **$\frac{1}{2}$**

4. What is the probability that the offspring of a hybrid-tall, hybrid-yellow pea plant and a hybrid-tall white plant will be short white? **$\frac{1}{8}$**

13-6

NAME _____ DATE _____ PERIOD _____

Enrichment

Combinations and Pascal's Triangle

Pascal's triangle is a special array of numbers invented by Blaise Pascal (1623-1662). The values in Pascal's triangle can be found using the combinations shown below.

1. Evaluate the expression in each cell of the triangle

		C(1, 0)	C(1, 1)		
		1	1		

	C(2, 0)	C(2, 1)	C(2, 2)	
	1	2	1	

C(3, 0)	C(3, 1)	C(3, 2)	C(3, 3)
1	3	3	1

C(4, 0)	C(4, 1)	C(4, 2)	C(4, 3)	C(4, 4)
1	4	6	4	1

C(5, 0)	C(5, 1)	C(5, 2)	C(5, 3)	C(5, 4)	C(5, 5)
1	5	10	10	5	1

2. The pattern shows the relationship between $C(n, r)$ and Pascal's triangle. In general, it is true that $C(n, r) + C(n, r + 1) = C(n + 1, r + 1)$. Complete the proof of this property. In each step, the denominator has been given.

$$C(n, r) + C(n, r + 1) = \frac{n!}{r!(n - r)!} + \frac{n!}{(r + 1)!(n - r - 1)!}$$

$$= \frac{n!(r + 1)}{r!(n - r)!(r + 1)} + \frac{n!(n - r)}{(r + 1)!(n - r - 1)!(n - r)}$$

$$= \frac{n!(r + 1)}{(r + 1)!(n - r)!} + \frac{n!(n - r)}{(r + 1)!(n - r)!}$$

$$= \frac{n!(r + 1 + n - r)}{(r + 1)!(n - r)!}$$

$$= \frac{n!(n + 1)}{(r + 1)!(n - r)!}$$

$$= \frac{(n + 1)!}{(r + 1)!(n - r)!}$$

$$= \frac{(n + 1)!}{(r + 1)!((n + 1) - (r + 1))!}$$

$$= C(n + 1, r + 1)$$

14-1

Enrichment

Misuses of Statistics

Statistics can be misleading. Two graphs for the same set of data can look very different from each other. Compare the following graphs.

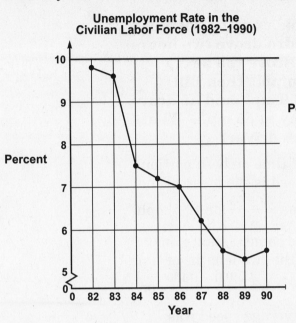

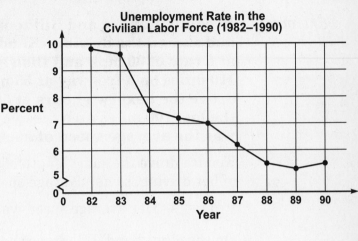

Notice that the two graphs show the same data, but the spacing in the vertical and horizontal scales differs. Scales can be cramped or spread out to make a graph that gives a certain impression.

1. Which graph would you use to give the impression that the unemployment rate dropped dramatically from 1982 to 1990?

2. Suppose that a car company claims, "75% of people surveyed say that our car is better than the competition." If only four people were surveyed, how many people thought that this company's car was better?

Suppose an advertiser claims that 90% of all the cars of one brand sold in the last 10 years are still on the road.

3. If 10,000 cars were sold, how many are still on the road?

4. If 1000 cars were sold, how many are still on the road?

5. Find an example to show how you think averages could be used in a misleading way.

6. A survey of a large sample of people who own small computers revealed that 85% of the people thought the instruction manuals should be better written. A manufacturer of small computers claimed that it surveyed many of the same people and found that all of them liked their manuals. Discuss the possible discrepancy in the results.

14-2

Enrichment

The Harmonic Mean

The *harmonic mean H* is a useful measure of central tendency in special cases of averaging rates.

Example Recently Kendra and Bill took a trip of 370 miles and shared the driving. Kendra drove two hours at a rate of 30 mph and then drove the next 110 miles on a freeway at 55 mph. Then Bill drove the next two hours at 50 mph and he drove the last 100 miles on a freeway at 55 mph. What was the average speed of each driver?

Kendra drove the same length of time on both portions of her driving, so her average speed is the mean of the two rates. Her average speed was $\dfrac{30+55}{2}$ or 42.5 mph.

On the other hand, Bill drove the same distance on both portions of his driving, but the two lengths of time varied. Actually, the time he drove was $\dfrac{100}{50} + \dfrac{100}{55}$, or approximately 3.82 hours. His average speed was $\dfrac{200}{3.82}$, or about 52.4 mph.

Bill's average speed also may be found by using the formula for the harmonic mean as follows.

Let n = number of rates x_i where $1 \le i \le n$. $H = \dfrac{n}{\displaystyle\sum_{i=1}^{n} \dfrac{1}{x_i}}$

We apply the formula to Bill's speeds. $H = \dfrac{2}{\dfrac{1}{50} + \dfrac{1}{55}}$

$H \approx 52.4$ mph

The mean, also called the arithmetic mean, is used when equal times are involved. When equal distances are involved, the harmonic mean is used.

Find the harmonic mean of each set of data. Round each answer to the nearest hundreth.

1. {3, 4, 5, 6}   **2.** {5, 10, 15, 20, 25}

3. Bev, Phyllis, and Gordon competed in a 375-mile relay race. Bev drove 40 mph, Phyllis drove 50 mph, and Gordon drove 60 mph. If each drove 125 miles, find the average driving speed of the contestants.

14-3

Enrichment

Percentiles

The table at the right shows test scores and their frequencies. The frequency is the number of people who had a particular score. The cumulative frequency is the total frequency up to that point, starting at the lowest score and adding up.

Score	Frequency	Cumulative Frequency
95	1	50
90	2	49
85	5	47
80	6	42
75	7	36
70	8	29
65	7	21
60	6	14
55	4	8
50	3	4
45	1	1

Example 1 **What score is at the 16th percentile?**

A score at the 16th percentile means the score just above the lowest 16% of the scores.

16% of the 50 scores is 8 scores.

The 8th score is 55.

The score just above this is 56.

Thus, the score at the 16th percentile is 56.

Notice that no one had a score of 56 points.

Use the table above to find the score at each percentile.

1. 42nd percentile _____

2. 70th percentile _____

3. 33rd percentile _____

4. 90th percentile _____

5. 58th percentile _____

6. 80th percentile _____

Example 2 **At what percentile is a score of 75?**

There are 29 scores below 75.

Seven scores are at 75. The fourth of these seven is the midpoint of this group.

Adding 4 scores to the 29 gives 33 scores.

33 out of 50 is 66%.

Thus, a score of 75 is at the 66th percentile.

Use the table above to find the percentile of each score.

7. a score of 50 _____

8. a score of 77 _____

9. a score of 85 _____

10. a score of 58 _____

11. a score of 62 _____

12. a score of 81 _____

Advanced Mathematical Concepts

14-4

Enrichment

Shapes of Distribution Curves

Graphs of frequency distributions can be described as either symmetric or skewed.

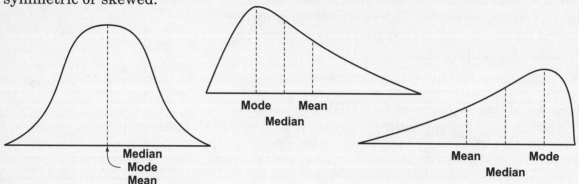

In a distribution skewed to the right, there are a larger number of high values. The long "tail" extends to the right.

In a distribution skewed to the left, there are a larger number of low values. The long "tail" extends to the left.

For each of the following, state whether the distribution is symmetric or skewed. If it is skewed, tell whether it is skewed to the right or to the left.

1.

2.

3.

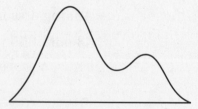

4.

5.

6.

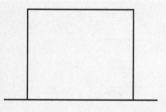

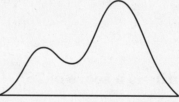

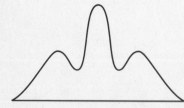

A vertical line along the median divides the area under a frequency curve in half.

7. Where is the median in a symmetric distribution?

8. Where is the median in a skewed distribution?

Advanced Mathematical Concepts

14-5

Enrichment

Binomial Expansion Coefficients

The picture at the right shows a device often used to illustrate a normal probability distribution. The device is filled with small steel marbles. The marbles roll past a series of hexagonal obstacles, collecting at the bottom in each of nine columns.

It can be shown that the number of paths from A to G is 1, A to J is 1, A to H is 3, and A to I is 3. For example, H can be reached by the way of E. Hence the number of paths to H is the sum of the number of paths to D and the number of paths to E. Likewise the number of paths to any point can be found by adding the number of paths to points diagonally above it. This is precisely the method by which the numbers in Pascal's triangle are obtained.

The numbers in Pascal's triangle are the coefficients in the expansion of $(x + y)^n$ where n is any positive integer. Therefore, the probability of a marble falling in any given column is proportional to the coefficient of the corresponding term in the binomial expansion of a power. The power is a whole number equal to the row being considered. For example, in the illustration above the columns are in the *eighth* row. Thus the probability of a marble falling in the *third* column is proportional to the coefficient of the *third* term in the binomial expansion of $(x + y)^8$.

The figure above at the right has equally-spaced vertical segments whose lengths are proportional to the numbers in the eighth row of Pascal's triangle. A smooth curve connecting the tops of these segments suggests the probable distribution of marbles in the column. Notice the similarity of this curve to the normal distribution curve.

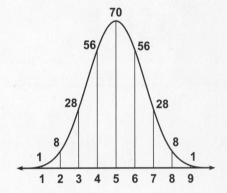

Solve.

1. Draw a smooth curve connecting the tops of the segments whose lengths are proportional to the coefficients in the expansion of $(x + y)^{12}$.

2. A teacher decided to mark 64 tests with the grades A, B, C, D, and F (A highest) in proportion to the coefficients in the expansion of $(x + y)^4$. How many tests received each grade?

Answers (Lessons 14-1 and 14-2)

14-1 Enrichment

Misuses of Statistics

Statistics can be misleading. Two graphs for the same set of data can look very different from each other. Compare the following graphs.

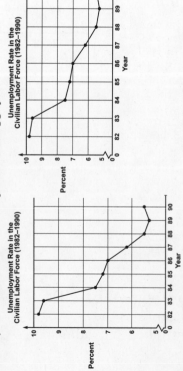

Unemployment Rate in the
Civilian Labor Force (1982–1990)

Notice that the two graphs show the same data, but the spacing in the vertical and horizontal scales differs. Scales can be cramped or spread out to make a graph that gives a certain impression.

1. Which graph would you use to give the impression that the unemployment rate dropped dramatically from 1982 to 1990? **the first graph**

2. Suppose a car company claims, "75% of people surveyed say that our car is better than the competition." If only four people were surveyed, how many people thought that this company's car was better? **3 people**

Suppose an advertiser claims that 90% of all the cars of one brand sold in the last 10 years are still on the road.

3. If 10,000 cars were sold, how many are still on the road? **9,000**

4. If 1000 cars were sold, how many are still on the road? **900**

5. Find an example to show how you think averages could be used in a misleading way. **See students' work.**

6. A survey of a large sample of people who own small computers revealed that 85% of the people thought the instruction manuals should be better written. A manufacturer of small computers claimed that it surveyed many of the same people and found that all of them liked their manuals. Discuss the possible discrepancy in the results. **See students' work.**

© Glencoe/McGraw-Hill   T157   *Advanced Mathematical Concepts*

14-2 Enrichment

The Harmonic Mean

The *harmonic mean* H is a useful measure of central tendency in special cases of averaging rates.

Example   Recently Kendra and Bill took a trip of 370 miles and shared the driving. Kendra drove two hours at a rate of 30 mph and then drove the next 110 miles on a freeway at 55 mph. Then Bill drove the next two hours at 50 mph and he drove the last 100 miles on a freeway at 55 mph. What was the average speed of each driver?

Kendra drove the same length of time on both portions of her driving, so her average speed is the mean of the two rates. Her average speed was $\frac{30 + 55}{2}$ or 42.5 mph.

On the other hand, Bill drove the same distance on both portions of his driving, but the two lengths of time varied. Actually, the time he drove was $\frac{100}{50} + \frac{100}{55}$, or approximately 3.82 hours. His average speed was $\frac{200}{3.82}$, or about 52.4 mph.

Bill's average speed also may be found by using the formula for the harmonic mean as follows.

Let n = number of rates x_i where $1 \le i \le n$. $H = \dfrac{n}{\displaystyle\sum_{i=1}^{n} \frac{1}{x_i}}$

We apply the formula to Bill's speeds.

$$H = \frac{2}{\frac{1}{50} + \frac{1}{55}}$$

$$H \approx 52.4 \text{ mph}$$

The mean, also called the arithmetic mean, is used when equal times are involved. When equal distances are involved, the harmonic mean is used.

Find the harmonic mean of each set of data. Round each answer to the nearest hundreth.

1. {3, 4, 5, 6}   2. {5, 10, 15, 20, 25}
   4.21   **10.95**

3. Bev, Phyllis, and Gordon competed in a 375-mile relay race. Bev drove 40 mph, Phyllis drove 50 mph, and Gordon drove 60 mph. If each drove 125 miles, find the average driving speed of the contestants. **48.65 mph**

© Glencoe/McGraw-Hill   T158   *Advanced Mathematical Concepts*

14-3 Enrichment

NAME _____ DATE _____ PERIOD _____

Percentiles

The table at the right shows test scores and their frequencies. The frequency is the number of people who had a particular score. The cumulative frequency is the total frequency up to that point, starting at the lowest score and adding up.

Score	Frequency	Cumulative Frequency
95	1	50
90	2	49
85	5	47
80	6	42
75	7	36
70	8	29
65	7	21
60	6	14
55	4	8
50	3	4
45	1	1

Example 1 What score is at the 16th percentile?

A score at the 16th percentile means the score just above the lowest 16% of the scores.

16% of the 50 scores is 8 scores.

The 8th score is 55.

The score just above this is 56.

Thus, the score at the 16th percentile is 56.

Notice that no one had a score of 56 points.

Use the table above to find the score at each percentile.

1. 42nd percentile __66__
2. 70th percentile __76__
3. 33rd percentile __66__
4. 90th percentile __86__
5. 58th percentile __71__
6. 80th percentile __81__

Example 2 At what percentile is a score of 75?

There are 29 scores below 75.

Seven scores are at 75. The fourth of these seven is the midpoint of this group.

Adding 4 scores to the 29 gives 33 scores.

33 out of 50 is 66%.

Thus, a score of 75 is at the 66th percentile.

Use the table above to find the percentile of each score.

7. a score of 50 __6th__
8. a score of 77 __72nd__
9. a score of 85 __90th__
10. a score of 58 __16th__
11. a score of 62 __28th__
12. a score of 81 __84th__

14-4 Enrichment

NAME _____ DATE _____ PERIOD _____

Shapes of Distribution Curves

Graphs of frequency distributions can be described as either symmetric or skewed.

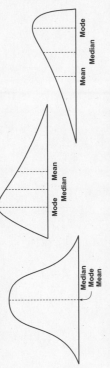

In a distribution skewed to the right, there are a larger number of high values. The long "tail" extends to the right.

In a distribution skewed to the left, there are a larger number of low values. The long "tail" extends to the left.

For each of the following, state whether the distribution is symmetric or skewed. If it is skewed, tell whether it is skewed to the right or to the left.

1. symmetric

2. skewed to the left

3. skewed to the right

4. symmetric

5. symmetric

6. skewed to the right

A vertical line along the median divides the area under a frequency curve in half.

7. Where is the median in a symmetric distribution?

in the middle of the range; it is the same as the mean.

8. Where is the median in a skewed distribution?

to the left of the mean if skewed to the right; to the right of the mean if skewed to the left.

NAME _____ DATE _____ PERIOD _____

14-5 Enrichment

Binomial Expansion Coefficients

The picture at the right shows a device often used to illustrate a normal probability distribution. The device is filled with small steel marbles. The marbles roll past a series of hexagonal obstacles, collecting at the bottom in each of nine columns.

It can be shown that the number of paths from A to G is 1, A to J is 1, A to H is 3, and A to I is 3. For example, H can be reached by the way of E. Hence the number of paths to H is the sum of the number of paths to D and the number of paths to E. Likewise the number of paths to any point can be found by adding the number of paths to points diagonally above it. This is precisely the method by which the numbers in Pascal's triangle are obtained.

The numbers in Pascal's triangle are the coefficients in the expansion of $(x + y)^n$ where n is any positive integer. Therefore, the probability of a marble falling in any given column is proportional to the coefficient of the corresponding term in the binomial expansion of a power. The power is a whole number equal to the row being considered. For example, in the illustration above the columns are in the *eighth* row. Thus the probability of a marble falling in the *third* column is proportional to the coefficient of the *third* term in the binomial expansion of $(x + y)^8$.

The figure above at the right has equally-spaced vertical segments whose lengths are proportional to the numbers in the eighth row of Pascal's triangle. A smooth curve connecting the tops of these segments suggests the probable distribution of marbles in the column. Notice the similarity of this curve to the normal distribution curve.

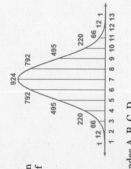

Solve.

1. Draw a smooth curve connecting the tops of the segments whose lengths are proportional to the coefficients in the expansion of $(x + y)^{12}$.

2. A teacher decided to mark 64 tests with the grades A, B, C, D, and F (A highest) in proportion to the coefficients in the expansion of $(x + y)^4$. How many tests received each grade?
   A = 4, B = 16, C = 24, D = 16, F = 4

T161

Advanced Mathematical Concepts

15-1

Enrichment

A Matter of Limits

There are many examples of limits in our world. Some of these are absolute limits, in that they can never be exceeded. Others are like guidelines, and still others result in a penalty if they are exceeded. Fill in the chart below.

Limit	How is the limit set?	Is the limit absolute?	Penalty or consequence if the limit is exceeded
1. speed limit on a highway			
2. height limit on a road underpass			
3. luggage limit on an airline flight			
4. temperature of a warm object placed in a cool room			
5. the speed of an accelerating space craft			
6. credit limit on a credit card			

*One special feature of mathematical limits is that they may be finite, infinite, or they may not exist. Classify each limit as **finite, infinite,** or **does not exist.** If the limit is finite, give its value.*

7. $\lim\limits_{x\to 0} \dfrac{1}{x^2 + 1}$

8. $\lim\limits_{x\to 1} \dfrac{x + 1}{x^2 - 1}$

9. $\lim\limits_{x\to 2} \dfrac{x^2 - 4}{x^2 - x - 2}$

10. $\lim\limits_{x\to 0} \ln |x|$

15-2 ## Enrichment

Powerful Differentiation

In Chapter 12, the series expansions of some transcendental functions were presented. In particular, the even function $y = \cos x$, was shown to be a sum of even powers of x:

$$\cos x = 1 - \frac{x^2}{2!} + \frac{x^4}{4!} - \frac{x^6}{6!} + \frac{x^8}{8!} - \cdots$$

and the sine function, being odd, was shown to be a sum of odd powers of x:

$$\sin x = x - \frac{x^3}{3!} + \frac{x^5}{5!} - \frac{x^7}{7!} + \frac{x^9}{9!} - \cdots.$$ Although differentiating

functions such as sine and cosine has not been presented, the power functions in these series expansions can be differentiated.

1. **a.** Find $\dfrac{d(\sin x)}{dx}$ by differentiating the series expansion of $\sin x$ term by

   term and simplifying the result.

   b. What function does this new infinite series represent?

   c. So, $\dfrac{d(\sin x)}{dx} = \underline{\quad ? \quad}$.

2. **a.** What would you guess might be the derivative of $\cos x$?

   b. Find $\dfrac{d(\cos x)}{dx}$ using the series expansion of $\cos x$.

   c. So $\dfrac{d(\cos x)}{dx} = \underline{\quad ? \quad}$.

3. **a.** The series expansion for e^x, $e^x = 1 + x + \dfrac{x^2}{2!} + \dfrac{x^3}{3!} + \dfrac{x^4}{4!} + \cdots$

   was also discussed in Chapter 12. Differentiate the series expansion of e^x term by term, and simplify the result.

   b. Thus, $\dfrac{d(e^x)}{dx} = \underline{\quad ? \quad}$.

Use the results of Exercises 1-3 to find the derivative of each function.

4. $f(x) = xe^x$ 5. $f(x) = \sin x^2$ 6. $f(x) = (\cos x)^2$

15-3

Enrichment

Reading Mathematics

There is quite a lot of special notation used in calculus that is not used in other branches of mathematics. In addition, there is often more than one notation for the same thing. You have already seen this in the case of the derivative.

1. Let $f(x) = x^2$. What does $\lim\limits_{h \to 0} \dfrac{(x + h)^2 - x^2}{h}$ calculate?

2. List several other ways of expressing this quantity.

Yet another notation for the derivative of a function $y = f(x)$ is $\dot{y}$. This was the notation developed by Isaac Newton. Each of these notations also can be used to indicate higher-order derivatives.

For example, $f''(x) \dfrac{d^2 y}{dx^2}$, and $\ddot{y}$ all indicate the second derivative of some function $y = f(x)$.

3. What is the order of each derivative?

   a. $f'''(x)$ **b.** $\dot{y}$ **c.** $\dfrac{d^4 y}{dx^4}$ **d.** y''

The Leibniz notation for the derivative $\dfrac{dy}{dx}$ is usually read "$d\,y\,d\,x$," or, more formally, "the derivative of y with respect to x." Note that $\dfrac{dy}{dx}$ is *not* a fraction of any kind. To indicate the value of the derivative at a specific value of x using the Leibniz notation, one might use the following: $\dfrac{dy}{dx}\Big|_{x = 2}$, read "$d\,y\,d\,x$ evaluated at $x = 2$."

Given $f(x) = x^3 + 3x^2 - 4$, find the value of each expression.

4. $f'(2)$ **5.** $\dfrac{dy}{dx}\Big|_{x = -1}$ **6.** $f''(0)$ **7.** $\dfrac{d^3 y}{dx^3}\Big|_{x = 4}$

                 Advanced Mathematical Concepts

15-4

Enrichment

Chain Rule

An alternate way to define a derivative is

$$\frac{dy}{dx} = \lim_{\triangle x \to 0} \frac{\triangle y}{\triangle x}, \text{ where } \triangle y \text{ is } f(x+h) - f(x) \text{ and } \triangle x = h.$$

Suppose $y = f(u)$ and $u = g(x)$. If both $\triangle x$ and $\triangle u \to 0$,

$$\frac{dy}{dx} = \lim_{\substack{\triangle x \to 0 \\ \triangle u \to 0}} \frac{\triangle y}{\triangle u} \cdot \frac{\triangle u}{\triangle x} = \lim_{\triangle u \to 0} \frac{\triangle y}{\triangle u} \cdot \lim_{\triangle x \to 0} \frac{\triangle u}{\triangle x} = \frac{dy}{du} \cdot \frac{du}{dx}.$$

This is known as the chain rule. It provides a short cut for finding some derivatives.

Example   If $y = (x^2 - 2x)^2$, find $\frac{dy}{dx}$ by the chain rule.

Let $u = x^2 - 2x$, then $f(u) = u^2$.

$$\frac{dy}{dx} = 2u \cdot (2x - 2) \text{ or } \frac{dy}{dx} = 2(x^2 - 2x)(2x - 2) = 4x^3 - 12x^2 + 8x$$

Check: $y = (x^2 - 2x)^2 = x^4 - 4x^3 + 4x^2$

$$\frac{dy}{dx} = 4x^3 - 12x^2 + 8x \checkmark$$

Use the chain rule to find the derivative of each function. If possible, check by expansion or multiplication.

1. $y = (x^2 - 1)^2$

2. $y = (\sqrt{x} + 2)^3$

3. $y = (x + \frac{1}{x})^2$

4. $y = (x^2 - 3x + 2)^2$

5. $y = \sqrt{2x + 3}$

6. $y = (3x - 1)^{-\frac{1}{2}}$

7. $y = \frac{1}{2x - 5}$

8. $y = \frac{2}{x^2 - 1}$

Answers (Lessons 15-1 and 15-2)

15-1 Enrichment

A Matter of Limits

There are many examples of limits in our world. Some of these are absolute limits, in that they can never be exceeded. Others are like guidelines, and still others result in a penalty if they are exceeded. Fill in the chart below.

Limit	How is the limit set?	Is the limit absolute?	Penalty or consequence if the limit is exceeded
1. speed limit on a highway	The government sets the speed limits.	no	speeding ticket, fine, and so on
2. height limit on a road underpass	Height limit is set for safe clearance.	yes	Damage is done to vehicle and/or structure.
3. luggage limit on an airline flight	Airline sets limit on amount of baggage allowed.	no	Passenger must pay for any luggage beyond limit.
4. temperature of a warm object placed in a cool room	can only get as cool as its surroundings	yes	not possible
5. the speed of an accelerating space craft	physical constant, the speed of light	yes	not possible
6. credit limit on a credit card	Set by bank issuing card.	no	Financial penalty set by bank, possibly may lose card.

One special feature of mathematical limits is that they may be finite, infinite, or they may not exist. Classify each limit as finite, infinite, or does not exist. If the limit is finite, give its value.

7. $\lim_{x \to 0} \frac{1}{x^2+1}$ finite; 1

8. $\lim_{x \to 1} \frac{x+1}{x^2-1}$ does not exist

9. $\lim_{x \to 2} \frac{x^2-4}{x^2-x-2}$ finite; $\frac{4}{3}$

10. $\lim_{x \to 0} \ln |x|$ infinite

15-2 Enrichment

Powerful Differentiation

In Chapter 12, the series expansions of some transcendental functions were presented. In particular, the even function $y = \cos x$, was shown to be a sum of even powers of x:

$$\cos x = 1 - \frac{x^2}{2!} + \frac{x^4}{4!} - \frac{x^6}{6!} + \frac{x^8}{8!} - \cdots$$

and the sine function, being odd, was shown to be a sum of odd powers of x:

$$\sin x = x - \frac{x^3}{3!} + \frac{x^5}{5!} - \frac{x^7}{7!} + \frac{x^9}{9!} - \cdots.$$ Although differentiating functions such as sine and cosine has not been presented, the power functions in these series expansions can be differentiated.

1. a. Find $\frac{d(\sin x)}{dx}$ by differentiating the series expansion of sin x term by term and simplifying the result. $1 - \frac{x^2}{2!} + \frac{x^4}{4!} - \frac{x^6}{6!} + \frac{x^8}{8!} - \cdots$

   b. What function does this new infinite series represent?   cos x

   c. So, $\frac{d(\sin x)}{dx} = \underline{\quad ? \quad}$.   cos x

2. a. What would you guess might be the derivative of cos x?   Answers may vary.

   b. Find $\frac{d(\cos x)}{dx}$ using the series expansion of cos x. $-x + \frac{x^3}{3!} - \frac{x^5}{5!} + \frac{x^7}{7!} - \frac{x^9}{9!} + \cdots$

   c. So $\frac{d(\cos x)}{dx} = \underline{\quad ? \quad}$. $-\sin x$

3. a. The series expansion for e^x, $e^x = 1 + x + \frac{x^2}{2!} + \frac{x^3}{3!} + \frac{x^4}{4!} + \cdots$ was also discussed in Chapter 12. Differentiate the series expansion of e^x term by term, and simplify the result. $1 + x + \frac{x^2}{2!} + \frac{x^3}{3!} + \frac{x^4}{4!} + \cdots$

   b. Thus, $\frac{d(e^x)}{dx} = \underline{\quad ? \quad}$. e^x

Use the results of Exercises 1-3 to find the derivative of each function.

4. $f(x) = xe^x$ $xe^x + e^x$

5. $f(x) = \sin x^2$ $2x \cos x^2$

6. $f(x) = (\cos x)^2$ $-2 \cos x \sin x$ or $-\sin 2x$

15-3 Enrichment

Reading Mathematics

There is quite a lot of special notation used in calculus that is not used in other branches of mathematics. In addition, there is often more than one notation for the same thing. You have already seen this in the case of the derivative.

1. Let $f(x) = x^2$. What does $\lim_{h \to 0} \dfrac{(x+h)^2 - x^2}{h}$ calculate?

the derivative of $f(x) = x^2$

2. List several other ways of expressing this quantity.

Sample answers: $\dfrac{d(x^2)}{dx}$, $f'(x)$, $\dfrac{dy}{dx}$, $\lim_{\triangle x \to 0} \dfrac{\triangle y}{\triangle x}$, y'

Yet another notation for the derivative of a function $y = f(x)$ is $\dot{y}$. This was the notation developed by Isaac Newton. Each of these notations also can be used to indicate higher-order derivatives. For example, $f''(x) \dfrac{d^2y}{dx^2}$, and $\ddot{y}$ all indicate the second derivative of some function $y = f(x)$.

3. What is the order of each derivative?

a. $f'''(x)$ **third**   **b.** $\dot{y}$ **first**   **c.** $\dfrac{d^4y}{dx^4}$ **fourth**   **d.** y'' **second**

The Leibniz notation for the derivative $\dfrac{dy}{dx}$ is usually read "d y d x," or, more formally, "the derivative of y with respect to x." Note that $\dfrac{dy}{dx}$ is *not* a fraction of any kind. To indicate the value of the derivative at a specific value of x using the Leibniz notation, one might use the following: $\dfrac{dy}{dx}\Big|_{x=2}$, read "d y d x evaluated at x = 2."

Given $f(x) = x^3 + 3x^2 - 4$, find the value of each expression.

4. $f'(2)$ **24**

5. $\dfrac{dy}{dx}\Big|_{x=-1}$ **−3**

6. $f'(0)$ **6**

7. $\dfrac{d^3y}{dx^3}\Big|_{x=4}$ **6**

15-4 Enrichment

Chain Rule

An alternate way to define a derivative is
$$\dfrac{dy}{dx} = \lim_{\triangle x \to 0} \dfrac{\triangle y}{\triangle x}, \text{ where } \triangle y \text{ is } f(x+h) - f(x) \text{ and } \triangle x = h.$$

Suppose $y = f(u)$ and $u = g(x)$. If both $\triangle x$ and $\triangle u \to 0$,
$$\dfrac{dy}{dx} = \lim_{\triangle x \to 0}\dfrac{\triangle y}{\triangle x} = \lim_{\triangle u \to 0}\dfrac{\triangle y}{\triangle u} \cdot \lim_{\triangle x \to 0}\dfrac{\triangle u}{\triangle x} = \dfrac{dy}{du} \cdot \dfrac{du}{dx}.$$

This is known as the chain rule. It provides a short cut for finding some derivatives.

Example **If $y = (x^2 - 2x)^2$, find $\dfrac{dy}{dx}$ by the chain rule.**

Let $u = x^2 - 2x$, then $f(u) = u^2$.
$$\dfrac{dy}{dx} = 2u \cdot (2x - 2) \text{ or } \dfrac{dy}{dx} = 2(x^2 - 2x)(2x - 2) = 4x^3 - 12x^2 + 8x$$

Check: $y = (x^2 - 2x)^2 = x^4 - 4x^3 + 4x^2$
$$\dfrac{dy}{dx} = 4x^3 - 12x^2 + 8x \checkmark$$

Use the chain rule to find the derivative of each function. If possible, check by expansion or multiplication.

1. $y = (x^2 - 1)^2$
$$2(x^2 - 1)(2x) = 4x(x^2 - 1)$$

2. $y = (\sqrt{x} + 2)^3$
$$3(\sqrt{x} + 2)^2\left(x^{-\frac{1}{2}}\right) =$$
$$\dfrac{3x^{-\frac{1}{2}}}{2}(\sqrt{x} + 2)^2$$

3. $y = \left(x + \dfrac{1}{x}\right)^2$
$$2\left(x + \dfrac{1}{x}\right)(1 - x^{-2})$$

4. $y = (x^2 - 3x + 2)^2$
$$2(x^2 - 3x + 2)(2x - 3) =$$
$$4x^3 - 18x^2 + 26x - 12$$

5. $y = \sqrt{2x + 3}$
$$\dfrac{1}{2}(2x + 3)^{-\frac{1}{2}}(2) = (2x + 3)^{-\frac{1}{2}}$$

6. $y = (3x - 1)^{-\frac{1}{2}}$
$$-\dfrac{1}{2}(3x - 1)^{-\frac{3}{2}}(3) =$$
$$-\dfrac{3}{2}(3x - 1)^{-\frac{3}{2}}$$

7. $y = \dfrac{1}{2x - 5}$
$$-(2x - 5)^{-2}(2) = -2(2x - 5)^{-2}$$

8. $y = \dfrac{2}{x^2 - 1}$
$$-2(x^2 - 1)^{-2}(2x) =$$
$$-4x(x^2 - 1)^{-2}$$